THE BLAIR REVELATION

'*My grandmother . . . gave me a Bible with her favourite texts written on the fly-leaf. Among these was "Thou shalt not follow a multitude to do evil". Her emphasis upon this text led me in later life to be not afraid of belonging to small minorities.*'

The Autobiography of Bertrand Russell, Vol.I, p.22

THE BLAIR REVELATION

Deliverance for whom?

Michael Barratt Brown
and
Ken Coates MEP

SPOKESMAN
for
Socialist Renewal

Socialist Renewal No.11

First published in Great Britain in 1996 by
Spokesman
Bertrand Russell House
Gamble Street
Nottingham, England
Tel. 0115 9708318
Fax. 0115 9420433

Publications list available on request

British Library Cataloguing in Publication Data available on request from the British
Library.

With grateful acknowledgements to Steve Bell for the use of his cartoon for the cover.

ISBN 0-85124-604-4 cloth
ISBN 0-85124-605-2 paper

Printed by the Russell Press Ltd, Nottingham
(Tel. 0115 9784505)

Contents

Introduction

What this Book is About

What really is New Labour?

The two authors of this book, both with many years of activity in the British Labour Movement, believe that the question has to be asked whether the transmogrification of Labour into New Labour might not augur ill for the great majority of the people of Britain, and, moreover, in spite of current opinion polls, might not even possibly deny to Labour that commanding victory at the next election which has been the overriding objective of the 'Blair revolution'.

New Labour has now published its 'Road to the Manifesto' and a stream of policy statements supported by speeches and interviews given by Tony Blair himself and his leading associates. These are marked by a quite astonishing degree of ambiguity, even in the so-called 'pledges' that have been made to the electorate. There is a desperate desire in the country to be rid of the Tories but a growing unease at what appears to be on offer in their place. The alternative has to be discerned through a mist of vacuous aspiration and moralising sentiment and does not seem to amount to anything very real.

[margin note: N. lab vacuveus]

This new manner of presenting political choices no doubt arises from the emergence of spin doctors who both clothe and doctor policy, so as to make it appear attractive to as many people as possible and unattractive to as few as possible. It means that the presentation and packaging become more important than the content, which may almost be made to disappear, if that seems convenient. It also means that the presenters take the place of ideologues in political leadership.

[margin note: presenters over political ideology]

The projection of the image of Tony Blair himself has become the ultimate aim of political campaigning. His Christian convictions — Anglican or Catholic *au choix* — his youthful conversion to Christian socialism, his devotion to his own family and belief in the nuclear family as the basis of society, his conception of a 'stakeholding' economy and

1

Emphasis is on Blair rather than Lab

commitment to a 'one nation' society driven by the dynamic competitiveness of the market to achieve world leadership — all appear as one man's personal vision.

This is what politics have come to in the age of television and the mass media, where charisma replaces character and the soundbite substitutes for sound argument. Yet arguments have to be addressed and policies have to be pronounced and from them we have to discover what the real intentions of the new party leadership might be. The leading spin doctor, Peter Mandelson, together with one of the founders of Dr David Owen's Social Democrats, Roger Liddle, two of Tony Blair's closest associates, have written a much promoted apologia, under the title, *The Blair Revolution: Can New Labour Deliver?* This is probably the nearest one can get to an argued case for New Labour. It is presented as 'part political philosophy, part social commentary, part history and part political analysis'.

New Lab distorts party history

Barratt Brown and Coates have concluded that, in spite of its evidently calculated evasions and absurd pretensions, the book has to be taken seriously; but they believe that it is based on a gross distortion of Labour's history and this urgently needs to be corrected. Mandelson and Liddle say that it was necessary for Labour to be 'reinvented'. In the process they have had to reinvent its history, and in particular the events leading to the defection of the Social Democrats from the Labour Party. Mandelson and Liddle emphasise the disagreements in the broad church that was Old Labour, but in doing so they fail to recognise the central fact that, whatever else the Party disagreed on, it was united in the belief that full employment was the basis of the freedom and security of the British people. Putting that back at the head of the political agenda would mean changing our conception of employment and work. But nothing less could establish it clearly as a party of labour.

Old Lab united around employment

The central message of Mandelson and Liddle's book and the justification for New Labour is that the world has changed, old policies no longer work, new ones are needed to respond to a moral, political and social crisis that faces not only Britain but the whole of mankind. We can agree with this and believe that the crisis is deeper than New Labour understands. But what has to be challenged is whether New Labour has in fact anything new to offer in meeting this crisis except some new packaging for the status quo.

Crisis new principle new lab, but it does offer anything new?

Having re-engaged with the Social Democrats, Tony Blair seemed set upon accommodation with the Liberals, but there are now key areas of policy where they begin to seem more radical than New Labour.

2

Advisers on social democracy, such as Professor Marquand and Will Hutton, are expressing their discomfort that the 'project' has moved too far to the right. Where Tony Blair once spoke of proposing policies to 'the left of centre', this became defence of the 'centre left'. Then in a recent visit to the United States he announced that Labour was the party of 'the Centre'. Enjoying this game some Conservatives have discovered that New Labour is 'too right wing' for them. Are we in the end being offered not new Labour but a new Conservatism?

hals
New Tory's?

How far has this political shift already gone, and where is it intended to go? And who will speak for all those people who have been left behind? The question that has to be asked, then, is not whether New Labour can deliver, but what it will deliver and to whom. Given the ambiguities and the silences as well as the pronouncements, it will be necessary to look behind the statements — about Tony Blair's Christianity, about New Labour's 'core values', about the several ideas of community, about the realities of 'stakeholding' in a capitalist economy, about the commitment to equality and welfare, about care for the environment, and about being at the centre of Europe, while firmly tied to the Atlantic Alliance.

several community

When all that has been explored in the successive chapters of this book, it should be possible to know better what sort of party this really is that is being presented as New Labour, and to suggest the basis for a real alternative to meet the critical needs of the much misgoverned British people.

N. Lab moved from left of centre, to centre left, to centre.

CHAPTER 1

The Spin Doctors Fabricating a Leader

'Communications means throwing your net much wider than publicity. It means deciding what we say, how we say it, and which spokesmen and women we choose to say it.'

(Guardian interview with Peter Mandelson)

Public relations is all today. Understanding the meaning of the 'Blair revolution' demands recognition of the role of the public relations people not only in the presentation, but now in the development of politics. Mrs Thatcher was the first British political leader to put her campaigning in the hands of an 'adman', Maurice Saatchi, who master-minded all her election campaigns. He is quoted as having said before he got the job that the Conservative approach came across as 'cruel and efficient' while Labour appeared 'caring but incompetent'. Peter Mandelson, who is co-author of the book on the Blair revolution, was brought in to make the Labour Party look competent and set out to 'modernise' it. Apparently, nobody told him what for. He came from a television background (LWT's *Weekend World*) to be appointed Labour's director of campaigns and communications after the 1983 election failure. He joined up with Philip Gould of Gould Matheson advertising agents to jolly up the Party's image with red roses and all. None of this could get Kinnock elected in 1987.

Mandelson, however, had wider ambitions. As he told the *Guardian* in the interview we have just quoted, he sees himself as much more than a publicist for New Labour. A profile of Mandelson by Nyta Mann in the *New Statesman* in March of 1996 quoted a former Party director's comment that 'it very quickly became apparent that he had a political as well as a technical agenda.' He appears, for example, to have done much to end the Party's commitment to nuclear disarmament. Labour's defeat in 1987 left Mandelson disillusioned with the Party and in particular with Kinnock. In self-justification he coined the sound bite

[handwritten margin notes: "modernise empty" and "Mandelson had own agenda"]

5

that Labour 'won the campaign but lost the election'. He left head office in 1990 and stood for Parliament in 1992. He was returned; but he was *persona non grata* with John Smith, we are told, and only bounced back with Tony Blair. He has taken over as Tony Blair's campaign manager — officially chair of Labour's general election planning group. His successor as director of communications, Joy Johnson, has resigned. Mandelson and his old friend Philip Gould, Alastair Campbell and Lord Hollick, we are told, now form the inner group around the party leader. It is from this vantage point that the book with Roger Liddle was written.

The Spin Doctors

The Mandelson and Liddle book has been seen as a public relations exercise for Blair. Certainly, references to the leader are never less than hagiographic. But Nyta Mann's profile suggests that the book is also a bid to consolidate Mandelson's own future. He wishes to be seen as more than the mirror of the Labour leader's thoughts and wishes. 'He is tipped', she says, 'to be the first of the 1992 intake to make it into a Blair cabinet — either as the Number Ten-based "minister for the *Today* programme", proposed in his book, or in some other capacity'. In a real sense today the medium becomes the message. Mandelson is currently Blair's front bench spokesman on the civil service. As such in government as a non-departmental minister he might appropriately be a member of the cabinet as the Lord Privy Seal — a splendidly fitting feudal title for a spin doctor, who carries the monarch's own seal of authority.

There is a wonderfully perceptive imagery around the concept of a 'spin doctor' — the spinning of a tale or other fabrication, the deceptive spinning of a ball, while 'doctoring' has always had the ambiguous meaning both of healing and tampering, even of emasculating. Politics becomes today like any other commodity, a product to be prepared, packaged and marketed with the appropriate brand image after careful market research by the advertisers and public relations experts into what people want. But it also must reflect what the producer has on offer. Politics is conducted through the media of press and television. It so happens that the media — newspapers and TV, apart from the BBC — are in the hands of a few great press magnates. Dennis Potter, the fiercely independent television playwright who died on June 7th, 1994, called his cancer 'Rupert' in honour of the tycoon who owns *The Times* and much else besides; and there is a profound sense in which the media has grown like a cancer in the body politic.

The media, as the word implies, is a two-way process, but there is an asymmetry of power involved. There is the message which the owners of the newspapers and private TV channels wish to communicate on their own behalf and those of the advertisers, giant companies in the main, whose adverts cover much of the costs of newspaper production. At the same time, for the product to sell, public opinion must be understood, assuaged and to some extent reflected. Taste can be formed with murder stories and page three ladies and the taste grows by what it feeds on, but in politics the public can be wilful. People have needs and aspirations which can only be manipulated within certain limits.

The task of the spin doctors is to manage that wilfulness. It is said that Labour lost the 1992 election in the last week, when the *Sun* newspaper mounted a massive campaign against John Smith's warning that improved services meant higher taxes. He should never have said it, say the spinners, and New Labour's leaders have since repeated *ad nauseam* that they will not raise taxes, but will make efficiency savings to shift the pattern of public spending, without increasing it. This is what is meant by 'communications being much more than publicity'. Under the Mandelson regime only what has already been agreed by the spin doctors will go out on the media. Clare Short will be taught not to say that Labour will renationalise the railways, when the sale of railtrack is announced for a song, but that 'Labour will bring the railways back into a framework that protects the public interest.'

Now, all the spinning and doctoring applies also to the words of the leader. These have to be prepared, packaged and presented. The result is that the man himself becomes increasingly an invention, an artificial construct made to the measure of the market. Not only are his speeches circulated to the press in advance without any of the comment they might have aroused in the audience, but even his 'impromptu' comments are prepared in advance and projected by his minders to the press, so that sometimes he has to strain his exchanges with audiences in order to say all the things which have been given already to the press outside the meeting, whether it is a private conference or the European Parliament.

In a *New Statesman* interview with Julia Hobsbawm, Peter Hitchens complained of her and all Blair's other PR people that they interfered with serious reporting. He quoted an incident when he found Mandelson reading over his shoulder at a Party Conference as he typed up his report and seeking to 'correct' it. Thus the leader does not write articles or books, he has them written about him. Mandelson or Liddle writes the book about New Labour's policies. The leader's views appear as interviews granted to chosen journalists. He is not seen attending Party meetings and committees unless they are staged for him with 'soundbites' arranged for the news flashes. His visits are arranged around the world for him to appear in photo calls shaking hands with national leaders. So, it is no surprise when he appears in Australia speaking at a businessman's convention as the guest of Rupert Murdoch.

Roy Hattersley in a revealing article in the *Guardian* (28-05-96) about the role of New Labour's spin doctors, very properly entitled 'Shoot the Messenger', gave examples of the doctoring that goes on. Apparently, each member of the shadow cabinet has a 'messenger' whose task is to interpret the Party's views to the press and to correct any statements that do not follow what the messenger believes to be the message. According to Hattersley these beliefs are not at all necessarily in line with agreed Party policy and often put forward only to enhance the position of the messenger's particular shadow minister. This is apparently what happened in the disagreement between Robin Cook and Gordon Brown over Brown's proposed changes in the pattern of Child Benefit. It was Brown's messenger who insisted that Cook was wrong. It was claimed that Brown had put forward one single change rather than a series of options.

Sometimes the difference between the shadow minister and the even more shadowy messenger is indeed a matter of interpretation in what appear to be deliberate ambiguities in New Labour's policies. When questions were asked about Blair's speech in Washington early in 1996, which was said to mark 'a historical repositioning of Labour' on the political spectrum, these words were found not in the speech itself, but in the communication from a member of Blair's office.

Thus New Labour was moved from Centre-Left to Centre, and the messengers seem not to have finished their push to the right. The only difference we have with Roy Hattersley on this score is that he politely assumes that these messengers are acting on their own behalf and without either their shadow minister or the leader's authority. Since they were appointed by the member they serve or by the leader, this seems hardly likely. But perhaps it explains why Peter Mandelson, who is called by Hattersley 'their spiritual leader', was summarily exiled by John Smith after Kinnock resigned, and why he came back as soon as Blair was appointed. John Smith was a man of great integrity.

N lab not
centre left

8

What Modernisation Means

Even Blair's critics from within the Labour Party agree that the Party needed to be modernised and made into an efficient machine that could win elections. But the Blair revolution went far beyond sprucing up the image. First, attention was given to the changing of Clause IV as the ultimate aim of the Party. This was presented as the ending of something that no-one believed in. This presentation was accepted by some old socialists like Stuart Hall, because, as Hall writes, the Party was never 'within a million light years of taking all of productive industry, of the full fruits of workers' labour by hand and brain, into common ownership.' Those who argued that this was not what the Clause said were told not to juggle with words. Nothing, they said, could alter the fact that this was the meaning which the media would take up. It is, however, a dangerous principle to accept that if the *Sun* says it three times, it is true. In fact, old Labour saw common ownership as the *basis* for ending exploitation of labour. This implied a large public sector, what Nye Bevan, echoing Lenin, called 'the commanding heights', ownership of which would strengthen the power of labour against capital. It did not entail the expropriation of 'all of industry' let alone the prohibition of individual enterprise. Without this *basis* in common property, the Labour Party ceased to be a socialist party, whatever the new words said, and the readers of the *Sun* newspaper could no longer be regaled with stories of Labour's supposed threat to end all private property.

In spite of the affront to thousands of old Party members this change in doctrine was not the half of it. Long before the assault on Clause IV, Blair as shadow Employment Secretary had argued in an article in *Marxism Today* for a new settlement between the individual and society through recognition of a 'public interest' that could regulate and reconcile the interests of capital and labour. How this was to be achieved was not made very clear, except that some government regulation was needed and government support

> 'to enhance the power of individual employees not just to protect their position from abuse, but also to grant them the capability to use or exploit capital'. (*Marxism Today*, October 1991)

This apparently revolutionary proposal was explained as meaning no more than that there would be government investment in training individual workers to develop their talents. The collective institutions of labour were dismissed as having failed to defend the individual,

9

becoming themselves vested interests exploiting labour, whether as government, state industry or trade unions. The radical New Right policies of Thatcher were commended for turning back from the collective to the individual but criticised for not seeing the citizen as part of a wider community, needing government regulation to protect him and her. Mandelson and Liddle were telling no more than the truth in writing that '[New Labour's] strategy is to move forward from where Margaret Thatcher left off'. Thatcherism is truly their chosen heritage, not socialism.

Modernisation and community go together as key words in New Labour speak. In a 1982 lecture in Australia Tony Blair described his search for 'a political philosophy . . . more sensitive, more visionary, in a word more modern, than Marxism'. With this empty nonsense, he welcomed the Social Democratic Party's attempt to 'offer some compromise between the overt callousness of Mrs Thatcher and the old-fashioned collectivism of Labour'. Blair was undoubtedly impressed with the success of the Liberals in retaining their national vote, by what they called 'community politics', which meant fighting on local issues to win seats on local government Councils, when winning seats in Parliament for a third party was ruled out by the electoral system.

He argued that 'A local party should grow out of a local community, the party having roots in that community . . . and involving themselves . . . in community groups or local campaigns . . .'

The Meaning of 'Community'

New Labour's concept of community is, however, highly ambiguous. It has in this passage a comforting local sense, which is by later sleight of hand extended to the whole nation and linked to the idea of a social market. Thus, when Mandelson and Liddle came to revise their presentation of social democracy, they did not exactly offer 'covert' callousness, but what they called 'a more rounded approach'. They recognised uncomfortably that David Owen's

> 'concept of the social market as essentially putting people in boxes . . . the combination of individualism in people's economic lives with social concern outside them . . . finds a parallel in the attitudes that Kenneth Clarke and Conservatives like him would strike today'.

And they are not yet, perhaps, ready to welcome Kenneth Clarke into their project. He might after all prove to be too far to the left for them. So the spin doctors offer something they call 'community [as] a robust and powerful idea . . . at the heart of the stakeholder economy New Labour wishes to create.'

This then is the 'more rounded approach':

'Notions of partnership and community should influence all aspects of our lives. Enterprise is applauded, but it has responsibilities. Social rights — for instance to greater equality of opportunity — are properly emphasised, but at every point rights go along with matching obligations. Unlike the Owenite SDP, New Labour marries the social market with more traditional Labour values of community and responsibility.'

This is not the place for a philosophical examination of the relationship of rights and obligations. But we have to notice that the word 'community' has different meanings which lead to ambiguities, possibly deliberate, in its use by Tony Blair and his spin doctors. The different meanings arise from the origins of the word passing from Latin through French into English, from a word meaning fellowship, literally oneness, to the wider notion of some corporate body but with a sense of common identity running through it all. The confusion arises because in its original sense a community is held together by norms of behaviour which are internalised and self-enforced. Usually, this is based on one variant or another of common ownership, as in a family or club or commune. No external rules or laws are needed to bind such an entity and therefore there is no special 'caste' of enforcers of norms, since these hold solely because of a shared perception of right and wrong. In the wider sense, people often speak of a 'community' when they mean a society, in which external rules and regulations are developed, and need to be policed by separate bodies of law-men. Then it is really misleading to speak of a 'community', if by this is meant a fellowship which is spontaneously regulated by shared values. Of course, people often use the same word for both senses, but this leads to confusion. Many sociologists use the word 'association' for the wider body, so as to avoid any muddle about two very different kinds of 'community'.

We have come to the conclusion that Tony Blair's script-writers may be deliberately seeking to muddle the wider association of a nation with the comforting sense of a close community, by flitting backwards and forwards between the two concepts, without ever specifying precisely which it is they mean. Thus, when Blair says that he sees 'a new settlement between the individual and society which determines both their rights and obligations . . . and protects individuals from the possibility of abuse by the very action [of government] supposed to assist them', the source of this settlement is not explained. But the reader is left with a fuzzy feeling that recognition of the wider community somehow settles the matter. The idea of a contract between citizen and state is something that social philosophers have argued about down the centuries, but it must be clear that the settlement is something that requires external rules and enforcement, and not just regulation on self-enforcing moral principles. So it exists, not in a true 'community' but in an 'association' in the sociological sense.

Tony Blair's appeal to ethical values as the basis of his concept of community will engage us in a moment. Here we have to note that his shift from 'old-fashioned' collective action to a supposed wider sense of 'community' has implied the abandonment by Labour not only of social ownership but also of its link with the Unions. Within a limited but more effective system of regulation than that of the Tories, it was propounded that the market would allow the individual to create a tide of wealth which in President Kennedy's phrase 'raised all boats, large and small'. That some would be found to be holed and unseaworthy or too small for their safety mattered not. Freed from old-fashioned trade union ideas of class struggle, of capital versus labour, of strikes and lock-outs, it would be possible to appeal to all to row together in the interests of a mythical 'community'.

The replacement of what Mandelson and Liddle call the 'infamous Clause IV' commitment to social ownership ended also the commitment to 'the most equitable distribution of the fruits of industry' and 'the best obtainable system of popular administration of each industry or service'. These were essential parts of the Clause omitted by Mandelson and Liddle when they came to quote from it. That leaves Labour without any commitment either to the redistribution of income and wealth or to industrial democracy.

The trick becomes clear when it is claimed that the so-called

'new conception of community . . . where all citizens have a stake and where a sense of social justice and fairness govern (sic) decision-making by those in power'

replaces any idea of opposition between capital and labour. This had to be done, it was argued, to make Labour what was called 'electable'. It was claimed by the modernisers, and accepted by the gurus of *Marxism Today*, for which Blair wrote about his vision of a new political settlement, that the links with the unions and with the nationalised industries were deeply unpopular and had caused the winter of discontent and the Social Democrats' defection. Even old socialists like Stuart Hall accepted this, but we shall show good reasons for rejecting the claim as wholly untrue.

A Party of Labour?

Without the old Clause IV and estranged from the unions, New Labour was ready to appeal to the contented classes, and to seek and win financial support from many rich men and women. Dinners at £500 a head are regularly organised by Eric Hobsbawm's daughter for people with that sort of money for a meal. There they can meet Mr Blair and learn what he plans to do about not taxing them. Above all, freedom from Clause IV meant that New Labour could hope to have Mr Murdoch's tabloid press on its side in an election. This offered a Faustian solution to all Labour's perceived problems at one stroke, but it meant, we believe, nothing less than a profound break in the history of the British Labour movement. Whether Tony Blair will actually get the prize he aspires to remains to be seen.

In the past, Labour governments and the trade unions can be criticised for not doing enough to protect the poorer half or three-fifths of the population, but without such a government, those working people who have no professional skills or property of their own will have lost their only protector. The community to which Mr Blair expects individuals to appeal is not simply an amorphous body; it is a fiction and a deception, like that contradiction in terms, Mrs Thatcher's 'Community Charge'. It is a false prospectus, the same trick that is perpetrated when it is said that disabled people will receive 'care in the community', because funds have been cut for proper care. As a result, we have schizophrenics jumping into zoo cages to play with tigers and deranged people committing random murders, because it is no-one's job to look after them.

There are of course some really caring communities in the original sense, where battered women, single parents, minority groups, old people, the homeless — may sometimes be able to find or create supporting groups. But most individual employees, the unemployed and even the self-employed need trade unions and other guilds or protective associations; not loose affinities or primary 'communities', but rule-governed associations empowered to negotiate on their behalf, to reach accords and to make rules which can be enforced. All these in turn need a protective framework of laws to uphold social care. It is the argument of this book that this cannot simply be a matter of responsive regulation but has to be an actively interventionary force, initiating policy. Otherwise, at least half the population will feel themselves to be, and will actually be, locked out. It was a symbolic moment when the Tory government abolished the one department of state which had a responsibility for the employees — the so-called Department of Employment. It will be a test of New Labour's values whether it is reinstated by a New Labour government.

It is not enough for Tony Blair to say that he will give to the TUC the same recognition as to the CBI. In a thousand ways the CBI already has recognition, not only by ease of access to government, but automatically by the power of owners to own and of managers to manage. There can be no evenhandedness between the strong and the weak, between the rich and the poor, between the securely employed or self employed and the insecurely employed and the unemployed. They cannot be said to belong to the same community. However much Tony Blair may appeal to Christian charity and to community feeling in its original sense, some are included and some excluded. And so there must be everywhere a Party to represent and champion the excluded as well as the more fortunate people in society. This has always been the rationale for a party of labour and beyond that for a democratic socialism with its roots in both Christian and humanist traditions.

Tony Blair frequently talks about the need for Labour to be inclusive, most recently in an article on 'Ideological Blurring' (in the June 1996 issue of *Prospect*), but the implication is that the inclusiveness should defer to the needs of top people rather than expressing those of the people at the bottom.

'The totalising ideologies of left and right no longer hold much purchase', he writes and continues, 'We have to solve our problems as a nation.'

We have never been much enamoured of the talk of ideologies except in their original meaning, that of offering false choices, but we are even less keen on rhetoric about the 'nation'. We do, however, recognise that the employers and the employed have different interests. This is not a matter of ideology but of fact. Sellers of labour want a high price; buyers a low one. And what could be more 'ideological' than the appeal that our problems should be solved within the framework of 'one nation'? To be fair, though, we need to start from Tony Blair's self-proclaimed first principles, by exploring the origins of his Christian socialist and communitarian convictions.

Tony Blair's Christianity

Here is what Blair himself and his spin doctors have to say about the leader as a Christian communitarian:

> '. . . my view of Christian values led me to oppose what I perceived to be the narrow self-interest that Conservatism — particularly its modern, more right-wing form — represents.' (Tony Blair. 'Why I am a Christian', *Sunday Telegraph*, 7-4-96)

This is clear enough but it is given a twist by the spin doctors:

> 'To create opportunities of self-fulfilment for all, which was the mainspring of his Christian sense of social justice, it was necessary to change people's social conditions. In other words, Christianity was not enough by itself — you needed politics and organisation, too, to improve society.' (Peter Mandelson and Roger Liddle on 'Labour's Leader' in *The Blair Revolution*, p.33)

When on Easter Day, 1996, the most holy day in the Christian calendar, Tony Blair published in the Conservative *Sunday Telegraph* a major interview entitled 'Why I am a Christian', this was a statement not only of a personal faith but of a public commitment. It demanded the most serious consideration from its readers and was heralded with much editorial comment. Very few political leaders of recent times can have presented themselves so strongly for religious endorsement. It is hard to think of another contemporary British politician of whom it might be said that the 'social commitment of Christianity' is his inspiration. One has to go back to a Cripps or a Gladstone to find an equal protestation of Christian commitment to politics.

In continental Europe things are different. All the Christian Democrats make this claim. This is possible because the Roman Catholic Church is *not* a state religion in the way that the Anglican Church is. In the modern secular world, there is something in the very idea of a state religion that invites scepticism. It is also the case that in a succession of Papal Encyclicals from *de Rerum Novarum* in 1891, through *Quadragesimo Anno*, 40 years on in the middle of the slump of 1931, down to *Centesimus Annus* on the centenary of *Rerum Novarum*, the Catholic Church has laid down a social policy of giving workers 'their due', while defending the family and private property, if not necessarily capitalism itself. This policy is held to guide all Catholics, even Prime Ministers. It has not always been seen to work very effectively.

For an aspirant to the British premiership, it was a bold thing for Tony Blair to do to present himself as something more than a nominal Christian. But since the *Sunday Telegraph* article he has acted even more boldly in allowing it to be known that he takes communion not only as an Anglican but also as a Catholic. How far is this the result of genuine uncertainty? Has Mr Mandelson seized the opportunity to please voters of both persuasions? If so, why stop at two?

According to John Rentoul, one of his biographers, Blair's ideas were developed in a circle of friends at Oxford chosen for their radicalism. Geoff Gallop came from the International Marxist Group, in which, he says 'Tariq Ali was my guru', Peter Thomson was an Australian Anglican Socialist, studying theology, and Olara Otunna was a Ugandan refugee. The reading of the group, reports Rentoul, ranged from Tawney and William Morris through to Gramsci and Isaac Deutscher. Such a menu might be expected to produce at least some less respectable thoughts than those expressed in the *Sunday Telegraph*, but, apparently, they led him to join first the Christian Church and then the Labour Party.

Some commentators on this interview and some reviewers of Mandelson and Liddle have suggested that the religious bits are purely for decoration. We doubt this. It is impossible to be certain, because the political programme of New Labour is founded on a whole number of ambiguities. There is a theology of ambiguity as well; it is a well developed one, but it hardly helps anyone to address serious moral questions. As for the politics of ambiguity, they can only in the end be interpreted in the light of the actions which they generate.

We think that we might have been more comfortably at home with the young man who was exploring the relationship between moral values and political action at Oxford in the early 1970s than we are with the present leader of a 'socialism' based on the dynamism of the capitalist market. Nonetheless, the rhetoric of Christian conviction, of moral values and community constantly recurs in Blair's speeches and in the statements of his acolytes diffused through a wide variety of newspapers and television presentations. We propose to take all this seriously and to examine it closely, alongside the inheritance that the new leader claims from the Christian Socialists and, in particular, from the Scottish theologian, John MacMurray.

The Influence of John MacMurray

In tracing the origins of Blair's socialism, Mandelson and Liddle tell us that

> 'it was MacMurray's interpretation of the social commitment of Christianity through the idea of community, rather than personal experience of extreme poverty and hardship, that inspired Blair's political awakening.' (M&L p.33)

We are told in this connection that Blair's father was a 'modestly well-off lawyer'. We know rather more from Martin Jacques about Blair's father. Before he joined the army at the outbreak of war, he had been the Scottish Secretary of the Young Communist League, having been brought up on Clydeside by a locally well-known Communist couple, a Govan shipyard rigger and his wife, who was widely known as a regular and very visible seller of the *Daily Worker*. At that time, the Scottish YCL Secretary, as a full-time post, was a key cadre appointment in the British Communist Party, then dominated by Scots. Blair senior followed youth leader John Gollan, and Gollan, of course, was to become the national Party leader. Doubtless, Britain's Communists saw leadership potential in Blair senior as well. They were to be disappointed. Leo Blair came out of the army a major and, after studying for a law degree, apparently became in time a Conservative of what his son calls the Thatcher-Tebbitt meritocratic mould. But did none of the Scottish revolutionary tradition rub off on the grandson?

One can only speculate about the attraction of MacMurray for the young Blair. Did he see in MacMurray some traits he admired in the father he so shocked at Oxford by appearing as a long haired, unconventionally dressed left-wing hippie? There is a curious similarity between the political evolution of the father and MacMurray's intellectual journeying over the years. MacMurray was also a Scot, whose early years coincided with the depths of the depression. The response of many Scots was to embrace communism and look to the Soviet Union as a wonderland, where there was no unemployment. As a Christian theologian, MacMurray sought to reconcile that undoubted fact with the atheism of Soviet society. Like other Christians of the time, faced by the inhumanity of capitalism, he was attracted to the Communist response and attempted to see it dialectically as a development of Christianity. He wrote a book on *The Philosophy of Communism* and contributed with a number of Christian socialists to a collection of essays published in 1935 on *Christianity and the Social Revolution*.

MacMurray went to the Soviet Union with Dr Hewlett Johnson, the 'Red Dean' of Canterbury, and visited the International Brigade in Spain. He genuinely believed that a new and more moral society was being built in Russia and discounted the stories of terror and of purges that were coming out of the Soviet Union at that time. He was not a traditional Christian socialist like Archbishop Temple or R.H. Tawney; his sympathies were more with what were then called Communist 'fellow-travellers'. After the war he abandoned his enthusiasm for Soviet Communism and his writings became more philosophical and increasingly concerned with personal moral problems of the family, as in his 1954 Gifford Lectures at Glasgow University. His interest remained in the area that seems to have much interested Blair — the problem of relating the community of fellowship to the political actions of the state. How, one wonders, did this particular man come to affect Blair so strongly, if Mandelson is to be believed? Blair never met MacMurray. Although he and his friend Thompson once set off to do so, Thompson met the old man but Blair did not.

Tony was the second child, adored by his mother, and as he was musical, he was sent to Durham Choir School, which is a fee-paying preparatory school, and then to Fettes, a 'public school' sometimes referred to as the 'Eton of Scotland'. We would be the last to question Blair's convictions because of the misfortune of his educational background, and we are told by one of his biographers that Blair was not happy at Fettes. What was the attraction to this man of ethical socialism? Was it his way of adjusting to his father's revolt against grandfather's revolutionary socialism? What was this 'ethical socialism' which Mandelson and Liddle tell us is

> 'the key to understanding everything about Blair and his determination to transform the Labour Party . . .
>
> 'an ethical socialism which draws on the ideas of Ruskin and Tawney, but is also a modern socialism which takes account of changes in society and the economy.' (M&L, pp.32-3)

So, let us look at this part of the socialist tradition.

CHAPTER 2

Tony Blair and Christian Socialism

'We cannot exist in a moral vacuum. If we do not learn and then teach the value of what is right and what is wrong, then the result is simply moral chaos which engulfs us all.'

(Tony Blair, speaking after the murder of the two-year-old Jamie Bulger by two young boys in February 1993)

'It was MacMurray's interpretation of the social commitment of Christianity through the idea of community, rather than personal experience of extreme poverty and hardship, that inspired Blair's political awakening.'

(Mandelson & Liddle, op.cit., p.33)

In these quotations we have two expressions of Blair's Christianity — the personal and the social. What kind of Christian is Blair the Labour politician? Christianity, like other religions has, indeed, two aspects to it — a sustaining personal faith and a church of worshippers, often associated with what is called a 'national community', Church of England, Church of Scotland, Greek, Russian, Serbian Orthodox and so on. In the church itself there is also a real community of the spirit, represented in the Communion. But extending this to the wider society, as Blair has sought to do, is not legitimate. Here he is following MacMurray, for whom religion was a social activity. It was the way in which human beings 'express their human nature' he believed and 'therefore that all religion is the expression of community'. But extending the Church's community of the spirit to something much wider is a fiction and a very dangerous one, as MacMurray understood when he continued:

'. . . every nation which claims independence as a historic group, has a religion of its own. There is no difficulty in understanding why, during the late war [1914-18], every nation appealed to its God for support and for victory. It was appealing, from the human point of view, to its own sense of national community.'

A State Church or Universal Religion

2 senses of community

Here we can see the real dangers which arise from confusing the two senses of community — the self regulating group and the outer regulated society. Along with this we can see the trick of extending the fellowship in Christ to the state church, against which so many dissident communities have rebelled, defending their ethical norms against external laws. But MacMurray also believed that St Paul had established Christianity as a 'universal religion' for all peoples, 'the universal community of mankind . . . not yet a fact of experience but still to be realised in the future.' This is the Christian vision, a far more ambitious perspective than that of Labour's Clause IV. In historical fact St Paul and the authors of the Acts of the Apostles succeeded only in creating the outer form of an inner community in a religion for the Roman Empire. This was difficult enough in itself, because it meant combining in the record of the sayings of Jesus both the message of the revolutionary Nazarene carpenter's son, preaching the kingdom of heaven on earth, when the poor shall have their inheritance, and the requirement of a citizen of Rome to 'render unto Caesar the things that are Caesar's'.

When Mr Blair in his *Sunday Telegraph* interview sympathised with the supposed dilemma of Pontius Pilate bowing to a Jewish mob and condemning the revolutionary to the cross in place of the common thief, he was accepting a story written up afterwards to assuage Roman feelings. It is an interesting fact that Blair's *Sunday Telegraph* interviewer should have been Matthew d'Ancona, who happens to be one of the few people who still believe that the gospels were written by those who had witnessed Christ's death. All biblical scholars, according to Graham Stanton (*Prospect*, April 1996) now accept that they were composed in the second century. It was anyway an incredible story that a Roman procurator with a reputation, according to the contemporary Jewish historian, Josephus Flavius, for being 'inflexible, merciless and obstinate', sent especially from Rome to stamp out a Jewish rebellion, should have suffered from any moral compunction in deciding on Jesus's crucifixion. But it has been grist to the mill of anti-Semites ever since to lay the death of Jesus at the door of the Jews.

Next year perhaps Mr Blair may find grounds for proposing the merits of Judas Iscariot. In the meantime, the story serves to reveal the dilemma of Christianity as both a state religion, with all the pomp and ceremony of the established church, bishops in gaiters with purple blouses and gigantic pectoral crosses, on the one hand; poor parish priests with a message of redemption, comforting dying men and women

and inspiring revolutionary struggles, on the other, along with monks
— and nuns too — agonising on their knees on the cold stone floors of
a tiny cell. It is from the Christian belief in the community of the spirit,
implying the equal worth of all men and women in the sight of God,
and contempt for the worthlessness of treasures laid up on earth, that
Christian socialism was born and drew its strength.

Christianity and Socialism

Christian socialism has a long history of dissident voices in England —
from John Ball's rallying cry in the Peasants Revolt of 1381, 'When
Adam delved and Eve span, who was then the Gentleman?' through
Bunyan's Pilgrim's Progress, the 'Levellers' in Cromwell's
Commonwealth and Blake's vision of Jerusalem, down to the Christian
Social Movement of Charles Kingsley, James Ludlow and F.D. Maurice
in the 1850s, John Ruskin in the 1870s, R.H. Tawney, the socialist
agitator, and Conrad Noel, the 'red vicar' of Thaxted, in the 1920s and
30s. By the 1940s this tradition even received the blessing of a great
prince of the Church, William Temple, as Archbishop of Canterbury
no less, in his commitment to the Labour Party, to eliminating the
'disease of unemployment' and elaborating a 'Christian social
programme, in the sense of one which seeks to embody Christian
principles', one that was far more radical than any subsequently adopted
by Labour.

At the beginning of Archbishop Temple's book *Christianity and the Social
Order* in which he says that he sets out to 'rebuild the shattered social
teaching of the Church', he recalls how, among the early Christians

> 'the institution of property was regarded as rooted in sin; for if all men love
> God with all their hearts and their neighbours as themselves, they would
> cheerfully labour for the common good and would take for themselves no
> more than their fair share . . . God wished the earth to be the common
> possession of all men, to produce its fruits for all men, but avarice created
> the rights of property.'

When Mr Blair in his Easter Day interview asked whether Tories could
truly be Christians, some of them were very cross and one Tory MP
replied that 'anyone who believed in original sin must be a conservative.'
This was perhaps not just a joke but a deep insight into the original sin
of private property. So it would have seemed to William Temple.

Early in this century Temple had argued in favour of common

ownership, long before Clause IV was agreed in 1918 and denounced in 1995. His words bear repeating at length:

> 'This is not an economic question. It is a question touching the human personality. It asks what are the deepest and most potent motives in the human soul. The question is not economic — to the Christian it is religious . . .
>
> If Christianity is to be applied to the economic system, an organisation which rests primarily on the principle of competition must give way to one which rests primarily on cooperation. . . .
>
> The question of the competitive principle is driven down into the labour market, so that men compete against each other for the right to live. Go and see it at work in the London docks [today we might say: in any job queue]. If one man is to secure the means of feeding himself and his family, he must be depriving another. Is that an exhibition of brotherhood? Such a system embodies no principle but selfishness and mutual antagonism . . .
>
> As citizens we are guilty of a whole system of oppression: it is there, we tolerate it, and so become responsible for its results. There is nothing inevitable in it: it is all the result of human choices. I do not mean that anyone deliberately put it there; it is the greatest fluke in creation. But it is the net result of innumerable human choices, and by human choices it can be modified. Here lies our duty — and our guilt.'

How are we to judge the claim of Tony Blair to stand in that tradition? We may remember how one of the Nineteenth Century Christian Socialists, Charles Kingsley, taught us, when we read his book *The Water Babies*, that there were two good fairies: Mrs Do-as-you-would-be-done-by, all radiant and gentle, encouraging good works, and Mrs Be-done-by-as-you-did, sternly admonishing all transgressions. The first is at the heart of socialist ethics and does not need a Christian justification, only that we should recognise all our fellow human beings as having equal rights with ours. The original words are put by Matthew into Christ's mouth:

> 'all things whatsoever ye would that men should do to you, do ye even so to them; for this is the law and the prophets.'

The second has an element of retribution in it, nearer to the Old Testament dictum: an eye for an eye and a tooth for a tooth. Christian forgiveness does not figure high on such an agenda.

It is to be supposed that when Mr Blair spoke of the need 'to be tough on crime and tough on the causes of crime', he was following Mrs Be-done-by-as-you-did, who put a stone in Tom's mouth instead of a

22

sweet because he had similarly abused the sea urchins, and who bricked Mr Grimes up in a chimney, because he had chased the apprentice sweeps into chimneys all his working life. Mr Blair is not at all alone in his interpretation, but some Christians believe that they should turn the other cheek when struck. Many Christians believe that they must be pacifists and renounce all wars and use of retribution and violence in human relations. They quote from St. Matthew's gospel, Jesus speaking to Peter:

> 'Lord, how oft shall my brother sin against me, and I forgive him? till seven times? Jesus saith unto him I say not unto thee, Until seven times: but until seventy times seven.'

Christianity, Humanism and Marxism

Do-as-you-would-be-done-by, however, is rather different from the principle of inevitable retribution in Be-done-by-as-you-did. It derives its strength as a practical prescription for social behaviour, not only from the scriptures but from the thought of Immanuel Kant, who, though a Christian himself, worked out a principle of ethics that did not require support from any otherworldly authority. Kant started from the assumption that our own humanity was the supreme good, so that the *golden rule* binding upon all of us was

> 'always to treat humanity in your own person and in others as an end in itself and never as a means merely.'

This was a universal principle, and behaviour could be based on this, because any dereliction would be destructive of humanity if it became universal. Generations of humanists have embraced this idea, so that it is by no means a Christian monopoly. But the 'golden rule' is, to say the least of it, difficult to uphold in the real practical world.

As humanists ourselves, we find that we are often in sympathy with Christians and troubled like them by the difficulty of applying Kant's rule to our economy. In present day capitalist society, all economic activity, all productive organisation is in fact based on the systematic violation of Kant's imperative. In every office, factory, mine and government department we find that men and women, far from being considered 'ends in themselves' are compelled to labour as 'means only', in order to realise goals that have been determined by other people. Often their work serves to destroy the very environment on which their long-term survival depends. Masses of employees who work for wages find themselves used as means to others' ends, augmenting the power and prestige of others, enriching others, and enlarging others' influence and status. Worse: employees are not only subordinates, but they find their subordination intensified by the fact that their interests and aspirations can be imposed upon and manipulated by social forces which are quite beyond their individual or collective control. The more they earn for others the more power this gives to others to range against them. We shall provide chapter and verse in subsequent pages to justify these assertions.

This, Blair might say, is a Marxist way of looking at alienation. It is; but it has a humanist as well as a Christian foundation. This was very clear to John MacMurray, whose early writings included a careful and sympathetic examination of Marx's youthful discovery of alienation. Blair says that he rejected Marxism after reading MacMurray, because he saw that

> 'Marxism was essentially determinist . . . it left out free will . . . it suppressed the individual by starting with society.'

In fact, this is not a criticism MacMurray made of Marx, as he engaged with him at the beginning of his academic career. Far from it, MacMurray was very excited by the ideas sparked in the young Marx's critique of Christianity through his argument with Ludwig Feuerbach. MacMurray's search for a synthesis as he saw it of Christianity and Communism preoccupied him throughout his writing in the 1930s:

> 'Throughout the history of Christianity the conception of the communist society in which property is held in common for the needs of all, and in which brotherhood, equality and freedom are the governing principles of social organisation, has emerged time and time again. There is nothing surprising in this . . . such a society is implied directly in the teaching of Jesus . . . Christianity is the source of communism . . . Communism, whatever its exponents say, has rescued the essential core of a real belief in God, which organised Christianity has in our day largely lost.'

There is thus an irony in the Christian-Communist source of Blair's conversion. Of course, MacMurray of the 1930s was not MacMurray of the 1950s, from whom Blair learnt to justify his own commitment later against socialism. For MacMurray had come to condemn the economic necessity which he later believed he found in Marxism, and it is this which Blair sees as

> 'obscuring the importance of personal responsibility, concentrating only on the social determinants that contribute to individual behaviour.'

'For the left of centre', Blair writes, 'the great rediscovery has been the early social-democratic view that better social conditions enhance personal responsibility; they are not a substitute for it.' (*Marxism Today*, 1991)

No Marxist ever said they were, although Stalin may have found some theologians to preach something of the sort in the distortion of Marx's humanism that became fashionable in MacMurray's younger days. Legions of Russian Marxists as well as Christians and other dissidents perished in Stalin's Gulag, in protesting against the betrayal of everything that Marx stood for. MacMurray was mistaken in his gullibility, to believe only the best of Stalin's Russia: Blair is equally mistaken in his gullibility in rejecting everything that MacMurray saw to be truthful in the Marxian vision.

Above all, Marx's humanism was to be practised. It had practical maxims that are still burningly relevant for all those who have work and for those who have not, such as 'The true economy is economy of labour time'. Thus, Marx welcomed the Ten Hour Day and the formation of cooperatives in the second half of the Nineteenth Century, as victories of the 'political economy of labour' over the 'political economy of capital' just because they gave priority to human needs over the return to capital and in so doing awoke new opportunities for working people. The freedom of shorter working time enhances *both* social conditions *and* personal responsibility, which Blair seeks to set against each other.

Blair's attempt to distance himself from Marx, like his attack on Marxists in the old Labour Party, will certainly win favour from those who truly fear the implications of either the Christian or the humanistic belief that human beings must be treated as ends and not as means. But the argument for individualism as the enemy of socialism has to be examined further.

Individualism and Socialism

Blair appeals to 'a sense of individual duty [from which] we connect the greater good and the interests of the community — a principle the Church celebrates in the sacrament of the communion.' It may do, but this is just the point at which Blair confuses the two senses of community. Individual duty rules the smaller community; it cannot rule the wider society, based as it is on private ownership. The humanist has equally a sense of individual duty, to do-as-you-would-be-done-by, which leads him to understand his social responsibilities and, if he is a Marxist, to see economic exploitation as the greatest and most widespread denial of men's and women's humanity. The humanist like the Christian seeks to 'treat people as of equal worth'. This is what Blair says is the crucial difference between his position and the Marxist and Tory extremes. But it requires positive social organisation in the wider society to protect those whose position in the market, and especially the labour market, is intrinsically weak. To talk of community while welcoming 'the rigour of competitive markets' is frankly double talk and runs counter to all the social teaching of the Christian churches.

Blair's emphasis on the individual reflects both the capitalist economic system of wage labour and the limits of the democratic state. An employee is taken on by an employer as an individual and recognised as such in the firm's records and accounts and in national statistics. But individuals are also persons. William Temple in criticising the economists' treatment of individuals as competitors in the market, distinguishes individuality and personality, quoting from the French philosopher, Jacques Maritain:

> 'Every person is an individual, but his individuality is what marks him off from others; it is a principle of division; whereas personality is social and only in his social relationship can a man be a person.'

It is so obvious in the origin of the two words: the one meaning quite materially something that cannot be further divided, and therefore, suitable for statistical enumeration; the other taken from the *persona* (the mask in classical theatre) which we wear and thereby show the character we are, necessarily in relation to others.

Mrs Thatcher wanted to count us all as individuals and families and deny the existence of society. That is true for statisticians and is the ultimate abstraction of 'economic man'. But for a Christian politician it is the final heresy, while for humanists it is a libel on the humanity which we learn from one another. So, Mr Blair says that he wants to put something he calls 'community' in the place of society, but what does he mean — the self-regulated community or the externally regulated community? He too, like Mrs Thatcher, starts from individuals and families. In speaking about the murder of Jamie Bulger, he said:

> 'I have no doubt that the breakdown in law and order is intimately linked to the break-up of a strong sense of community. And the break-up of community in turn is, to a crucial degree, consequent on the breakdown in family life . . . It is largely from family discipline that social discipline and a

sense of responsibility is learned . . . [Public policy should] help create the best circumstances for the family to prosper.'

Reinforcing the family may well be one of the aims of public policy. Each in his own way, Hitler, Stalin and Mussolini all tried. We are left asking where the rather forbiddingly phrased 'family discipline' is to come from if it is not internal. Family policy externally applied, whether draconian or liberal, can hardly overcome the kind of social breakdown which follows when unemployment lays waste not only families but whole villages, towns and regions. It leaves unanswered what public support should be given in the most crucial matter of all, the guarantee of the right to work for a living. This is not a matter which individuals can solve by 'getting on their bikes'. If some do and move to new areas to work, families are disrupted, single parent families proliferate, and without public action mass unemployment remains.

If individuals cannot solve their economic problems on their own, still less can they hope to act politically as individuals. Mr Blair's guru, John MacMurray, was particularly clear about the limitations of what he termed 'bourgeois democracy'.

> 'The idea of this democratic state is expressed in the formula: "One man, one vote". That is its symbol of freedom and equality. In other words, the man appears in the state organisation as an *individual*, and therefore, all men are equal. The equality, however, is purely formal, almost a numerical equality, which is only achieved by separating his legal existence from his social existence as this particular person leading this particular life in society . . . The fact that he may be unable to take advantage of his freedom owing to poverty, or the condition under which he earns his living has nothing to do with the matter, because it belongs to the sphere of his *private* life.'

Could Tony Blair have possibly remembered this passage from his reading at Oxford, and turned it around to serve his political purpose in re-forming the Labour Party from a party of particular (and often disagreeing) persons searching for a socialist democracy into a party of individuals which could be managed for a political project which was to stay firmly within bourgeois democracy? But it is persons who exist, and as Temple said, 'the richer his personal relationship, the more fully personal he will be'. It grates on the ear today that the gender is always masculine but Temple's next sentences have great political importance:

> 'For these relationships exist in the whole network of communities, associations and fellowships. It is in these that the real wealth of human life

consists. If then it is the function of the state to promote human well-being, it must foster these many groupings of its citizens.'

If Blair's Christian beliefs have led him to see community as well as family in this manner, then we can test the result as Temple did:

> 'A democracy which is to be Christian must not only tolerate but encourage minor communities as at once the expression and the arena of personal freedom; and its structure must be such as to serve this end.'

And in the very next paragraph Temple wrote

> 'It is impossible to say how much we owe in our own country to the schooling in democratic habits provided, first by the old Trade Guilds, then, when the fellowship of trade had been broken up from the release of individual acquisitiveness, by the Trade Unions, and ever since the seventeenth century by the dissenting congregations.'

Mr Blair has continuously sought to distance himself from the unions, which were Labour's foundation. What lessons has he taken from the dissenting congregations which nourished an early Christian socialism and what can his politics of Christian community deliver to the English, Scottish, Welsh, Irish and Caribbean and Asian and other national 'communities' in Britain? At the heart of his answer to this question must be his understanding of the meaning of equality.

Tawney on Equality

In contributing an essay to a collection of Christian writings for the Student Christian Movement in 1993 (*Reclaiming the Ground*), Blair wrote of

> 'equality as the main concern of democratic socialism — for the sake of the proper relationships between human beings, community is central to Christianity — inherent in it are the demands for personal and social change and hopes for a better world.'

Ronald Preston reviewing the essay for the Institute for Economic Affairs, commented that it showed either a certain optimistic blandness or blindness about the realities of capitalist society.

Had Blair attended to the warnings of R.H. Tawney, one of the ethical socialists he is supposed to model himself on, he would have been warned about these realities. In Tawney's famous book on *Equality*, dedicated to Sidney and Beatrice Webb, 'with gratitude and affection', Tawney wrote:

> 'The inequality which they [the socialists] deplore is not inequality of personal gifts, but of the social and economic environment. They are concerned not with a biological phenomenon but with a spiritual relation and the conduct to be based on it. Their view in short, is that, because men are men, social institutions — property rights, and the organisation of industry, and the system of public health and education should be planned, as far as possible, to emphasise and strengthen, not the class differences that divide, but the common humanity which unites, them.'

And, lest it be supposed that the rejection of class difference as a basis of social policy implied any doubt in Tawney's mind about the wasteful and oppressive nature of such divisions between the few owners and the many workers, it is only necessary to read Tawney's detailed examination of the concentrations of economic power in his day and their effects on the liberty of the subject. He rejects all the arguments of the coal owners and the industrialists for the retention of capitalist enterprise.

> 'In an industrial civilisation', he writes, 'the great Leviathan is not the State . . . It is the sleek, serviceable but still not wholly domesticated monster, which sprawls heavily over colliery villages and factory towns . . . "When he raiseth himself up, the mighty" — and how much more mere cabinets! — "are afraid. Darts are to him as stubble". Indeed, as he owns five-sixths of the press, he is a principle purveyor of darts himself.'

We shall show in the next chapters that little has changed. When Tawney tackles the old argument that inequality is inseparable from freedom, and that all attempts to reduce inequalities end up only in reducing freedom, he builds an alternative contrary argument on Professor Pollard's aphorism that 'There is only one solution of the problem of liberty and it lies in equality.' And the equality he turns to is equality in the work place. In his last major political essay (reprinted in 1966 in *The Radical Tradition*) Tawney appealed for 'a systematic attempt to democratise the routine of industrial life.' This attempt was in vain; all those social democrats from Bill Rodgers to Shirley Williams, who lionised him and reprinted his book, then strode off purposely in the opposite direction. Has there now been a change of heart? And do Blair's phrases about community and fairness mean the same thing as Tawney meant by equality? Hardly.

Capitalism has to be ended).

Our Standpoint in our Critique of New Labour

It is the firm belief of socialists that the system of capitalism has to be ended. Christians believe similarly that Christ's kingdom of heaven is to be on earth, not immediately by some messianic deliverance, but in good time, by steadily working towards that end. Kant thought his imperative followed logically from our common humanity, but we are bound to conclude from experience that no such logic has asserted itself. Common humanity does not exist yet, and to bring it about we must first bend all of our efforts to reduce and overcome the power of one person over another. Only then might that beneficial logic take effect and rule all human action and all social institutions, so that human potential may begin to be realised for all. Until then, as William Morris had it: 'No man is good enough to be another man's master.' And socialist women will agree that this maxim should be blind to gender.

It is not enough, however, to reiterate that every effort should be made to diminish the power that one man or woman can exercise over another or even to insist that we must seek to establish an equality more profound than that of mere material means. Moral equality would surely mean to treat every life as an end in itself, rejecting the subordination of people so that they become mere instruments of others' ambitions or desires.

We need to recognise that the present inequality, which follows from the systematic flouting of such a morality, far from being eased, has been made consistently more intransigent by economic and technical 'progress'. Such progress perfects material objects, but adds up to moral decline. As William Temple wrote echoing William Morris's *News from Nowhere*

> 'The immense possibilities opened up to industrialisation so fascinated men that they ceased to ask what was the purpose of this vast mass of production. It tended to be an end in itself. It was no longer subordinated to the general scheme of a complete human life in which it should be a part.'

So we are going to judge Tony Blair and his New Labour by what is common in the highest Christian and humanistic standards. This is what his promoters have asked for and he deserves no less.

CHAPTER 3

What's Wrong with Capitalism?

'The 1990s will not see the continuing triumph of the market, but its failure.'
Tony Blair, London Review of Books, 1987

'Consequently, it [capitalist society] finds itself in times of stress with masses of unemployed on its hands, whom it considers not as persons having certain needs which must be supplied, but as unwanted material for which there is no present use. Its fundamental value principle, whatever it may be, is certainly not the absolute value of the individual person, but a principle incompatible with this. Such a society may profess to believe in the ultimate value of the individual, but its belief is idealist and illusory. It is divorced from social action. It is not a controlling motive. Instead its principle is the instrumental value of the individual to the social organisation.'
John MacMurray, Creative Society, *p.160*

Here is Tony Blair's chosen mentor telling him straight out that it is just impossible in capitalist society for people to be treated as values in themselves and therefore in this respect of equal worth. Does Mr Blair practice what MacMurray used to preach? He can be forgiven if he does not, since the dereliction is not personal, but lies in the system. He should not then, however, claim that capitalism is compatible with respect for the individual worth of every human being, or that 'socialism' might result from the dynamism of the market. MacMurray knew better. The political economy of capital subordinates humanity to money, quite cynically as in the case of such pretended laws as the Non-Accelerating-Inflation-Rate-of-Unemployment (NAIRU), as if the unemployed could be treated as numbers in a mathematical equation and not as human beings. But the witch doctors who promote such doctrines dominate the thinking of his shadow cabinet.

The Exploitation of Labour

Mr Blair and his promoters make much of the fact that the world has *change led to subservience*

changed and new responses are needed to global capital employing the new technology. It *has* changed and new responses *are* needed. But it has changed for the worse and New Labour's responses are wholly subservient. Today's transnational corporations suck profits out of employees stationed in every part of the world, and, if they are efficient in competition with their rivals, they will invest these profits in ways which will enrich them still further, while diminishing or destroying the expectations of others and, quite possibly even of some or many of their own employees. In this condition great surges in labour productivity only ensure that smaller workforces are able to accomplish greater efforts, often in shorter periods of time, while vast masses are excluded from work and are denied any proper livelihood.

Computers which could liberate men and women from burdensome toil are used instead to intensify that toil for some, while marginalising others. Airline passengers in some European countries may not know that their tickets are now commonly processed 'over the wires' by low paid Indian women working on the other side of the world, and the results flashed back to the automatic printers which issue the tickets in the metropolitan centres. So much of the work that goes into the goods we buy in the supermarkets is unknown to us — the work of families growing and collecting the coffee beans and cocoa beans for our coffee and chocolate, and receiving a single penny for the £'s worth of goods we take from the shelves; the work of young girls in Asia assembling the parts of our TV sets and videos and personal computers, whose eyes give out after a few years of working always through a microscope; the work of women in the poorer regions of Europe itself working long hours at home, as well as bringing up a family, so as to earn money from sewing together the pieces of the jumpers and jerseys we wear. For the Christian these are all our brothers and sisters, and 'in as much as ye do this unto the least of these my brethren, ye have done it unto me'. For humanists, all this pain diminishes mankind and prevents the whole of human society from becoming what it has in itself to be.

By contrast the political economy of labour would share work and incomes, so that none are overworked and none are marginalised even though it is claimed that it might be 'uneconomic' to do so. A political economy of labour invents new institutions such as life-long education with paid educational leave, parental leave, sabbaticals for approved social work. All of these assert the primacy of the human commitment over the money economy. A party of labour may not be able to introduce all such inventions at once, but the aim of full employment with the full

~~~me'LP.~~~

use of such supporting mechanisms would be in the manifesto of any true Labour Party. In New Labour's actual preliminary Manifesto, although the Tories are censured for their cynical creation of unemployment and modest proposals are made for assisting the young unemployed and the long-term unemployed, the aim of full employment does not appear. Neither do any of the new supporting mechanisms which this would require in today's conditions. At its best, this pathetic document is quite simply irrelevant to the solution of the major problem of the day.

This is not surprising in a capitalist party. Do-as-you-would-be-done-by is not a rule which any of the great entrepreneurs of capitalism could dream of applying. If they did so, they would find their task negated, because the organisation of modern industry is dominated by competitive markets which punish Christian tolerance and generosity and reward miserly behaviour. The economy of capital is based on the laws of accumulation, which in turn rest on the realisation of profit, and this can only come from paying workers less than the value of what they produce. Mr Blair's appeal for cooperation in a society of stakeholders implies that the stakes must be at least roughly equal. They are not; and an entrepreneur with a social conscience, seeking to follow the golden rule, would have to say:

> 'If I followed your advice, then I could not work my employees in anti-social shifts, since that is not a pattern of working life which I myself would wish to adopt. Neither could I myself exist on the wages which are paid in my establishments. But if I sought to introduce methods of work which I would easily accept, and standards of remuneration which fit my own style of life, then I would go bankrupt.'

In the event of such a bankruptcy, the livelihoods of everyone concerned would be placed in jeopardy, so that even the effort to act upon the Kantian categorical imperative would result in its infringement. That is why we need a new system without this fearful dysfunction. In the meantime, if we cannot yet live by the golden rule, we can at least act consistently to reduce the power of one man or woman over another, until no power at all exists without freely given consent. This implies industrial as well as social democracy. But this cannot be achieved if competition is put before cooperation.

The Nature of Capital

The conclusion to be drawn from these thoughts is that the attempt to regulate capitalism will always prove transitory. If the regulations 'work' for a time, they will tend to generate efforts to evade, and ultimately to annul, them. And even while they operate, they will never establish the objective rule of do-as-you-would-be-done-by. To do that, the power of private capital has to be challenged and in the end it has to be destroyed. This is because of something in the very nature of capital as the motor of the economy.

Unlike the ownership of land or slaves or gold or precious stones, capital is not accumulated because it gives immediate or direct pleasure in itself. But, although it does not either give any direct physical power, it confers, as Adam Smith recognised, 'a certain command over all the labour or all the produce of labour that is then in the market.'

Capital produces nothing, but can set labour to work to produce not only goods and food and raw materials, but buildings and plant and machines which are then called capital assets. While all these products of labour confer power on the owner of the capital, without labour the capital is of no value. For, while the labourer produces commodities or sells his own power to labour for money so as to buy commodities, with which to live, this is not enough for the owner of the capital. If his money were all used up, he would be no better off than the labourer who has no capital. But by employing labour the capitalist can make more money. This is because the labourer can produce more in value than he or she is paid, and this surplus will accrue to the owner of the capital.

The capitalist does not do this just out of wickedness, but because he is in competition with other owners of capital who are also employing labour. If his labourers do not produce as well as these others, he will find his capital is leaching away. If this situation were to persist, the capital would soon be all gone. So, competition forces capitalists to accumulate a surplus and that accumulation results in capital becoming concentrated on a larger and larger scale; the owners of capital seeking through every means to get their workpeople to produce more surplus whether by the sweat of their brows or by deploying more productive machines or more efficient organisation. There is no way round this on a world scale. Within a single country the surplus of all capitals can be taxed by government for its own needs and to fund the country's services and defence. But there is a limit to this; taxes in one country cannot be much more than in others or the country with the higher taxes will become uncompetitive in world markets, in bidding for new investment.

Unfortunately for capitalist accumulation the goods that are produced from the accumulation have to be sold back to the producers, and if too much surplus has been taken from them, and if too little is recycled through taxes and benefits, they cannot oblige. This is a fearful contradiction for which Keynes proposed the solution of extra government spending from more taxation of the surplus and of those living on it. This worked very well on a national scale for many years, but it collapsed once multinational companies extended their influence under the Keynesian regime, and came to dominate the national economies, switching their surpluses and the location of their activities internationally to wherever taxes or wages or overheads were lowest.

Inevitable Inequality

The natural tendency of capitalism is to generate and deepen inequality. Capital is continuously concentrated. Competition inevitably creates winners and losers. The rich get richer. In the UK less than half a million people, the top one percent of adults, own over twice the resources of all the lower fifty percent. At the very bottom, ten million people live on Income Support. 20% of households, according to government definitions, live below the poverty line and this includes 36% of British children. There is a differential of 1000 to 1 between a few thousand people with millions a year and millions with a few thousand a year. One percent of households now own yachts and other motor vessels, while 40% cannot afford a holiday or celebration — and this last figure has not changed in 25 years.

The distribution of income was once famously likened by the Dutch economist, Jan Pen, to a procession marching past a stand, beginning with the smallest people, representing those with tiny incomes and ending with such millionaire giants that their heads were lost from sight. The figures at the start were mere ants, followed by midgets and dwarfs. The whole march past took one hour and it was not until 45 minutes had gone past that people of our own height, that is on average incomes, appeared. In the last eight minutes the top ten percent arrived, the first over two metres (6 foot eight) but followed by figures soaring above us, the chairmen of private companies twenty yards high.

'During the last seconds,' as Jan Pen tells the story, 'the scene is dominated by colossal figures: people like tower flats . . . these are still people with salaries . . . [and after them] figures whose height we cannot even estimate: their heads disappear into the clouds and probably they themselves do not even know how tall they are . . . super rich people . . . almost all heirs, and the tallest of them have managed to multiply their inheritance . . . The last man . . . is John Paul Getty . . . His height is inconceivable: at least ten miles, and perhaps twice as much.'

Capitalism - inequality ambitions of socialism

We have retold this story because it is surely impossible that any socialist or any Christian should not be profoundly concerned with such grotesque inequalities in our society. Mr Getty has passed on, but his successors are even taller. Some of these inequalities are recognised by Tony Blair and his associates, but they do not influence his activities, still less form the driving force of his campaigns. This is concentrated quite frankly on the people in the middle of the procession, on what has come to be called 'Middle England'. Their's is an uneasy mix of prejudice and tolerance, greed and generosity, arrogance and timidity, laced with a strong element of chauvinism and dislike of foreigners. Mr Blair has recognised that Middle England is afraid and insecure and has determined to win it for Labour. Negative equity in the housing market and economic adversity have tarnished the once brazen dreams of Thatcherite individualism, so he has had some success. But an appeal to their prejudices will not open the door to social renewal. It is only when their idealism and generosity can be awakened that real changes will come.

Increasing Inequalities

It was the decision of the monetarists to unleash the full brutality of competition which brought us to our present miserable constraints. Any Christian should know that the cure for this condition is not more competition, still less more market dynamism, but more cooperation, more mutual support, more loving kindness. Yet again and again we are told that the new words in New Labour's Clause IV embracing the 'enterprise of the market and the rigour of competition' were insisted upon by Mr Blair as the hallmark of what is new and what has changed from old Labour to face a changed world. But what has changed lies not in any changes in the real nature of capitalism.

cooperation not competition needed

While there has been material progress, there has been moral retrogression, some of which Tony Blair understands. But the central target of any new labour programme must be the inequalities of our society that have become much greater and not less since Jan Pen wrote of the British condition more than 30 years ago. The abandonment by governments in the 1980s of Keynesian demand management and the acceptance of monetarist dogma has seen the reversal of those, albeit modest, corrections to earlier inequalities that used to be made in the 1950s, 60s and early 70s, which led a distinguished British economist, Professor Austin Robinson, to describe these years as the 'Age of

36

Equality'. According to the experts, writing in the *Oxford Review of Economic Policy* (Spring 1996)

> 'all European countries saw a long-term trend towards greater equality checked in the late 1980s. The largest and most sustained episode of increasing inequality during the 1980s was in the UK.'

Just to list a few figures of income distribution and capital ownership in the UK is to show how great has been the reversal. In the last twenty years the top fifth of income earners have seen their incomes increase by 40% in real terms, while the bottom fifth have actually become poorer. As a result the top fifth of households were taking 51% of all original income in 1994 compared with 43% in 1979. Most of this change was caused by the rise in unemployment. The unemployed in the 1970s averaged around 700,000; in the 1980s and 90s there have rarely been less than two and a half million of them and on the old basis of calculation over 3 million — nearly 15% of the workforce. More than a million of those registered for work have been without work for over a year. Even among those employed, some 13 million, over 60% of the workforce, receive pay that is below half the national average, the average being pulled up by the smaller number above them, but with much higher incomes, as in Jan Pen's parade.

At the same time that salaries and wages have risen at the top end of the scale, there has been a shift from such labour income to property income. In 1995 while wages and salaries rose by 4% before tax, income from dividends and interest is estimated to have grown by 38% in money terms before tax. In revealing these figures, another group of economic experts writing in the *National Institute Economic Review* (May 1996) commented

> '. . . it is clear then that there has been a sharp shift in the distribution of national income . . . [but] it is not yet clear whether this is a structural shift or a change associated with the recession of the early 1990s and its aftermath in high unemployment. Either way, it appears that there has been a weakening in the power of labour such that workers in aggregate accept lower rewards relative to their productivity.'

This, of course, shows the importance for capital accumulation of the constant replenishment in periods of slump of the reserve army of labour.

There was always a difference of view in old Labour between the so-called socialist 'fundamentalists' and those followers of Tony Crosland, who believed in the 1960s, as Blair seems to believe in the

1990s, that capitalism had been transformed: employers no longer sought to maximise profit and the task of labour was to make more equal the distribution of income among the employed. Crosland's belief was challenged then and must be challenged more surely today, as one of his surviving followers has come to recognise. Roy Hattersley it is, writing in the *Guardian* (25.7.96), who argues for equality of outcome and not just equality of opportunity as the lodestone of New Labour policies. He evidently found it too much to read reports of a speech by Blair, in which he said that he wanted to build a dynamic economy which constantly created new millionaires.

Capital Ownership

The fact is that figures for capital ownership reveal even greater inequalities than in the distribution of income. It is said by Tories and New Labour alike that there are millions of new shareholders, amounting in the UK to almost a quarter of all households; and we are never-endingly told that two-thirds of all shares in companies now consist of the savings of the masses in pension funds. In fact the proportion of households owning shares has fallen from nearly 30% to just over 20% of the total since the first privatisation sales took place and these small holdings of shares do not confer directorial powers on their owners. Others will deploy the votes which are linked to these shares: the stakes are illusory. The employers remain a very small number.

The actual control of capital, indeed, remains more concentrated than ever in the hands of controllers who own or have access to large-scale private capital, which in turn gives power through gearing ratios to all the rest. Less than 15% of owners own nearly 90% of all companies' shares and a similar proportion of all the land other than private houses and gardens. Take-overs and mergers in 1995 and 1996 returned to the huge scale of the late 1980s, amounting to around £30 billions a year. Fewer and fewer companies control the management of British business. Bankruptcies of small businesses are rife and the small shopkeeper is becoming almost an extinct species.

In industry and commerce world-wide, we are down to similarly small numbers. A few hundred giant companies now mine and manufacture at least a half of the world's total output. Three or four transnationals now market 80% to 90% of each of the world's commodities — that is the traded raw materials that go into our food and other consumer goods. While the transnational companies may retain their head offices and their research and development and some capital assets in the country of their origin, most of the labour including the great numbers working for sub-contractors is employed outside the home country.

We can learn something of these companies' operations from the annual *World Investment Reports* on Transnational Corporations (TNCs) published by United Nations Conference on Trade and Development (UNCTAD). The dominant position in world production of transnational companies has become overwhelming. Some 40,000 companies with 250,000 foreign affiliates are responsible for global sales of $7 trillions. In the export of goods and services these companies supply $1.6 trillions in intra-firm movements and another $1.6 trillion to non-affiliated firms, while exports by all other firms amount also to $1.6 trillion. But within these huge totals the top 100 transnational companies account for about a half of the foreign sales and they sell twice as much in domestic sales. In the most modern industries the proportions are much higher. 23 electronics TNCs account for 80% of estimated total world sales, just five for half of all the foreign sales.

The advance of this predominance of the transnationals is unrelenting. International production is now more important than international trade. Global sales generated by the foreign affiliates of TNCs now exceed world-wide exports of goods and services. The foreign direct investment of transnational companies has been growing since the early 1980s at twice the rate of exports. One has to imagine behind the giant figures in Jan Pen's procession the massive assets that these men control. The polarisation of wealth and poverty which Marx so accurately predicted over a hundred years ago is being realised to a degree that would have surprised even him.

While we were writing this chapter, the United Nations published their Development Programme (UNDP) report on *Human Development*. It dramatised a finding that left us staggering:

'The wealth of the world's 358 billionaires exceeds the combined annual incomes of countries which are home to nearly half the world's people'.

And it went on to tell us that

'In 70 countries average incomes are less than they were in 1980 and in 43 less than they were in 1970 . . . Whereas the richest 20% of the world's population were 30 times better off than the poorest 20% in 1960, they were now 61 times wealthier.'

The head of UNDP, James Gustave Speth, added his comment:

'If present trends continue, economic disparities between industrial and developing nations will move from inequitable to inhuman.'

On the same day as this study was released the *Guardian* also published a report on the business affairs of Mr Rupert Murdoch, who must surely be one of the 358 giants who share the same income as do half the world's population. It appears that his businesses have been able to avoid paying some £76 millions in taxation, and it is suggested that most of this vast sum of money will accrue to his family fortune. And this is the man whom Mr Blair goes to meet after commuting all round the world to visit his private island.

Such vast concentrations of power and the capacity of these giant companies to manipulate world prices and avoid taxation, by their movements of capital and processing arrangements, through transfer pricing and shifts of location, render the powers of most individual national governments almost nugatory. Governments become the clients not the governors of companies, even of those registered in the territories over which they exercise formal sovereignty.

On Regulating Capitalism

After twenty years of continuous reversal of all earlier trends towards greater equality, it might be thought that a reforming Labour government committed to the values of equality and social justice, would have plans for a major strategy to get back on to trend. If capital and the rich cannot now be taxed effectively by national governments, for redistribution to correct the system's inequalities, then an international tax agreement is required between governments. Something like this was in fact proposed by Keynes for the Bretton Woods agreements, but the nearest to it that followed, after Marshall Aid from the USA to Western Europe and Japan, was some little overseas aid for the poorest countries, overseen by the IMF and the World Bank to collect the debts.

In the international arena, governments of the rich countries made promises to transfer 0.7% of their annual national incomes to the poor countries and some, particularly the Scandinavians, the Dutch and Canadians, fulfilled their promises. The USA and UK were not among the more generous and, when the fear of the Soviet Union and the Communist challenge subsided, the motivation to make concessions to popular demands collapsed. Nonetheless, within the European Union a structure was established for distributing aid to regions of declining industry and traditional poverty. The future of this structure is now in question, as we shall have to notice in a later chapter.

A new alternative to income redistribution is now being peddled. This is the concept of 'regulation'. Tony Blair among others believes that the multinational companies can be persuaded by appeals to the stakeholding principle and Christian charity, to moderate their propensity to accumulation. It is the latest fashion among the tycoons of British industry to refer to the reports of Christian employers like Adrian Cadbury on business ethics as justification for leaving business to reform and regulate itself in what is called 'modern corporate governance'. The City of London was allowed to regulate itself, and the result was the Barings collapse and the Maxwell, Barlow Clowes and other pension fund scandals. This nonsense about self-regulating capitalism appears, with the usual ambiguity of phrasing, to have been accepted by Mr Blair on behalf of New Labour. In a statement to *The Times* of 18-06-96, he filled out the intentions behind New Labour's *New Industrial Policy for Britain*:

> 'Our central vision is of an inclusive economy which motivates each and every one of us to work for its success as stakeholders in our society . . . Labour is convinced of the need to foster competitiveness by harnessing the power of the market economy [polite word for 'capitalism']. This means ensuring that our domestic markets are running smoothly and efficiently and fairly. It means promising a higher quality and quantity of investment in our industry and in our people and in ideas. It means enabling the success of the smaller business sector. It means encouraging modern workplaces and modern corporate governance structures.'

It is not clear who is to do the fostering, harnessing, promising, enabling and encouraging, but then perhaps it is not intended to be clear. Moreover, in answer to the Tory accusation against Labour that it is the party of regulation, Blair replied that New Labour's Manifesto envisaged only minimal regulation on such matters as safety, although in the case of the former public utilities there is to be a little help from a regulator for each industry concerned This is what Mandelson and Liddle proposed for the giant international companies that now own the telephone, electricity, gas, water, petroleum, railway and other public utilities in the UK, which once served to fuel government public expenditure and now enrich the private shareholders and the fat cats who head up these companies. A once-for-all 'windfall tax' is to be

41

imposed upon them, to take back some of the sweeteners which were provided by Tory governments to ease their privatisation, but thereafter.

> 'Regulatory reform should be high on the New Labour agenda, offering fair but not excessive returns for the genuine natural monopoly; promoting a proper framework for competition wherever feasible; establishing mechanisms for fulfilment of the special social obligations of the utility sector (for example energy conservation and help for the fuel-poor); and ensuring that regulators are properly accountable for their decisions.' (M&L p.83)

Phrases like 'fair but not excessive', 'wherever feasible' and 'properly accountable' hardly suggest a very tough regime, but prices to consumers of the products of the utilities might be reduced and that might help some people. But we need to ask whom.

This new concern for the consumer in New Labour's programme has to be looked at carefully. Most of the consumption of public utilities is by businesses and the richer households. And how they spend the money saved tends to be on the goods which the big companies find it most profitable to supply. This is the second great fault in capitalism after its propensity to continuous accumulation at the expense of the workers. It is that the growth path of a capitalist economy follows where profits and surpluses are highest and that will be in the richer markets and for goods which can be produced most productively — that is with least labour. When governments previously owned the major utilities and increased their taxation of private capital, they could increase the public provision of services like health and education and measures of conservation, which are all labour-intensive, and therefore counteract the capital-intensive unemployment-generating tendencies of the private sector. This they cannot now do. It has been estimated that the sell-off of nationalised industries is costing 2% of national income a year in lost revenues (equivalent to over 10% of central government total revenue); and North Sea oil operating companies hardly pay any taxes at all (Larry Elliott, *Guardian*, July 8, 1996).

There is no alternative for correcting the faults of capitalism except provision outside the requirements of capital accumulation — and that must be through public authorities. No amount of regulation will alter the capitalist growth path; it has to be stopped. Of course, New Labour spokesmen are right to bewail the misspending of so much public money on payments to the unemployed, when what workless people need is work. Where they are wrong is in believing that training for the long-term unemployed, plus work-fare for the young unemployed, will of themselves create new jobs. We shall show later, we believe conclusively, that only public spending can overcome the lag in job creation, since the connection between economic growth and expansion of employment has been decisively broken. More than this, because of the globalisation of capital and its opportunistic location of investment in production, governments will need to agree on joint or common programmes to make any effective response.

Exploitation of Natural Resources

Capitalism cannot exist without the exploitation of labour — that is of men and women, and especially of those including minority groups and whole peoples least able to defend themselves. And capital accumulation continuously weakens the position of such people, while its growth path enriches those whose pull on the market is strongest. But capitalism is also ruthlessly destructive of nature as well as of humanity. Because the Soviet planned economy was destructive in both cases, such destructiveness is said to be a human failing which can be regulated. What both systems manifestly suffer from is a lack of democratic control, but, whereas a planned economy might have been more or less democratically controlled, the power exercised by private ownership in capitalism defies democracy. Within limits some of the worst features of capitalism might be corrected by government regulation, and this is particularly the case regarding the using up of irreplaceable energy resources and the destruction of the environment. Such regulatory measures would not make capitalism unworkable. Indeed, it can be argued that they are essential for its survival.

If capitalism would not survive without the exploitation of labour, but could survive if the exploitation of nature were to be made sustainable, this would still require the almost unimaginable agreement of all capitalists. After years of delay the use of gases which are destroying the ozone layer are being phased out. The prohibition of less universally damaging chemicals like DDT and other toxic pesticides is only effective where public opinion is alert, and prohibition in the North has not prevented their continued use by international companies operating in the South. Serious measures of conservation of oil and natural gas are simply non-existent.

John Ruskin, who is claimed as one of Tony Blair's inspirers, was, like William Morris and other early socialists, always conscious of the destructive force of capitalism, both on our natural environment and on our humanity. Who can deny that Ruskin's message about capitalist

43

industry still stands, give and take some changes in the example from pin making to electronics circuits and in the gender of the human souls? Can Mr Blair deny such a message?

> 'We have much studied and perfected, of late, the great civilised invention of the division of labour; only we give it a false name. It is not, truly speaking, the labour that is divided, but the men: divided into mere segments of men — broken into small fragments and crumbs of life; so that all the little pieces of intelligence that is left in a man is not enough to make a pin or a nail, but exhausts itself in making the point of a pin, or the head of a nail. Now it is a good and desirable thing, truly, to make many pins in a day; but if we could only see with what crystal sand their points were polished — sand of human soul, much to be modified before it can be discerned for what it is — we should think there might be some loss of it also. And the great cry that rises from all our manufacturing cities, louder than the furnace blast, is all in very deed for this — that we manufacture everything there except men; we blanch cotton, and strengthen steel, and refine sugar, and shape pottery; but to brighten, to strengthen, to refine or to form a single living spirit, never enters into our estimate of advantages.' (p.21)

There is, however, no pledge about labour conditions nor about protecting the environment in New Labour's Manifesto. As we shall see in later chapters such provisions are all subordinated to the demands of competitiveness. They constitute what Mandelson and Liddle call, in reference to such European provisions: 'overprescriptive regulations.' This is a telling phrase that says much about New Labour's concept of the regulation of industry — general admonishment but no precise prescription. We shall try to show in this book that the project of New Labour for regulating capitalism, rather than replacing its workings by social ownership and democratic control, even bit by bit, cannot be expected to succeed. Regulating the very worst excesses of child labour and poisonous working conditions may be possible, as might be the regulation of industrial pollution and the introduction of conservation measures in crop production, mineral extraction and the cutting down of forests. But even to achieve these changes in capitalist conduct will require a direct and imaginative challenge to capitalist power and to capitalist ideology, which has survived for so long because it blinds its victims to the true nature of its power.

44

CHAPTER 4

Success or Failure?
Labour in Government

'. . . the reality of the past 25 years is that each period of Labour in office in the 1960s and 1970s produced an improvement in the balance of payments and in manufacturing investment, whereas each period of Conservative government resulted in a deterioration'.

Lewis Minkin, The Contentious Alliance

'Modernisation of Labour is about a fundamental reinvention of what Labour offers to the British people, not abandonment of Labour's basic principles and convictions'.

Peter Mandelson & Roger Liddle, The Blair Revolution

The Labour Party was the offspring of an earlier marriage of Humanist democracy, Marxism and Christian socialism with a rapidly advancing trade union movement at the end of the Nineteenth Century. This story has been chronicled in detail elsewhere (Ken Coates and Tony Topham, *The Making of the Labour Movement,* Spokesman, 1993). The aim of the Party that emerged was not only to provide representation in Parliament for those people recently enfranchised and simply to win the vote for all those still excluded from the body politic. It was to defend and advance the interests of working people, to release them from all arbitrary powers, including above all those of capital.

The Labour Party has in the past been a broad church able to hold together democratic socialists from many tendencies and traditions, united by their belief in the equal humanity of all men and women. Its two wings, the unions and the Parliamentary Labour Party, were held together by the socialist societies, which in the beginning often formed the core of local party branches. In Parliamentary elections in the 1920s, in the war-time coalition, in 1945 and again in the 1960s and 70s Labour formed governments with the strong support of a trade union movement, whose growth continued up to 1979. After that year the unions came under ferocious attack from Mrs Thatcher and for four elections running Labour was defeated at the polls. It was said by some that the cause of this was the link with the unions, and that people had changed. Now they wanted to be treated as individuals and not as collectivities. We will seek to challenge this assertion, which has been advanced without any real evidence.

The central claim of New Labour, according to Mandelson and Liddle, is that it is concerned to 'modernise' the old Labour Party. 'Modernisation', they write in the preface to their book, 'is about more than developing a package of attractive propositions that can win Labour power.' In case any one could conceivably have imagined such a thing, or that principles were being abandoned, they go on to reassure us that

> 'In carrying out its radical shift, the Blair revolution is not creating a Labour Party without principles. On the contrary, it is rescuing the party's traditional values of cooperation and social solidarity and putting them to work to respond to the challenges facing Britain as we approach the new century'. (M&L, p.viii)

The onslaught that Mandelson and Liddle then launch upon Old Labour is introduced with a small filial touch of respect and a large rewriting of history. It is necessary to quote from their book to sort out the truth from the fiction. Like Blair himself, the authors claim that their 'political outlook was shaped by the strong ethical values of [their] respective parents'. They remain, they say, 'intensely proud of Labour's historic achievements.' But their experiences in the late 1970s working respectively in the economic department of the TUC and as a special adviser to the cabinet minister responsible for Transport, Bill Rodgers, led them to become

> 'disturbed by the extent to which Labour was trapped in its past and a prisoner of an outdated ideology . . .'
>
> 'The question', as they both saw it, 'was whether to stay and reclaim Labour from the grip of its *political madness* [emphasis added] or to decamp in order to build the party afresh on more fertile ground.'

Bill Rodgers was one of the 'Gang of Four' who 'decamped', i.e. deserted the Party, taking with him Roger Liddle, his assistant, and the others who followed the 'Gang of Four' to form the Social Democratic Party in 1981, thus dividing the Labour Party before the election in 1983. Mandelson and Liddle tell us that, though Mandelson stayed with

46

Labour, 'Throughout, [they] have not stopped being friends . . .' (M&L, p.ix) and can now work happily together again to build New Labour.

'Modernisation' or Destruction?

'New Labour', according to Mandelson and Liddle, 'has set itself a bold task: to modernise Britain socially, economically and politically . . .' It seeks to 'move forward from both the postwar Labour Party of Wilson and Callaghan and the Conservative Party of Thatcher and Major', adding that, 'its strategy is to move forward from where Margaret Thatcher left off . . .' (M&L, p.1)

> 'Modernisation of Labour is', let us repeat what they say, 'about a fundamental reinvention of what Labour offers to the British people', not 'abandonment of Labour's basic principles and convictions' but 'a sharper definition of those core aims and values, and their thorough reapplication to the circumstances of the modern world.'

Labour, according to Mandelson and Liddle, has been more resistant to change than the Conservatives:

> 'The last time Labour reinvented itself was in the 1930s. Then in the aftermath of its 1931 electoral disaster, Labour reconstituted itself under Hugh Dalton's intellectual leadership and Herbert Morrison's strategic decisions and laid the foundations for eventual victory in 1945. (M&L, p.2)

Mandelson and Liddle draw the parallel today in their next sentences:

> 'Labour's current phase of reinvention was started by Neil Kinnock and continued by John Smith. But, essentially they were engaged in a ground clearing operation — first, to rid the party of the Bennite excesses that had led to the SDP split and to its worst ever postwar defeat, and then to restore its unity of purpose and to democratise its internal procedures. Tony Blair has built on that solid inheritance to lead the party in the restatement of its values and the wholesale modernisation of its policies.' (M&L, p.2)

This paragraph involves the reinvention not only of Labour but of the history of at least the last 65 years. There has never been just one 'Old Labour'. As Eric Shaw, summarising his book *The Labour Party since 1945*, has written:

> 'In reality, there were many old Labours — Fabians and quasi-Marxists, ethical socialists and revisionists — a colourful tapestry woven of many threads. But uniting them, there were common objectives to which all could subscribe: the drive for distributional justice, a more equitable apportionment

47

'of income, wealth and power; full social participation, to be realised by a universal welfare state financed by a progressive system of taxation; the eradication of mass unemployment; and social arrangements which institutionalised the norms of fellowship, communal responsibility and public service.' (Shaw, NS&S, 26.4.96)

Eric Shaw concludes, 'Labour governments after 1950 fell short of these ideals. They were, however, regarded as a beacon of light which set the Party's course. That beacon has been extinguished'.

Shaw seeks to show that each one of the objectives of Old Labour has been abandoned by Mr Blair. To cloak him with the mantle of Tawney and the Christian Socialists is in that case to cover up a total apostasy. Certainly, for Mandelson and Liddle to place him in a kind of apostolic Labour succession from Dalton and Morrison is to confuse everything. The foundations for Labour's victory in 1945 were laid by many people. 1931 and 1981 do have one thing in common. A group of leading members of the Labour Party defected, MacDonald and one or two others to a Tory-dominated National Government in 1931, the 'Gang of Four' to alliance with the Liberals in 1981, and disaster followed for Labour through a split vote at the polls.

The recovery of Labour after 1931 has beyond doubt to be attributed to Ernest Bevin, leader of the Transport and General Workers' Union, who then regarded himself, according to his biographer, as the personal custodian of the rights of British working people.

The Party and the Unions

Labour was above all, in Keir Hardie's phrase, a 'great alliance' of socialist organisations and trade unions symbolised at first in a common home in Bevin's Transport House. But the alliance was always, in Lewis Minkin's phrase, 'contentious'. If Bevin saw the party as 'essentially the instrument of trade unionism', the alliance was, contrary to much Blairite criticism, one that was regulated by what Minkin calls a 'deeply ingrained protocol [that] governed policy and financial consultations.' There were clearly accepted rules of solidarity and unity but also of autonomy that governed the relations of the Party and the unions, although these were established more by convention than by written agreement. The central 'rule' developed in the inter-war years was the freedom of the unions from government control and equally the autonomy of the Parliamentary Party.

This 'rule' implied a certain demarcation of roles and spheres — the industrial and the political. Yet, in Minkin's view, while the industrial was affirmed by the unions to the point of having direct access to government, the 'political was much more ambiguous'. Minkin quotes Gaitskell speaking to the TUC before opening Labour's election campaign in 1959:

> 'We are comrades, but we have different jobs to do. You have your industrial job and we have our political job. We do not dictate to one another'.

And Gaitskell added: *Gaitskell asserting independence from unions.*

> 'And believe me, any leader of the Labour Party would not be worth his salt if he allowed himself to be dictated to by the unions.'

For many years, the National Council of Labour and later the Liaison Committee kept the two parts together, although both fell out of use when Labour was not in government.

The freedom of the Parliamentary Labour Party was always respected, the election of the Party Leader and Cabinet resting entirely in the hands of the PLP until the establishment of the electoral college for choosing the leader in 1981. The unions had predominant voting power in Conference which was the Party's sovereign body and which elected its national executive committee from a balance of sections — unions, constituency branches, the Cooperative Party and women. Yet for long that power was used primarily to sustain the Party leadership and only quite exceptionally against it.

Conference decided policy but the 'rule' ever since 1907 had been that the PLP had 'time and method discretion' in giving effect to Conference decisions. It was always adhered to. The role of the party Conference was both a factor for discipline and for stability. Minkin quotes from L.Hunter's *Road to Brighton Pier*:

> 'Firmly based on the millions of workers organised in the trade union movement, the Labour Party could always survive so long as it exercised self-discipline based on full democratic discussion and unswerving obedience to majority decisions once they had been taken.'

During the years when this rule applied, Conference in fact usually voted with the National Executive platform, and when it did not, as in the vote for unilateral nuclear disarmament, then just as usually the votes were reversed the following year. The unity and solidarity of the Party and the unions were seriously weakened, however, during the Wilson-Callaghan administrations of 1974-79, when the government entered into conflict with the unions. A rehearsal of these tensions had been held in the late sixties, with the launching of Mrs Castle's industrial relations programme, 'In Place of Strife'. But during the Thatcher years the unions became more than ready to seek renewal of their older relationship with the Labour Party. After the ending of Michael Foot's leadership of the party, this became more and more difficult. It was strongly restored by John Smith, with the firm promise to give top priority to full employment. But the subsequent leadership has brought the relationship to a new low level.

The idea of the unions dominating the Labour Party has to be most sensitively examined. First of all, it was not the TUC which represented the unions at Conference, but a large, if declining, number of individual unions, each with their own sectional interests. Secondly, the 'rules' governing union and Party autonomy were firmly adhered to and it was not the unions which sought to change them in the late 1970s and early 1980s. Thirdly, the towering position of Ernest Bevin in the 1930s and 1940s was never replicated, even by the 'Praetorian Guard' of big union leaders formed against the Left in the 1940s and 50s. But Bevin's role in the 1930s does have to be understood. He was not only the leader of the largest union, but the one who saw most clearly the necessity for the unions of non-skilled workers to promote government action to maintain full employment. It was Bevin who was among the first to grasp the importance for labour of Keynes's ideas. Dalton and Morrison, Mandelson's heroes, far from offering such intellectual leadership, trailed far behind.

The Defining of 'the Left'

What is missing from Mandelson and Liddle and also to a less extent from Minkin's study, is any analysis of 'the left' and the role of socialist ideas in the Labour Party. Mandelson and Liddle regard the left as an 'aberration' of the 1970s. Minkin concentrates his attention on the struggle between 'the left' and 'the right' for domination of the Party Conference in the 1970s, with only minimal distinctions being drawn between different kinds of 'left' in the unions. Yet the Labour Party was the product not only of the unions and a Parliamentary Labour Party but of the coming together of a number of socialist societies. Communists and Trotskyists were always formally excluded, though there were 'fellow travellers' and 'entrists' at all times. 'The right', especially in the union leadership, was ever vigilant in its concern to keep out what were called 'subversive elements'. Apart from 'entrists' this exclusion could be effective in the Party but not in the unions.

Many of the most powerful British trade union leaders like Arthur Horner or Will Paynter of the Miners in the 1940s and 60s, had been Communists. Even more were ex-Communists, including some of the main union leaders of the 1970s; Hugh Scanlon of the Engineers, Laurence Daly of the Miners, Richard Seabrook of the Shop Workers. There were 'rules', formal and informal, to exclude non-Labour Party members from representing unions at Party Conference and the Party selection conferences for choosing Parliamentary candidates. For part of the 1930s and after the first years of the 1939-46 war, the Communist Party of Great Britain adopted a policy of unity with Labour and later threw its weight behind the leftward moves in the Labour Party in the 1970s. At certain periods this was welcomed by Labour leaders — by Cripps in the 1930s and by Benn in the 1970s.

There were always major differences inside 'the left', but these were not necessarily to be categorised as between Communists and Labour or even as between Marxists and Liberals. Differences over resistance to fascism in the 1930s, over membership of the European Community, over incomes policy and over workers' control, to take four key examples, crossed over the Party distinctions. This made for great difficulties in the left over reaching a united position on issues inside the Labour Party. The central unifying force among socialists was their belief that the capitalist system had to be ended if the humanity of all was to be respected. This, as we have seen, was a conviction shared by Christians, Marxists and humanists. But differences over short-term compromises for long-term aims remained, and were to produce fatal divisions in the 1970s.

These differences cannot be put down to personal antipathies, though these existed, as between Bevin and Cripps. They often reflected power groupings and depended on the organising agency of a newspaper. Ernest Bevin promoted the *Daily Herald*. Aneurin Bevan used the *Tribune* to expound his views. In the '70s the *Voice of the Unions* papers, especially *Engineering Voice* spoke for the emerging democracy in the unions. But this journal failed to overcome differences over incomes policy which reflected the Communist Party position of Ken Gill on the one side, and the more flexible policies of Jack Jones on the other, with Hugh Scanlon caught between them. But this is to anticipate. Even in the heyday of Labour in 1951 a left group of Ministers — Aneurin Bevan, Harold

Wilson and John Freeman — could resign from government on cuts in the Health Service to pay for rearmament, and form a left factional opposition — the Bevanites.

The Road to 1945

Liberal Democrats and other kinds of liberals like John Gray may claim that Keynes and Beveridge and the Liberal summer schools of the 1930s were the architects of 1945. But Bevin's influence on the unions, GDH Cole's on Fabian summer schools and discussions among academics and other groups like Political and Economic Planning and the Next Five Years Group did most to transmit the ideas of Keynes and Beveridge into Labour's post-war programme. Dalton, as we have said, was not a Keynesian and though he did much to concentrate the mind of the Labour Party on medium-term Parliamentary objectives, the intellectual leadership came from elsewhere. Inside the Labour Party, much of it was provided not only by Cole but by Tawney, who lectured widely under the auspices of the Workers' Educational Association, of which William Temple was for a long time the President. It was also provided by a generation of Marxists, famously preserved in the works of the Left Book Club, whose editors included both Harold Laski and John Strachey.

The organisational power of Labour after 1931 came from the unions and from Bevin more than from anyone else. It is an understandable filial (or rather, grandfilial) tribute that Mandelson makes to Herbert Morrison, but he was only one of many who decided the strategy that laid the foundations for victory in 1945. Morrison was the most determined of Labour's leaders in pressing that Labour should leave the war-time Coalition in advance of the election, while at the same time plotting to replace Attlee as leader. Morrison did also have a major influence on the design of the nationalised industry boards as closed public corporations. Ironically, these are of all the elements in Old Labour policy the one which his grandson most derides. And they were certainly responsible for most, if not all, of the disillusionment later occasioned by public enterprise.

Thus the fact is that, contrary to the assertions of Mandelson and Liddle, in their attempt to deny credit to the left and to the unions for Labour's past successes, the unions and the leftist intellectuals were central to Labour's advance to 1945. Neither Dalton nor Morrison made any lasting impression on the intellectual climate of their times, although both were gifted 'fixers'. As intellectuals, Cole, Tawney and the Marxists together with Stafford Cripps, Nye Bevan, Michael Foot, George Orwell and others from the *Tribune* left have to be seen as the ones who built the road to 1945. Nor should we overlook Clem Attlee himself for his intellectual contribution to the Party's development as well as for the way he modestly but firmly led the Party to victory. Both Dalton and Morrison were in semi-permanent conspiracy against him, fortunately none too competently. The greatest number of those who made the 1945 victory possible were, of course, those in the forces and the factories who voted for a programme of full employment, social housing, longer education and a universal health service.

When Mandelson and Liddle come to review the achievements of the 1945 Labour Government, these are regarded very coolly as completing 'the work that Lloyd George and Churchill had begun a generation before. However,' they continue, 'despite its magnificence, the 1945 achievement was never as universal as its present day defenders sometimes imagine.' (M&L, p.140) Their roll call is a depressing one. The NHS never became a salaried service. Pensions and family allowances were less than Beveridge had proposed. Top-quality free education was never extended to all, and the public schools were left intact. Unemployment insurance and family credit instead of being a right became part of a means-tested social security system.

All these criticisms which Mandelson and Liddle make of old Labour are true, but come ill from this source, unless it intended that New Labour will correct them? In fact, most of the disillusionment with the Welfare State so far has been caused by persistent Tory underfunding and the Tories' encouragement of private provision especially in relation to pensions and private health insurance. The one outstanding success of the post-1945 Labour Governments that forced all Conservative Governments to follow suit was that they created and maintained full employment — until Callaghan broke the spell and Thatcher pressed home the resultant advantage for capital against labour. Far from opposing this fatal reversion, the founders of the Social Democratic Party were zealously implicated in it.

Full Employment: Labour's Main Objective

This is not mentioned in the list of aims of New Labour, only that it is 'not practicable to return to some 1945 'New Jerusalem' that never was.' (M&L, p.143) This reference to Blake's 'Jerusalem' draws on a study by Elizabeth Durbin, entitled *New Jerusalems: the Labour Party and the Economics of Democratic Socialism*, published in 1985. This book describes the work of those Labour thinkers in the 1930s — Tawney, Cole, Gaitskell, Dalton and Durbin — who with Keynes drafted the plans for the post-war Welfare State, which Correlli Barnett in his *Audit of War* has attacked with all the venom at his command:

> 'New Jerusalem itself, a dream turned to a dank reality of a segregated, sub-literate, unskilled, unhealthy and institutionalised proletariat hanging on the nipple of state maternalism.' (Barnett p.304)

Barnett's intemperate language does not reappear in Mandelson and Liddle, but the story of a 'dream that never was' and the accusation of 'short changing' against Old Labour must be designed to create the belief that Old Labour's aims were unrealistic and to prepare us for Blair's apostasy. The emasculation of the Welfare State is blamed upon the health workers' unions in the 'winter of discontent' and on the teachers' unions' strikes of the 1980s, which together, it is said, led so many middle class families to take out private health insurance (7 million contributors by 1995) and send their children to private schools (over 600,000 children by the same year). We shall examine this claim in a later chapter.

It is frequently argued — and New Labour seems to have accepted what is a right-wing argument — that the post-war full employment was the result of special circumstances that cannot be repeated: first, the demands of reconstruction after the war and the possibilities of catching up with US technological advances; second, the accumulated war-time savings — private and government — and Marshall Aid from the USA that made possible rapid growth without inflation; third, the Bretton Woods system of inter-national exchange rates tied to gold through the US dollar, that made possible national economic management within a firm international framework; fourth, the regular excess of US foreign expenditure financed by gold sales that maintained world-wide demand at a high level. All these elements sustaining economic growth, it is argued, came to an end in the mid-1970s with the oil price hike creating inflationary pressures, with the ending of demand from US gold sales and with the increasing challenge to national policies from transnational capital movements.

That all these things happened cannot be doubted, but the response of governments in exchanging the economic theories of Keynes for the monetarist ideas of Friedman was to end all forms of state intervention in the economy and place increasing reliance on the market, which had become more globally integrated than ever before. The result has been not to expand development but to slow down growth nearly everywhere, damage business confidence and create unacceptably high levels of unemployment. The UK has suffered worst of the developed countries, despite the North Sea oil bonanza, because Mrs Thatcher made monetarism into a weapon to destroy the trade unions, thus undermining the purchasing power of their members; and because British capital, partly for that reason, partly for historic reasons, migrated overseas.

The UK economy has been dominated, and has been increasingly dominated, to a far greater extent than others by transnational companies, and their domination was further extended under the Thatcher regime. UK employment was thus hit hardest by lack of investment at home, and by the competition of manufactured goods and manufacturing companies coming from outside. It need not have happened, had investment of British capital been maintained in the home economy, as it was by other national capital in the economies of the rest of Europe.

Economists writing recently in official and semi-official publications like the National Institute *Economic Review* and UNCTAD's annual *Trade and Development Report* have been looking back to the post-war years and identifying active government intervention as a key factor in maintaining full employment. As the CLARE group of UK economists put it, writing in the *Economic Review* for February 1995, about 'the confidence engendered by the full employment policy itself.'

> 'The knowledge that governments of all political parties were committed to full employment, and would adjust their fiscal and/or monetary policies to offset any general contraction of the aggregate demand for goods and services, must have downgraded one important element in the risks attached to spending money on capital projects.' (Note: 'fiscal' means government spending and taxing)

In contrast with these years of positive government intervention in the economy to maintain full employment, the authors of the UNCTAD *Report for 1995* write as follows:

> 'The generally restrictive monetary policies implemented in the last two decades have shunted economies into low-growth paths in which low demand growth and low potential output growth have fed back into one another. Frequent underutilisation of the existing productive capacity has

made for slow capital formation. The slow growth of potential output has, in turn, provided justification for persisting in macro-economic policies that limit demand growth to that of the potential output growth. These policies have thus created a weak economic growth dynamic, and generated an increasing imbalance between the labour force and the tools — i.e. capital — to employ labour productively.'

These authorities we cite, first, in order to contrast their argument with New Labour's analysis, and secondly to rescue the efforts of Old Labour to ensure full employment from the charge of 'Bennite excesses', or 'Bennite aberrations'. These are said by Mandelson and Liddle to have come from an 'extremist fringe' that Benn supposedly encouraged to 'increase support for his own brand of centralised state socialism.' The Mandelson/Liddle critique of Labour's economic policies in the 1960s and 1970s, apart from complaint at these 'aberrations', is the following (M&L, pp.10-12, with our comments in brackets):

— lack of a 'stable macro-economic framework' (the nature of which is not specified, except in terms of 'partnership with business');

— inadequate 'industrial strategy in addressing fundamental weaknesses of competitiveness' (mainly seen as supply side weaknesses of excessive wages in relation to productivity and of poor education and training in the work force, not of any lack of positive government action to encourage capital investment);

— 'retreat from "In Place of Strife" and industrial relations modernisation, which left trade unions powerful and unreformed' (the so-called 'dictatorship by the unions', to be rectified by the planned separation of New Labour from the unions following Thatcher's legislative onslaught on some of their most essential powers to protect working people);

— 'resistance to modernisation throughout society — from the hold of vested interests . . .' (i.e. from professional unions, not, however, to be applied to the interests of the owners of capital);

— excessive 'public spending plans', which led to higher taxes and 'the alienation of Labour's better off supporters among the skilled' (who could, however, have been encouraged to understand the benefits of public spending in ways that New Labour does not appear to recognise);

— finally, Labour governments accepted the TUC's proposed incomes policies which involved 'horse-trading with the unions for favours', as part of a 'centralised, statist' solution to problems in a manner typical of a 'corporatist' state.

This last is such a distortion of the facts and so central to the ambiguities at the heart of New Labour that we now need to pay it due attention. We shall particularly have to notice that the accusation of state corporatism was used by the left against the right as well as the other way round, according to who was being incorporated.

Planning for Full Employment

When Labour was returned to power in 1964, after 13 years in opposition, a Ministry of Economic Affairs was set up headed by the deputy Prime Minister, George Brown, who was instructed to draw up a National Plan. Far from being imposed from the centre this was worked out in a National Economic Development Council (NEDDY) drawing upon the work of sub-committees for each industry. The NEDC had been established by a Conservative administration on the initiative of Selwyn Lloyd. This was continued and developed by the Wilson Government, in the hope that it might play a catalytic role in the stimulation of investment and enterprise. The NEDC and all of the committees, which came to be called Little Neddies, were tri-partite in composition, comprising government ministers, industrialists and trade unions.

The aim of Labour's 1965 National Plan was quite modest — to raise the rate of economic growth from just under 3% a year to just under 4%, and to ensure that this was sustained without booms or slumps over a five year period. The method was to encourage business to believe in faster and more continuous growth by working out in detail what this would mean for each industry. Unfortunately, competition in the market failed to ensure that what actually happened bore any close relationship to what had been planned, especially as concerned imports and exports. Nowhere was this more obvious than in the case of over supply by the fuel industries. Labour's 1965 National Plan was not in any way a compulsory plan. Government could not give orders. The plan failed as uncontrolled imports moved rapidly ahead of exports.

Some thought that the Plan might have succeeded better if the minister in charge had been a less volatile character, but no-one could have called George Brown left-wing. It was more significant that the Treasury had rigidly opposed devaluation to solve the export-import imbalance and had set its face inexorably against any other government department than themselves being involved in economic management, while Treasury officials held to a firm non-interventionist stance.

By the 1970s it was becoming clear to a number of left-wing economists, notably Stuart Holland and Robin Murray (Holland, 1974, Murray 1975), that the old anarchy of the market was being transformed by the internal planning and operational integration of giant companies, conducting their business transnationally. These transnational companies were becoming major producers of goods and services. The top 100 British companies increased their share of UK manufacturing output from one-fifth to two-fifths in the 1960s and they were beginning to produce as much outside their country of origin as inside. As a result, they could overcome the risks of failures in demand or supply, and of government intervention, by their own integrated operations and systems of transfer pricing. They formed what Stuart Holland called the 'meso-economy' in between the 'macro-economy' of the state and the 'micro-economy' of the small firm or enterprise. Governments would need to deal with them in future, using all the fiscal instruments at their command but also developing the efficiency of their own 'meso-economy', which existed in the public sector of nationalised industries and state services.

The problem for governments was that the more capital-intensive industries, mainly in the private sector, yielded increased profits and a very proper demand from workers for their share. At the same time, workers in the more labour-intensive services, mainly in the public sector, could make no such immediate claim. The traditional Labour response had been that both company profits and the wages of workers receiving higher payments in the capital intensive industries could be taxed, and higher payments could then be made in the public sector of health and education and social services.

This policy had, however, become much more difficult to effect for two reasons: first, companies' profits were much less susceptible to taxation when companies operated transnationally and could transfer their profits, through transfer pricing, to countries where tax levels (and trade union demands) were lowest; secondly, slower rates of growth and higher rates of inflation, following the oil price-hike, meant that tax increases left workers, even in the capital-intensive industries, with no increase in real take-home pay. The position of workers in the labour-intensive industries was that they were actually worse off. As productivity began to grow, without compensating wage increases, unemployment rose. By 1975 and 1976 it moved beyond the post-war figures that had hitherto ranged between 300,000 and 800,000.

The crisis of the mid-1970s, which is simply not explained by Mandelson and Liddle in the list of Labour's failures quoted earlier, did not arise, as they suggest, either from the age-old power of the City of London or from the new and 'unreformed' power of the trade unions. It arose from the increased freedom of movement of the location of production of the giant transnational companies particularly: and by increased international lending by banks as large amounts of volatile finance were made available from the huge new incomes of the oil states. This new money did not stay in the UK. By 1977 the overseas capital transactions in the UK balance of payments accounts had steadily moved from ten years of mainly net inflows to enter upon ten years of consistent net outflows, averaging over £4 billions a year. The capital resources at British companies' disposal, including funds made available by government, were being employed so that jobs were created abroad and not at home.

It was to deal with this problem of the lack of public control over the public funds supplied to industry that the proposal for making planning agreements with the large transnational companies had been put forward by Stuart Holland, who had at one time been in Harold Wilson's office in Downing Street and was later to become an MP. There had been a long history behind this of work by the left in the Labour Party not just to extend public ownership, but to extend the accountability of industry. In particular, there was the work of the Public Sector Group formed by the Party's Industrial Policy Committee during the Heath Government from 1970 to 1974. This group consisted of Judith Hart and Ian Mikardo, left-wing members of the National Executive, Lord Balogh, Wilson's economic adviser, Margaret Jackson MP (later Margaret Beckett), a metallurgist and now a member of Blair's shadow cabinet, Lord Delacourt-Smith, who had been a Post Office Engineering Union general secretary, Jim Mortimer, another one-time union official, then Labour Relations Director of the London Passenger Transport Board, later to be General Secretary of the Labour Party, Tony Banks, a researcher with the AEUW, Derek Robinson, an Oxford economist, Richard Pryke, another academic who had served briefly in Wilson's office, alongside Stuart Holland, who was responsible for drafting most of the papers. The Group was never more than an offshoot of the Industrial Committee, to which it had to report, and which was a body representative of the whole Party, consisting of never less than a third of the cabinet members and all the major trade union general secretaries or their assistants (Michael Hatfield, *The House that the Labour Left Built.* pp.87-90, 156).

The chairman of Labour's Industrial Committee until Benn took over late in 1972 was John Chalmers, a boiler maker and a right-wing trade union member of the National Executive. Members at different times included Tony Crosland, Barbara Castle, Harold Lever, Roy Mason, Reg Prentice, Robert Sheldon and Jeremy Bray; also Edmund Dell and Bill Rodgers who would later break away from Labour to form the Social Democratic Party. It would not seem likely that the Public Sector Group would necessarily have the support of the rest of the Committee, but it is wrong to assume that the later defection of the Social Democrats was already dividing the Committee. Crosland was never at one with Rodgers, and Rodgers himself was not opposed to a 'para-government agency' for economic development. In January 1972 he actually introduced a Bill in Parliament for a Regional Development Corporation. Edmund Dell, the other Social Democrat to be, had earlier proposed a similar motion and Roy Jenkins, who was then deputy leader of the Party, had asked Stuart Holland in May 1972 to help him to write a major speech on public ownership for a conference of the National Union of Mineworkers (Hatfield, p.108), a speech which appears as a programme for government action in a chapter of Jenkins' book, *What Matters Now*.

This little book was prepared by Roy Jenkins in 1972 in connection with his bid to become leader of the Labour Party. When this failed, he resigned to become a European Commissioner. The programme in the book should, however, give a picture of the policy commitments, which would have bound a social democratic leadership, had one been possible. In fact, in it Jenkins proposes almost all those measures which the defecting Social Democrats, supported now by Mandelson and Liddle, turned down as 'Bennite excesses' — 'more government intervention' to maintain full employment, a 'major State Holding Company . . . supported by a Regional Development Bank equipped with substantial initial resources . . . to embark on its extensive programme of acquisition and diversification', 'the extension of collective bargaining to encourage industrial democracy at shop floor level', 'an extended state pension service', 'increased official aid for Developing Countries to 1% of UK GDP', 'price restraints' and 'a national minimum wage' as elements of an incomes policy, 'a serious reduction in car use, especially in Central London' by withholding planning permission for private or public underground garages, 'rapid municipalisation of the private rented sector of housing'. (Jenkins, pp.34-6, 51,91, 92-3, 106, 111) Finally, Jenkins concluded that 'both wings of the alliance [in the Labour Party of the trade unions and the socialists] are as necessary to each other now as they were when the Labour Representation Committee was founded 72 years ago.' (Jenkins, p.117)

With that kind of support, it was not surprising that in fact, as Michael Hatfield shows, the Party's Industrial Committee did agree on the need to set up a State Holding Company, which came to be called the National Enterprise Board, just as Jenkins recommended, on the lines of the Italian IRI as a vehicle for a state holding in a number of industries, without nationalising a whole industry. Already, as Jenkins pointed out, the state held 49% of BP shares, 100% of Rolls Royce, 69% of Short Brothers in Northern Ireland, and a stake in International Computers Ltd. A further state holding in the motor industry such as existed in Germany, Italy and France seemed to be a natural extension. But the mythology of 'taking over' 25 companies or even 100 was invented afterwards. Even in the rhetoric of Tony Benn, it was only intended to take shares corresponding to the government's financial contribution, what would now be called its 'stake'.

Where then was the disagreement? The right-wing on the Industrial Committee, including the social democrats, disagreed with the mainly left-wing Public Sector Group on the purpose of the Holding Company and the number or names of firms to be brought within its holding. Crosland, Lever, Sheldon and the social democrats were opposed to any large scale extension of public involvement in industry and saw the holding company as a way of injecting public money into private companies, and exercising some control over the use of the funds, while encouraging competition. The Group, who were quite inaccurately sometimes referred to as 'the Marxists', according to Hatfield, saw a Holding Company as a means for extending public involvement to control monopoly power and for the exercise of more comprehensive economic planning to ensure full employment. Roy Jenkins appears from his book to have taken a middle position.

Planning Agreements, not Nationalisation

The Industrial Committee, nonetheless, succeeded in agreeing upon a proposal not only for a National Enterprise Board as a state holding company but also for 'programme contracts' with large companies to be incorporated in Labour's 1972 *Programme for Britain* launched officially by Wilson, Callaghan and Benn. (Hatfield, p.128) Such contracts, in Holland's words, were to be 'more than indicative, less than imperative'.

The key element was a commitment of the next Labour Government to planning on a *continuing* basis 'through a ministry armed with interventionist teeth', which would be 'impossible without the basic information, with the plans of leading companies being provided on a continuing and rolling basis.' This was the beginning of the Party's commitment to a Planning Agreements system. Added to the need for influencing large companies' plans for investment was the need for some control over price formation in order to establish a 'social contract' with the unions over wages policy.

This social contract was indeed a new development in government-union cooperation — a 'macro bargain' between the unions and the state, as John Hughes has described it, involving a voluntary instead of a legally imposed incomes policy resting on the collective authority, i.e. the self-discipline, of the unions, and redistributive measures by government including a wage freeze on top incomes and a rise in state pensions, plus planning agreements to direct company investment towards competitive industrial employment.

The 1972 Programme was largely incorporated into the next year's *Labour's Programme 1973*, on which the 1974 election was fought and won. But Mr Wilson had obtained the deletion of the much debated reference to the top 20 to 25 companies to be brought within the scope of planning agreements. According to Stuart Holland it was John Chalmers and not Tony Benn who had wished to set a number to indicate their serious intent. Wilson also deleted all references to replacing the Treasury as the central ministry for economic affairs. Wilson knew that, while there was strong support for an extension of public ownership and for government involvement in industry in the ranks of the Party and among union activists, this was not popular in the country at large. The reason was partly the strength of the prejudice against the government expressed in the media and partly the bitter opposition coming from the Confederation of British Industry. (Hatfield, pp.214ff.)

Since the failure in 1966 of George Brown's National Plan based on a Department of Economic Affairs, the Treasury was more firmly esconced in power than ever in all economic and financial matters. Benn had promised

> 'a fundamental and irreversible shift in the balance of power and wealth in favour of working people and their families',

but he had the whole apparatus of the British state working against him, as was to become clear when parts of the state security organs turned their sights onto Wilson himself.

When Labour came to power again in 1974, it was with a very small majority, not the massive endorsement for radical change like 1945. Tony Benn was given the Department of Industry, with a strong supportive left-wing team. But he soon lost Wilson's confidence. An industrialist was given the chair of the National Enterprise Board, planning agreements were shorn of the compulsory powers they were to have been given for obtaining information from large companies. Within a year Benn was demoted to the Ministry of Energy and his number two, Eric Heffer, had resigned.

So, when Mandelson and Liddle write of the 'Bennite fantasies of compulsory planning agreements', they are wrong on a number of counts. They had not been invented by Benn, but came from 'Labour's Programme for Britain' drafted for Labour's National Executive Committee by Geoff Bish of the Labour Party head office staff on the basis of proposals discussed and agreed in a broadly representative Industrial Committee of the Party, and endorsed at several Party conferences. They were not 'fantasies', but very largely copied from similar agreements already working successfully between government and big companies in France, Italy and elsewhere, covering information disclosure and agreement on investment policies (see Stuart Holland, ed. *Beyond Capitalist Planning*). In planning agreements to be reached with a number of large UK companies, there was to be a compulsory element to disclose information and to enter into agreements. Otherwise, the agreements would have been no more than a paper exercise. The carrot and the stick consisted in the granting or the withholding of government financial aid.

In the event, all compulsory elements were withdrawn from the Industry Bill, when it was presented to Parliament, and only one agreement was ever signed — by Benn's successor at the Department of Industry, Eric Varley, with the Chrysler Car Company to enable their take-over of the Rootes Group. This became a dead letter. The left had already been outmanoeuvred by Wilson in 1975 in relation to the Party's industrial policies. The Social Democrats were still apparently comfortable: they did not defect from the Party until six years later.

The Charge of Corporatism

It is a gross distortion of history to claim that Benn's Industry Bill and corporatist ideas for industry were the cause of Old Labour's failure or of the secession from the Party of the Social Democrats. *Labour's Programme 1973* stated that 'we reject the philosophy of the corporate state' and Benn had launched a major attack in a *Sunday Times* article in 1973 on the corporatism of the Heath Government's use of state intervention in support of private industry. He wanted public investment to be registered as a public stake, and in this respect might reasonably be seen as a pioneer of the stakeholder concept. This article of Benn's evoked an interesting riposte from Bill Rodgers in *Socialist Commentary*, the Social Democratic paper. After ridiculing Benn's comparison with Mussolini's Italy, Rodgers wrote:

> 'In our corporate state, the story goes, Parliament is increasingly by-passed as governments hob-nob with pressure groups outside and divest themselves of day-to-day responsibilities. But the fullest consultation at every stage with people most affected by decisions is highly desirable as a defence against bureaucracy.' (Hatfield, p.164)

The key question about corporatism is who is incorporated. Andrew Shonfield, director of Chatham House, writing in his *Modern Capitalism* (pp.122-3) about different brands of planning in Western Europe in the 1960s, distinguished three: indicative planning, as in the National Plan; planning based upon the state controlling a large part of industry, as in Eastern Europe at the time; and corporatist planning which brings together the major interest groups to conclude a series of bargains to move the economy in the direction they all agree upon. Labour was doing no more than ensure that the unions were involved as a major interest, to which Rodgers appeared then to have no objection.

So what was the problem for the Social Democrats like Bill Rodgers? We are bound to conclude that it was the change in the leadership of the unions. This was a shift from the exercise of arbitrary bureaucratic power, in the style of the old union bosses like Lord (Bill) Carron, to relatively open and democratic leadership. Suddenly, as it seemed at the time, the real opinions of members began to count as votes.

This was accompanied by a movement from the right to the left on industrial questions, but there is no evidence that membership political attitudes were changing. It was simply that they weren't being misrepresented any longer and a number of more or less right-wing union leaders like John Chalmers had become convinced of the need for more state intervention in industry. Concurrently the Social Democrats, who had supported planning agreements against further nationalisation, began to lose their support in the Parliamentary Party. With that gone, it was clear that none of them could look to lead the Labour Party; they looked instead to become leaders of a new party.

Regulating Investment and Prices

Full employment was still Labour's central aim, but maintaining it required new means for state intervention, not for more nationalisation, as Mandelson and Liddle pretend, but for planning agreements with big companies to extend democratic control of industry with union participation. It was an important addition to continental practice in state intervention that the British model had a democratic element. Even after Wilson had removed the compulsory powers under Planning Agreements, limited as they were to obtaining information, the 1975 Industry Act included the introduction into two existing institutions of important new powers to monitor and investigate private and public sector investment and pricing policies. These were the Industrial Development Advisory Board (IDAB) and the Prices Commission. Far from these bodies being either 'corporatist' or 'state socialist', they attempted to regulate business in the public interest. But this meant effecting some real control over monopoly pricing and the unaccountable investment of national resources. Whatever the rhetoric, this was what Tony Benn was actually doing — nothing 'mad' or 'aberrant'.

Such regulation, however, became too effective for the larger companies with monopoly or semi-monopoly positions and these two institutions were on the first list for abolition, as soon as Mrs Thatcher came to power. John Hughes, who was appointed by Tony Benn to IDAB and by Roy Hattersley as Deputy Chairman to the Prices Commission, has described 'thousands of millions of £s worth of selective assistance for urgently needed manufacturing investment', that went through their hands. This all ended with Thatcher, leaving Britain with declining capital investment in manufacturing and in the end virtually de-industrialised. Far from this state assistance being used indiscriminately to support 'lame ducks', as Mandelson and Liddle now aver, the Prices Commission was at the same time, according to Hughes, acting as an 'investigatory agency, able in a continuing way to scrutinise business pricing and other aspects of corporate policy . . . The price scrutiny is also part of the dialogue and bargaining over development: what does business want increased resources *for*? (is it seeking to develop in the UK?) . . . price controls are best understood by trade unionists as the extension of . . . bargaining with larger firms. The large firms, on examination, turn out to be not simply responding to 'pure' market forces, but to be engaged in power bargaining in various directions . . . This is true of both sectors, public and private . . . The investigatory process which the Price Commission developed systematically included direct contact with the trade unions involved in the enterprise . . .'

And Hughes goes on in responding critically to a 1982 Labour Party report on *Economic Planning and Industrial Democracy*, to conclude:

'In all these ways the "lessons of the past" were more positive than the "relative failure" . . . these most recent developments in planning under Labour Government . . . were not unfortunately part of a more general strategy of economic advance, and were undermined by the policies of economic management . . . of the Treasury/Bank of England.'

These measures to check rising unemployment by selective investment were only 'aberrant' in their moderation. Three million unemployed in 1933 led Clement Attlee to propose that 'all the major industries will be owned and controlled by the community', even while small enterprises could be 'carried on individually'. Mr Roy (now Lord) Jenkins commented in 1953 that Attlee 'said some things which now sound very odd indeed'. But Jenkins and his fellow Social Democrats writing in *Socialist Commentary* in 1956 still believed in

'planning to maintain full employment . . . no scaling it down to "a high and stable level of employment", no playing with the idea that a small dose of unemployment might be good for production.'

And twenty years later, Jenkins was still happy to seek help from Stuart Holland in the sections on economic planning for full employment in his book, *What Matters Now* and, as we have just seen, to propose in it extended measures of state intervention.

Was it the reality of a new and much stronger trade union movement and a new trend to joint government and union economic planning in the 1970s or just that they were losing influence in the Party, that made them want to 'break the mould'?

The Accusation of Trade Union Sectionalism

Planning agreements and other measures to reestablish full employment were strongly supported by the unions and pressed for in the annual Economic Reports prepared in the 1970s by the TUC. These have to be understood in relation to the growing numbers and strength of an increasingly educated trade union membership. Michael Foot at the Department of Employment in 1974 had established not only a Commission on Industrial Relations and a Health and Safety Commission, but an Employment Act which for the first time gave a statutory right to trade union representatives at the workplace to paid release for education and training. The major change which had taken place in the late 1960s and early 1970s in the leadership of British trade unions was in large part a result of democratic movements among the growing number of shop stewards. By 1974 there were 250,000 such trade union work-place representatives in a total trade union membership of nearly 12 million.

Contrary to Eric Hobsbawm's picture of the 'Forward March of Labour Halted' in the early 1970s, when Labour's vote declined, trade union membership continued to grow right up to 1979. Trade union power was indeed considerable in the 1970s, but it was mainly 'negative' power, in that it could sometimes veto unpopular decisions. It was not truly 'constructive', because it could not normally initiate beneficial change, determine new investment or shape industrial policy. Indeed, it had very little consistent influence over such positive decisions. It looked to Labour Governments for effective action, not as Mr Blair says for 'favours', but for productive investment to generate new employment opportunities in Britain. Thus the 'social contract' was a new departure in government-union cooperation:

> 'a prearranged agreement', as Stuart Holland has described it, 'to defend employment, social spending and welfare in return for a degree of wage restraint.'

But would the workers respond when they were called upon? The answer is that they did. The social contract held until the end of 1978, but it was in many respects a new trade union movement. Hobsbawm's criticism was actually addressing an important sociological change which was taking place in the 1970s, later accelerated by Mrs Thatcher's work of de-industrialisation. A manual working class which in 1911 comprised three-quarters of the population was reduced by 1976 to little over a half. Moreover, despite the increase in centralisation of capital through mergers and takeovers, the concentration of workers in plants of over 1000 — a quarter in plants of over 2000 in the 1960s — was for the first time since the Industrial Revolution being reduced. In the place of industrial manual workers, there had been a great increase in public sector employment, mainly of non-manual workers. A growing proportion of these were women. What Hobsbawm noted as a result, and lamented, was the spread of sectionalism — just when the need for unity and solidarity against the monopoly of capital was greater than ever.

Unions have always had sectional interests and the divide between skilled and unskilled, manual and non-manual and between competing industries like coal and oil, had for long been a fact of trade union life. It was the independent left, like the Institute for Workers' Control, which tried to overcome this sectionalism, while Hobsbawm's Communist Party tended to reinforce it. The remarkable feature of British trade unionism is that there has continued to be one central organisation for all unions, unchallenged until the 1980s and then not for long.

What Hobsbawm misses is that, despite the changes in employment, trade union membership in Britain grew and grew. As membership of manual workers declined, non-manual workers and especially women took their place. There is no doubt, however, that sectional strife was a serious problem in the 1970s. Despite the unity in resisting the Industrial Relations Act of 1971 and sympathy for the miners' strikes of 1972 and 1974, industrial action was sectionally driven. The miners' strikes were themselves sectional strikes in which the miners' leaders (some of whom were Communists) had not sought to involve either the oil workers and power station workers or the opencast miners. Even the dockers' strike which led to an upsurge of solidarity action, when five dockers were carried off to prison for defying court orders, was a strike against the spread of dock work to other transport workers at new containerised port terminals.

Redistribution of income and work within the working class is not popular with those who lose out, but it can sometimes be accepted within a general increase in employment and income. Redistribution of power is a bigger question and this was becoming *the* big question in the 1970s, as shop stewards began to challenge boardroom decision making powers.

Whatever their flaws, the policies of the TUC and the unions during the 1974-9 Labour government were strictly calculated to cut across sectional divisions and to create the most unified response. Such policies governed the work of the Liaison Committee — a tri-partite body of the PLP, NEC and TUC — which shaped a broad understanding on policy and procedure as part of what was truly seen as a social contract. They were given a powerful socialist drive from left-wing MPs on the NEC.

Hobsbawm rightly puts much blame for Labour's loss of votes after 1966 on the Wilson Governments. In spite of numerous desirable reforms which were enacted, it is on the great questions of social and political organisation that they may be judged to have been wasted years. The real democratic upsurge in the trade union movement in these years was consistently resisted by Wilson. New democratic experiments in participative forms of administration were explored in public sector enterprises, some of which were given government support, particularly in the Post Office, the nationalised steel industry and in local government. They suffered from the tendency to centralising union power, but at the same time other experiments emerged particularly in the development of workers' cooperatives. One set of experimental proposals from shop stewards at Lucas Aerospace won world-wide acclaim, and its authors were proposed for the Nobel Prize.

Industrial Democracy: An Aberration?

New trade union democracy threw up new leaders, who supported proposals for industrial democracy. There was a ferment of ideas after 1968 coming from the universities, which merged with the thinking about workers' involvement in management among trade union students, and some of their tutors on Day Release courses. This gained expression in the founding of the Institute for Workers' Control. IWC meetings attracted many from the new social movements of feminists, environmentalists and those concerned with Third World issues. All sorts and shapes of socialists and anarchists and liberals went to IWC conferences, including some 'loonies' like Harry Newton who were put there by MI5. But they were also attended by MPs, including, yes, Tony Benn, and Michael Meacher and more importantly by leading trade unionists. Among these were the leading members of the two largest unions, including Bill Jones, Chairman of the T&GWU and Hugh Scanlon, General Secretary of the AEUW. Mandelson and Liddle refer to trade unions in their day as the 'aberrations of the 1970s'. But the truth is that those unions represented the most advanced and systematic democracy achieved by the Labour Movement in Britain, on the strength of three decades of full employment.

The union leaders in Britain in the 1970s could only be called 'aberrant', if by this it is meant that they were straying away from the right-wing hierarchies of the previous two decades and the corporate norms of obedience that were then expected of trade union leaders by Labour Governments. What was true was that the Labour cabinets of this time included several members who were to leave Labour for the Conservatives or the Social Democrats, or later the Liberals. But the new union leaders were certainly not aberrant in relation to earlier trade union leaders like Ernie Bevin or Tom Mann. Jack Jones was probably the most perspicacious, and he tried hard to create conditions propitious for Labour Government, which would also meet the needs of his members. This he did in two respects: first, in designing an incomes policy that gave relatively more to the lower paid, since it gave an absolute sum per hour and not a percentage increase — this was at the heart of the 'social contract' — and secondly in arguing for a measure of industrial democracy to complement political democracy.

A Committee was set up by the government under the chairmanship of Professor Alan Bullock, vice-chancellor of Oxford University and Ernest Bevin's biographer, to recommend a scheme for workers' participation in company management. The proposal which emerged was not particularly radical, certainly not as radical as the IWC conferences had been asking for, not even as radical as that which had already been canvassed by the TUC. The Labour cabinet, however, turned it down, after referring it for a long period of procrastination to a cabinet sub-committee. The cabinet members assigned to the task of shelving it were Shirley Williams and Edmund Dell, who subsequently both left the Labour Party for the Social Democrats on the grounds that Labour was moving towards a corporatist centralised state. Mrs (now Lady) Williams, lacking any developed sense of shame, subsequently announced her conviction that Britain's problems could only be cured by the introduction of industrial democracy. Mr Liddle refrains from recording the thoughts of his boss, Bill Rodgers, who was convinced that such a corporatist state was a good idea. (Michael Hatfield, *The House the Left Built*, p.164).

Without an instalment of industrial democracy — what could be called real 'stakeholding'— and without a wider framework of government planning for industry, to maintain full employment — such as Mr Blair is shying away from — by 1978 the Labour Government was set on course for disaster. But it was not, as we shall see, the left that brought it down.

CHAPTER 5

Who Failed Old Labour?

'What happened to the Labour Party in the late 1970s and early 1980s is that its intellectual temple was stormed and captured by a generation of politicians and academics who thought that values and concepts like community and social justice were too weak to guide the party . . . the Party went through a period when because for many it justified itself solely in terms of nationalisation, it became divorced from the people it claimed to represent and at the same time subjected itself to continual debate about betrayal. Tragically it turned its back on an entire strain of thinking within the Labour Party — the tradition of ethical socialism.'

Tony Blair, 'My Vision for Britain' in Giles Radice-(ed.) What Needs to Change, *Harper Collins, 1996*

We have already suggested that there are reasons for doubting Mr Blair's ethical socialist convictions, but the statement quoted at the head of this chapter encapsulates almost all the dishonesty about the past and ambiguity about the future, which characterises New Labour pronouncements. We have shown how ambiguous are the concepts of community which Mr Blair has advanced and which we would certainly argue were an inadequate guide for any party. Nor did we think that the values of social justice were the same as those of equality and respect for the worth of all human beings which lies at the heart of the traditional Labour concept of socialism. But the idea that Labour in the late 1970s and early 1980s 'justified itself solely in terms of nationalisation' is too ridiculous to be taken seriously. Nobody reading the Party discussions of that period could come to that conclusion. Such discussions of nationalisation as did take place then were around how to reform it to make it more democratic and participative, and they received absolutely no supportive input from those who later founded the Social Democratic Party. But let us first take the accusation which lies behind Blair's statement that it was the left in the Party which brought down the Labour Government in 1979.

The Winter of Discontent

It is the accepted norm among New Labour speakers to blame the unions for the fall of the Labour government in what is referred to as the 'winter of discontent of 1978-9'. The accusation against the unions has somehow become merged in New Labour talk with accusations against 'Bennite aberrations'. The Social Democrats certainly did defect after Labour's defeat in the 1979 election, but can that defeat really be blamed upon actions of the left in the Party during that winter?

The facts of that unhappy winter are not difficult to relate. The profits of the big UK companies had benefited from Denis Healey's tax concessions, made in order to help them over the oil price rises, to an extent that left them hardly paying any tax at all. In 1977 the top 25 companies paid £400 millions on profits of over £4,000 millions. This was becoming clear to the unions which had agreed to a policy of wage restraint. Then in the autumn of 1978, the Ford Motor Company, having had a rather profitable year, granted a large wage increase to its workers, to fend off a threatened strike. At the same time the government, headed, after Wilson's resignation in 1976, by James Callaghan, with a parliamentary majority like Mr Major's today dependent on the votes of the Ulster Unionists, proposed to impose a ceiling of 5% on wage increases for public sector workers. This was proposed while the annual rate of inflation was ranging from 17% to 25% and unemployment was rising. It meant for many a swingeing cut in what were already poverty wages.

Not surprisingly, public sector workers went on strike. They included the London dustmen, and soon the streets of London were piled high with rubbish. Mr Callaghan, facing a further problem of demands for decentralisation of government, failed to make the necessary concessions to the demands coming from Scotland, Wales and, more importantly, Northern Ireland, and lost his majority in Parliament.

Now, it is said that the unions should not have pushed their luck in the capital-intensive private sector where productivity was rising. Nor should others have followed suit in the labour-intensive public sector, where increases in labour productivity are hard to achieve, without the excessive hours of work and abandoned safety provisions that became a feature of 'deregulation' and 'union bashing' in the years that followed under Mrs Thatcher's rule. The fact is that the unions had for three years held to the social contract and the Wilson and Callaghan governments had not. Labour was being penalised, capital let off lightly. The agreement made by a Labour Government to cut public spending

including no increase in old age pensions was the last straw — a part
of the Treasury's agreement with the IMF on the terms for a loan to
cover the balance of payments deficit.

Moreover, there were countervailing measures which could have
been introduced to advance union participation in company investment
decisions and to compensate for wage restraint. These had been
proposed by the unions, and were rejected not by Mr Benn and his
'activists', but by Messrs Callaghan and Healey with the full support of
the defectors to social democracy, some of whom now adorn the ranks
of New Labour in the House of Lords.

The unions were demanding not just an egalitarian policy inside the
working class to help up the low paid, as Jack Jones's lump-sum increase
for all was designed to do, but a more egalitarian policy between capital
and labour. In the event the skilled tool-room engineers had seen their
differentials reduced during the first 'social contract' and then watched
their wage increases being wiped out by inflationary price rises while
post-tax profits in the advanced private industrial sector boomed. At the
other end of the scale, the IMF-driven wage freeze hit the poorest public
sector workers the hardest. A 5% wage increase offered against inflation
at five times that amount was what resulted at the 1979 Election in
Labour's worst ever share of the votes of trade unionists. Who then
should be blamed for these transfers of votes? Those who felt let down,
or those responsible for creating such feelings? There are no bad soldiers,
we would think, but only bad generals.

Wasted Chances

Support for the Bullock Report might have put some pressure behind
the redistribution of income and of power from capital to labour,
through what might now be called 'stakeholding'. One other proposal
had been bruited about by the unions, but without any interest being
shown by the Labour Government. This was a scheme adopted briefly
in Sweden at the suggestion of a Swedish socialist finance minister,
Rudolf Meidner. It involved paying a lower wage increase to workers
in capital intensive industries than was justified by their increased
productivity and setting aside the unpaid surplus into an employees'
fund, in which union members could share control either of investment
in the company or for local social investment. The profits were then to
be fed into the workers' pension funds.

A similar proposal to that of Meidner was made by John Hughes to place the tax reliefs allowed to UK companies in 1974, to compensate for oil price rises, into

> 'blocked balances (company level investment funds) to be released with the agreement of the planning authorities to assist in financing future investment.'

The scheme was resisted by the British Treasury and the Bank of England. So what could have been a powerful planning and investment process linked to selective industrial aid was stopped. Much the same happened in Sweden where the workers, not having a majority of the voting rights in any company, could not in fact prevent an outflow of capital, which sent the Swedish economy into crisis. In the UK at that time with a larger state sector of industry more might have been done.

Introduction of a Hughes-Meidner-type scheme could have not only restrained the outflow of capital from the UK but reduced the pressure for wage increases in some capital-intensive industries. These were naturally copied in the labour-intensive service industries, mainly in the public sector, where, as we have seen, productivity increases are relatively slow and wages are often desperately low. Thus, some check could have been exercised on that element in price inflation that was being caused by a general rise in wages. Of course, the main element was the increase in oil prices. If such a scheme had been successfully introduced into the UK manufacturing industry, the whole tragedy of the 1978-9 winter might have been avoided and the subsequent years of Thatcherite redistribution of income from the poor to the rich and deliberate destruction of the British trade union movement could have been prevented.

The conclusion has to be drawn that, far from the Bennite left and the unions having been responsible for the collapse of the Labour government in 1979, the onus must fall fairly and squarely on the right wing of the Party, which undermined what had been a written contract between the government and the unions. Benn was removed from his influential position at the Ministry of Industry, where planning agreements were to have been initiated, and replaced by Eric Varley, who was to end up as the chairman of the Derbyshire based transnational company, now known as Anglo United, owners of Coalite. The trade union involvement in the National Enterprise Board, established to manage the companies in the public sector including the main British motor group, had a strong representative in Harry Urwin. But his colleague Jack Jones was black-balled by the Intelligence

Services, because he had fought against Franco with the International Brigade in Spain. The Board was handed over very largely to private industrialists who had no interest even in maintaining a British presence in the world motor industry.

Bennery: Father of Stakeholding?

There was, indeed, something which both the owners of capital in the UK and the British Civil Service had to complain about in Tony Benn's conduct at the Ministry of Industry. The complaint is best illustrated by a particular story. A large United States agricultural machinery manufacturer, International Harvester, with a major plant in Doncaster proposed to close down its UK operation and transfer to Germany, because it claimed that the British plants were losing money. The shop stewards at Harvesters took their case to Benn. This was that the firm had raised very sharply the internal transfer price charged to Doncaster for the tractor engines imported from Germany for assembly with the other parts manufactured in Doncaster and Ireland. This had made it impossible, they said, for the UK plant to be profitable and was a way of transferring capital for new investment from the UK to Germany. Benn consulted his civil servants who assured him that the new German engine was a much improved and more costly model. So Benn invited the shop stewards to the Ministry to confront the civil servants and representatives from import control at Customs and Excise. The stewards brought drawings with them, which showed the new engines to have only the most minor modification, which did not justify increasing the transfer price.

This kind of action came to be called 'Bennery' in Whitehall and led to complaints being made to the Prime Minister. Today, it might be called giving the workers a 'stake' in their company in the 'stakeholder' partnership of owners, workers, consumers and government which New Labour proposes to introduce. If that is what stake-holding means, then 'Bennery' will prove not to have been such an 'aberration' after all. Or was the problem with Benn that he tried to make his rhetoric into a reality? His rhetoric sometimes ran ahead of reality, but it is not true that the Party's policies and direction were ever captured by that, as Mr Blair and his associates are now pretending.

The Response to Thatcher: Labour and Social Democrat

Labour's response in the aftermath of Mrs Thatcher's victory at the polls in 1979 is said by New Labour to have been the real disaster for

Labour. What are the facts? A left majority had been established on Labour's National Executive Committee since the rise of the 'terrible twins', the Jones-Scanlon partnership, at the beginning of the 1970s. Towards the end of this ascendancy came Tony Benn's challenge for the deputy leadership of the Labour Party. By that time the trade union left was already fracturing. Scanlon was replaced by Terry Duffy, who had strong support from those who were about to defect from the Labour Party. Nonetheless, the Social Democrats deserted the Party claiming that they were hemmed in by a left bloc in the Party and the unions. They must have known that the left majority in the Party Conference was in fact tenuous. Benn failed in his bid for the deputy leadership in 1981, because he opposed an incomes policy and believed that that must lead him to oppose a minimum wage. This lost him the vote of the National Union of Public Employees, who so soon after the winter of discontent could not have failed to give a large majority to any advocate of a policy of raising low wages. And it was this which lost him the election.

The 1983 general election following the SDP breakaway was the most serious reverse for Labour since the defection of Prime Minister MacDonald in 1931. Labour's vote fell to 28% of those cast. The result of this defeat was a decline in the left's influence in the NEC and in Parliament. The unions began to suffer the ravages of unemployment and new hostile legislation. Yet there was no breakaway of unions, for which the SDP had been waiting. No others followed the electricians in leaving the TUC, and none at all severed their connection with Labour. The SDP withered, until Blair came to raise them from the dead, by giving their veterans new life in his office.

There was, however, a strengthening of Labour in the 1980s — in local government. During the first two Thatcher administrations, local government elections bucked the trend of the national vote. Labour won the Greater London Council (GLC) and in a number of the new Metropolitan Councils in the Midlands and North, Labour consolidated its control. A whole range of innovative programmes for employment creation and environmental improvement were introduced in an attempt to alleviate, if not to offset, the mass unemployment and deindustrialisation which Mrs Thatcher's policies had generated.

Some Old Labour Successes

Ken Livingstone, as the GLC Labour leader, became for a time outstandingly the most popular Labour politician. And the success of the GLC and the Labour led Metropolitan Councils was so great that Mrs Thatcher felt the need to root out their authority. The subsequent opprobrium that was attached to them as the 'Loony Left' was a right-wing media slander which Mandelson and Liddle have found it convenient to repeat. But it is a travesty of the truth about the caring and innovative work of these Labour authorities in job creation, care of the elderly, training for the young, encouragement of the arts, ending smoking on the Underground and many other popular initiatives. It is a particularly nauseating slander in relation to the attempt of these Labour Councils to remove the stigmata from those who were most disadvantaged in society — blacks, Asians, single parents, pensioners, the disabled.

It is simply a distortion of history for New Labour spokesmen to complain that throughout the 1980s the left and the unions were too powerful, so that nothing could be done to develop a renewed Party, more in tune with a changed workforce and new concerns for the position of women and for consumer and environmental issues. Let Lewis Minkin sum up from his comprehensive examination of the period:

'Consider the innovative record revealed in this study of changes in procedure and institution which have either involved the unions or entailed their acquiescence since 1979; new Joint Policy Committees and Joint Policy Review Groups; new procedures for candidate selection and leadership elections; a reorganisation of the Women's conference and of Women's Executive representation; acceptance of the principle of women's quotas; a new campaign strategy committee; a new organisation for the political mobilisation of trade unionists; TULV transmuting via TUCC into TUFL; new financial arrangements; a new relationship with sponsored MPs involving a new category of 'political officers'; broad agreement on a major reduction in the union vote at Party Conference, and on a wide ranging overhaul of the procedures of policy making including the procedure of the Party Conference and a new National Policy Forum; a major change in the role of the (much misunderstood) Labour Party-TUC Liaison Committee from a central position in 1982 to a point in 1990 when it had virtually disappeared.'

And all this took place before the Blair 'revolution'. It did not, however, win the 1992 General Election, when the tabloid press turned against Labour in the last week before polling day. It was in this that the residual forces of Labour failed, and in having no convincing answer to mass unemployment. But will New Labour do any better?

And we must not forget Old Labour's successes in government. Unemployment was kept below the one million mark until the very end of the Wilson-Callaghan administrations, when it is true that Old Labour was defeated by the concessions it made (in the end unnecessarily) for the IMF loan. Lewis Minkin sums up the comparison of Labour's last years in government from 1974-9 with the years that followed under Tory rule:

> 'It did better in terms of unemployment, particularly against the background of world trade (rising world oil prices). The adjusted growth rates now make the Labour Government's record better than that of the Conservatives since 1979 — in spite of the direct and indirect advantage of North Sea oil. Further the reality of the past 25 years (to 1990) is that each period of Labour in office in the 1960s and 70s produced an improvement in the balance of payments and in manufacturing investment whereas each period of Conservative government resulted in a deterioration.'

What kind of failure was that? The truth is that Labour governments by and large managed the economy rather better than their opponents did. What they did not do was to transform social relations, or lift up the spirits of those who supported them. Does New Labour have the desire to do the one or the capacity for the other?

CHAPTER 6

*Will New Labour 'Deliver'?
And to Whom?*

'Next year will be the 50th anniversary of the 1944 White Paper on Employment. That White Paper said: "The Government accept as one of their primary aims and responsibilities the maintenance of a high and stable level of employment". Today, I reaffirm that aim. The goal of full employment remains right at the heart of Labour's vision for Britain'.

John Smith addressing the 1993 Trade Union Congress

'There is no rash promise of full employment tomorrow and ultra-high growth every year thereafter, but New Labour does offer policies to produce something much better than the despair and cynicism we see now — lasting security, and increased hope and opportunity for the future.'

Peter Mandelson and Roger Liddle, The Blair Revolution: Can Labour Deliver?

Enemies of Labour frequently claim that it is too much to expect either 'full employment tomorrow' or 'ultra-high growth', which would be a different thing altogether. But the promise of 'something much better' than what we see now is surely the very least that any Party challenging a dying government could propose. And do New Labour's policies indeed offer 'lasting security and increased hope'? Not-Very-Old Labour, under the leadership of John Smith, really did offer hope, because it was firmly committed to full employment. Now the situation is quite dismal.

Parties in opposition have two tasks to perform — one is to design and promote a set of alternative policies to win a major part of the voters at the next election, but the other is more important: to sustain the morale and raise the aspirations of their supporters even before the government can be changed, in order to bond them together as an opposition capable not only of defending its interests, but of expanding them. 'I have come', James Larkin used to say, 'to stir you not to be contented with a little.'

What New Labour Promises to 'Deliver'

The so-called 'Road to the Manifesto', *Labour's Contract for a New Britain* is full of fine words about the better life we could have, but with very few precise commitments of government action to get us there. Even the 'five pledges' lack precision, as we indicate in our comments in brackets. Some will be discussed at greater length later. The five pledges are:

● using money saved from phasing out the assisted places scheme at private schools, to cut class sizes to 30 or under for 5, 6 and 7 year olds; (how much money and when? how will this be implemented with local management of schools?)

● bringing in fast track punishment for persistent young offenders by halving the time from arrest to sentencing; (to what? new prisons?)

● cutting NHS waiting lists by treating 100,000 patients by releasing £100m. saved from NHS red tape; (which managers will be sacked?)

● getting 250,000 under 25-year-olds into work by using money from a windfall levy on privatised utilities; (how much money and at what rates of pay?)

● setting tough rules for government spending and borrowing: ensure low inflation, strengthen the economy so that interest rates are as low as possible.(Does this mean continuing the Tory policy of putting control of inflation ahead of full employment?)

The only other fairly clear statements, that are not general hopes and aspirations, are the following (again with our queries in brackets):

● proposing a cash tax rebate for employers who take on long term unemployed (does this mean creating short term unemployed by replacing existing employees?)

● abolishing the 16-hour rule that deprives the young unemployed of educational opportunities; (with what money for their education?)

● creating a publicly owned, publicly accountable railway system as economic circumstances and the priorities of transport policy allow; (when will that be and with what subsidy to compete with road?)

● retaining the key elements of the (Tory) trade union legislation of the 1980s; (does this include sympathy strikes?)

● introducing a minimum wage decided according to the economic circumstances of the time and with the advice of a Low Pay Commission (how will the wage relate to social security levels?)

● constructing a system of post-11 education to acknowledge different abilities, but within comprehensive schooling; the future of the

remaining grammar schools is up to the parents affected; (does comprehensive schooling mean the same as comprehensive schools?)
- retaining SERPs with a new framework for funded second-tier pension provision (will this be with state or private funding and will it, like SERPs, be redistributive in favour of the poor?)
- the costs of pollution should, as far as is possible, be borne by those who pollute; (how far is this possible and what measures will be employed to ensure payment? As of today, in spite of rhetoric to fill a decade, the polluter almost never pays.)
- Reforming the right of hereditary peers to sit and vote in the House of Lords (Does that mean ending it?)
- QUANGOs will be made properly accountable to the people (how?)
- Crude Council tax capping should go (but what about less crude?)
- A directly elected strategic authority for London with the consent of the people of London (with what powers and how to obtain consent?)
- In Scotland a parliament with law making powers, and seeking the people's approval for giving the parliament defined financial powers to vary revenue (which people? how much power?)
- A Freedom of Information Act (with what powers?)
- Our security will be based on the North Atlantic Alliance and we will retain Trident and press for multilateral negotiations on nuclear, chemical and biological weapons (and in the meantime make what offers of disarmament?)
- target our resources to help the poorest people in the poorest countries (but what resources? up to the internationally agreed 0.7% of GDP, which the Tories have reneged on? The 0.7% was not a figure plucked out of the air, but was based on careful calculations made by Professor Tinbergen to allow for an optimal rate of development. Before he died he informed us that it should be revised to a figure three times higher if the IMF depredations in the Third World in the 1980s were to be offset)

What Sort of Opposition is New Labour?

For a party of labour, the task of an opposition is indispensable. It is to do everything possible to organise people to defend themselves, and to protect those who live solely by the sale of their labour and those who are too young or too old to work, as well as the unemployed and disabled. Since they make up a large majority of the total population, it is important for a Labour Party to show all the time it is in opposition that it is unsleeping in its defence of their vital needs. Even if there were no elections at all, this would be imperative. When democracy is at work, it remains crucial. Other parties know this. It was their local community politics that kept the Liberal Democrats alive through long years in the wilderness.

Mandelson and Liddle tell a story of Tony Blair occupying his office in Parliament as Opposition leader and being questioned why it was so drab, without pictures or any decoration. Blair's reply was that he was not in politics to oppose but to get on with doing something useful: 'My job is to get out of this office as quickly as possible, not to make it my home.' (M&L, p.31) This is, of course, a natural ambition in any politician, but 'doing something useful' is just as necessary in opposition as it is in government. Labour has not had the opportunity to fail in government since 1979, although it made a good fist of failure then. But it would not have stayed in opposition so long if it had acquitted itself better in the tasks of opposition. In fact there is a strong case for the view that it has been a bigger failure in opposition than it ever was in government. Labour politicians tend to think that opposition is an act performed at the dispatch box. It is not. It is affirmed in the theatre of the mind: it is either an act of public persuasion, or it will prove a comprehensive disappointment.

There has always been some fear among parliamentarians, particularly in the Labour Party, of 'extra-parliamentary' activity, which takes the form of country wide campaigns, marches, lobbies and demonstrations. Only in moments of national crisis — over reform bills, wars like the Suez War or the development and testing of nuclear weapons — have Party leaders encouraged such activity. It has evidently not been thought a proper activity for New Labour, although the level of unemployment amounts to a national crisis.

In Parliament itself, there is, nevertheless, a whole range of issues where the Major government's wafer-thin majority might have been challenged by Blair in the interest of ordinary people. Even more important, the Party could have campaigned to change media-induced public opinion, rather than conforming to it and in doing so reinforcing those trends most antipathetic to the traditional Labour aims of equality and humanity. Where inequalities have been challenged, the challenge has been half-hearted at best, the desire to placate what is called 'Middle England' being put first for electoral considerations — 'Middle England' standing for what the polls reveal as the more selfish and more short-sighted concerns of the more affluent third of the population.

Why have the following issues not been challenged more strongly and resisted more continuously:

- first, the steady erosion by the government of the rights of the unemployed, especially to refuse unsuitable work, and their replacement by job-seekers' allowances, with benefit sanctions and means-tested social security provision;
- second, the abolition of Wages Councils without any alternative protection for lower paid workers;
- third, the cut in the standard tax rate across all incomes, which gives most to the richest, nothing to the unemployed;
- fourth, the renewal of the Prevention of Terrorism Act, and its reinforcement with new powers for the police to stop and search with impunity — a denial of civil liberties established over the centuries;
- fifth, the Home Secretary's mad requirement of more and harsher custodial sentences, despite the doubts of the judges, and the consequent need to build more prisons — a policy that has failed dismally to reduce crime in the United States;
- sixth, the Tory government's actions in the Vienna talks on arms control, which were openly claimed to be to 'ensure a level playing field for British industry', i.e. arms industry, no matter what the nature of the political regimes to which the arms are sold;
- seventh, the steady cut-back in aid to less developed countries and lack of support for the cancellation of the foreign debts of the least developed;
- eighth, the increasing discrimination in financial provision in favour of opted out and selective schools and the steady erosion of the student grants for higher education;
- ninth, the railway privatisation plans and their adverse implications for public transport;
- tenth, the reduction of the employment and health and safety rights which in the past gave trade union representatives some power to protect their members;
- eleventh, the relentless introduction of market forces into the National Health Service, as it was;
- twelfth, latest but not least important, the dismissive attitude shown by New Labour itself to consultation with the unions, especially in the lack of advance discussion of the Blair plan for a direct appeal to individual members of the Party — One-Member-One-Vote — on a referendum for a centrally prepared election manifesto.

Why has Mr Blair Dropped the Unions?

There are still eight million union members, although the membership has been very severely run down as a result of the massive reduction of employment in production industries and in the public sector under Mrs Thatcher's administration. Between 1979 and 1994 the number employed in these industries was reduced by 3.3 millions. Over the same period, the number employed in the public sector, mainly in service industries, was cut by a further two million. These two together somewhat exceed the fall in trade union membership from 13 million to 8 million over these years. There will be some double counting in the public sector reduction because one million of these jobs were lost in the nationalised industries. Unemployment, which rose from one million in 1979 to over three million in 1995 (Labour Force Survey count; the OECD count totals four million) more than makes this up.

Apart from the deliberate creation of unemployment, a direct assault on the unions was launched by Mrs Thatcher. Ballots were imposed for all elections and before strikes could be called. The number of pickets permitted was reduced, and flying pickets were outlawed together with sympathy strikes. The closed shop was made illegal and the strongest union in the country, the National Union of Mineworkers, was divided and crushed. This was achieved by encouraging the defection of the Nottinghamshire miners and by attempts to isolate the NUM leadership through the active intervention of the state security services.

Very soon after Mrs Thatcher was elected to form a government, she had speeded up the introduction of natural gas from the North Sea as a third power station fuel in addition to oil and coal. After the miners' defeat, huge resources of coal were left in the ground and flooded at the bottom of shafts from which it will be impossible to work them again. Tragically, the defence of the coal industry by Labour's leaders and social democrats alike was luke-warm or non-existent. It is one thing to criticise the miners' leadership, but we now know that some of the more provocative behaviour was introduced by people having close associations with certain security agencies. Is this all to be forgotten by New Labour and no recompense made to the devastated mining areas?

Given the assault on the unions which was launched by the Thatcher Government and continued under Major, it is surprising that the fall in trade union membership has not been greater. The effect of such a reduction in numbers has inevitably been a concentration of minds on mere survival and the defence of members' redundancy payments and other rights on discharge, with little time to devote to thinking about alternative policies. But the reception by New Labour of such thoughts as they have emerged has been cool and often actually negative. In his maiden speech in the House of Commons, Tony Blair said that he stood for 'cooperation, not confrontation, for fellowship not fear.' Yet, in reviewing Blair's role as shadow Employment Secretary between 1990 and 1992, Mandelson and Liddle comment:

> 'The confrontation with the trade unions was difficult for Blair, because he was fresh in the job when the argument started and he was a relatively junior member of the shadow cabinet to be taking on the unions in that way.'

What was 'that way'? Tony Blair had already spoken out against the closed shop. He then argued that most of the Tory legislation on the unions should stand. Some trade unionists have now accepted ballots before strikes and for executive elections, and some might accept restrictions on mass and flying pickets, but the general outlawing of sympathy strikes has challenged the whole principle of solidarity. Not only have no similar restrictions to those applied to the unions been brought into force in the much less democratic terrain of company law, but none are contemplated. Managerial prerogatives are safe with New Labour.

Taking over from Thatcher? The End of Old Labour

Mrs Thatcher had hoped to reduce the political activities of the unions by requiring union members to ballot at ten-year intervals if they were to maintain a political fund (essential if they were to finance the Labour Party), instead of having a once-for-all ballot to initiate such a fund in perpetuity. She was much disturbed when overwhelming majorities voted to confirm their political funds in every trade union which had hitherto maintained a fund, and in quite a number which had not. The result was an enlargement of the numbers contributing and Labour retained its strong links with the unions.

Blair's policy for the unions has truly taken over — 'from where Margaret Thatcher left off', as Mandelson and Liddle put it. He has set about changing the whole nature of the Labour Party, which had been established as a federal party of membership branches and trade unions, jointly agreeing on policies at an annual conference, which Labour in government would normally try to follow.

In broad constitutional terms, the new leader has sought to change the position of the unions in New Labour by putting them on a par with the representatives of the employers. An effort to write hints about this into the new constitution was beaten off in the negotiations with the National Executive Committee of the Party. Nonetheless, the union role has already been downgraded. Consultation is now minimal. Union leaders are frequently disparaged, even publicly slighted. Spin doctors give hostile, unattributed, briefings to the press against those who are thought to be 'obstructive'. There has been a considerable reduction in the power of union leaders to engage along with the constituency representatives in making Party policy. Not only has the voting strength of the unions at conference been greatly reduced but Conference itself has been losing its power of policy making. Hitherto this has always been exercised under the guidance of the National Executive of the Party, elected by and answerable to the same Party Conference.

At the 1996 Trade Union Congress the ultimate strategy was revealed, in an open threat of a formal divorce between the Labour Party and the unions. Stephen Byers' alleged 'indiscretions' were, of course, deniable. He said that if a wave of strikes broke out after the election of a Labour Government, the divorce would follow. Firstly, this presumably means that a Blair administration might be planning to stimulate a wave of strikes by swingeing cuts in public and welfare expenditure, since it is entirely possible that the Conservatives will leave public finances in a very troubled state. Let us suppose that such cuts might provoke protests. A 'divorce' from the unions would be the very worst imaginable response. It would rub salt in all the wounds. The second point is that trade unions should pay special attention to the very limp denials of Byers' warning. The general impression that was given was that this statement was wrong because it was premature. Any legislation would come 'later'. How reminiscent of Tony Blair's own handling of Clause IV! During the Labour Leadership contest of 1994, when David Frost asked him about plans to get rid of Clause IV, Blair said '. . . I don't think that anyone is saying now, looking ahead to the next two years in the run-up to an election, that this is what we should focus on'. In the light of all this, it is completely understandable that many Labour members suspect that they are being softened up for the next onslaught.

Today the Labour Party's policy statements are ostensibly drawn up within the shadow cabinet, chosen by Labour Members of Parliament. In fact, some shadow cabinet members read about them in the newspapers. This showed very clearly when the double referendum was announced from on high, for controlling the progress of Scottish devolution. Policies are now presented to a National Policy Forum and to regional forums of representatives of individual members, but chiefly for endorsement, as Austin Mitchell has been complaining.

Trade union members are encouraged to become individual members of the Party and take their part in discussing, but not in fact deciding, policy through these forums. As for the Members of Parliament, they have always had the power to elect, if not subsequently to influence, members of the Shadow Cabinet. But in the summer of 1996 there was even an attempt to postpone such elections on the pretext of a forthcoming General Election. When this attempt was foiled, there was some highly questionable use of members' proxy votes in order to prevent the defeat of candidates who are close to the leader but unpopular with MPs. The strengthening and expansion of the leader's office is the salient fact in this story. The vanguard is to the right of centre and the leader leads. Although the trade unions still dominate the NEC with the support of women trade unionists and could theoretically veto a manifesto and influence a leadership vote, this power must be regarded as under threat from the Blair offensive.

In effect, all this represents an attempt to put an the end to the old Labour Party, built as it was on a unique federal alliance of trade unions and local party branches. The 'bourgeois democracy of "One-Member-One-Vote"', as John MacMurray, Blair's inspirer, called it, has triumphed. This is the nature, of course, of representative democracy. A bare majority of individual voters can determine the lives of the rest. Indeed, under the British system, the party with most votes can do this and it does not even need to have won a majority of the actual voters still less of all those eligible to vote.

The old system of democracy in the Labour Party sought to add something to 'One-Member-One-Vote', by drawing upon the group interests of unions and the group discussions of branches. As MacMurray would have said, individuals can be counted, but only persons can participate. There were criticisms to be made of the old system, where the total vote of each union was cast in line sometimes with a bare majority decision of the union delegates and where many party branches were thinly attended. Most have not recovered under New Labour's dispensations, and it is fair to say that often the situation has got worse, with more and more organisations finding it difficult to raise a quorum in their meetings.

But the old aim was a good one — allow for each union or branch to have a view and then seek to composite these views. The system had not been invented in the unions, but was copied from the non-conformist churches, who sometimes voted by size of congregations, in order to ensure that large chapels were not over-ruled or hijacked by small ones. As a new wave of union democracy emerged in the 1970s, there was real membership involvement in decision making. This, as we have shown, was not at all to the liking of those Party leaders who had relied on the union 'barons' to muster the 'feudal host' on their behalf, and resulted in the defections to the Social Democratic Party. What Mandelson and Liddle describe as 'a huddle of half a dozen men' from the unions did sometimes determine party policy. But none of those who left the Party for the Social Democrats complained when the half dozen were of their opinion.

It is also true that composited resolutions often failed in the end to represent the views of all of those whose resolutions had been composited. But the compositing was almost always in the direction of caution and policies had first been hammered out in thousands of small meetings of branches and hundreds of constituencies and in unions where personal experience and opinion counted. There was a real sense of a Labour Movement, and that now seems be drawing to a close, with the withering away of the role of the delegate Conference and of its National Executive drawn from unions and branches. Will Hutton is not the only one to have detected a 'distinctly centralist tone' in the preparations being made by New Labour for government. (Hutton, *Prospect*, March 1996, p.50)

New Labour: The Party for 'Middle England'?

New Labour is said to 'reflect the needs and aspirations of individuals and not of interest groups acting for them'. There is no room now, say Mandelson and Liddle, for 'trouble makers and extremist groups'. The 'leadership', we are told, 'is more in control of the Party.' Policy statements prepared from on high by a leader and his parliamentary shadows, however much they may afterwards do to present them and to count the carefully pre-structured votes, are no substitute for discussion rising from below. 'One-Member-One-Vote' is representative democracy at its minimum. The old Labour Party really was a 'broad church', in which many voices could be heard and some acted upon. A more united and more disciplined party may just possibly win an election, but how then will it govern? That must depend upon the way it responds to the felt needs, not only of the most vocal, better off population in the south and east of England, where New Labour claims

88

to have drawn much of its new support, but also of the overwhelming majority of the people everywhere whose lives are now impoverished or desperately insecure.

The foundation rock of the Labour Party has always been the unions. A Social Democratic party, such as New Labour, aspires to be a national party that appeals beyond the ranks of organised labour. Old Labour had the same aspirations, and as reflected in the membership of the PLP, was 'unique among major parties', according to Lewis Minkin,

> 'in the closeness it came to the national profile of the British people. It brought together valuable but different life experiences. And in the diversity of its profile, it came near to its aspiration of being a people's party of workers by hand and brain' (Minkin, p.14)

The question which New Labour is raising is whether the separation from the unions and the insinuation, even amounting to imposition, of candidates from the higher paid professions will not disturb that profile. It has always to be remembered that in a democracy the importance of the position of people adds nothing to their numbers when we are considering a party's representativeness.

Nearly half of the British population is still made up of manual workers and less skilled non-manual, service and clerical workers and their families, old and young. Trade union membership remains at over eight million, nearly half of them women. Without this army of relatively solid supporters, where will New Labour be? The SDP, we saw, tried and failed to win trade union support. New Labour's desire to distance itself from the unions brought on its head a fierce legal action from the Engineers' union, recently its most reliable supporter, following the questionable conduct of a parliamentary selection conference in Swindon, where it was announced that a favoured media-person and not a local engineer had 'won'.

The distance that Tony Blair and Gordon Brown are putting between themselves and the unions must raise questions about the solidity of the traditional Labour vote. If they hold it once — to oust the hated Tories — can New Labour, as Mandelson and Liddle ask, 'deliver' enough to win a second time? What the British people are being offered is no longer the 'sword of justice', as David Metcalf called the Labour-union alliance, nor the 'bulwark of democratic freedom against tyranny', as Francis Williams called the unions, nor the 'basis of social ownership' and 'popular administration' of the old Clause IV, but a 'stakeholding' in a capitalist society. What does it really mean?

The Stakeholder Economy: Who are the Stakeholders?

New Labour's concept of a 'stakeholder economy' is introduced in its manifesto by phrases recognising the globalisation of economic activity, the rapidity of technological change, the power of what are called 'dynamic markets' (polite word for transnational capital), the poor economic performance of the UK under the Tories and especially the educational backwardness of Britain's workforce — all leading up to insistence on the absolute necessity of fostering British industrial competitiveness by all pulling together as one nation. Getting down to detail, it turns out not to be so very different after all from central Tory policy. When Tony Blair unveiled his plans for a 'stakeholder economy', speaking to businessmen in Singapore in January of 1996, the *Financial Times* correspondent Martin Wolf summarised it as follows:

> 'Mr Blair gave support to low inflation and sustainable public finances; inward investment; internationally competitive tax rates; minimum labour standards — though not ones that "lead to rigidity or inflexibility in labour markets"; no repeal of the main parts of 1980s trade union legislation; partnership between the public and private sectors to "revitalise our infrastructure", education reform; and an active role in Europe, including participation in the social chapter.'

This was, of course, a speech to businessmen and in Singapore, which of all the four Asian 'tigers' has relied most on the investment of transnational companies for its development. Was that perhaps the reason why Tony Blair's first speech on 'stakeholding' was made there? Inward investment is included as the second main item in his programme, which exudes reassurances for transnational capital. With the exception of the reference to Europe, the speech could have been made by Mr Major. Is Europe to be the 'blue water' between the parties? If so, New Labour will have to do some solid educational work before election time to convince the British population about the benefits of economic union, and will have to bring the European dimension much more centrally into its thinking especially on common policies for reducing unemployment.

Noel Thompson in *New Left Review* (no.216, March-April 1996), discussing 'The Political Economy of New Labour' examined a number of New Labour's publications since 1993 and showed the similarities between New Labour and New Right economic discourse. No-one can say that New Labour does not publish. Thompson's quotations are taken from *Made in Britain*, 1993, *Making Britain's Future*, 1993, *Labour's Economic*

Approach, 1993, *Winning for Britain: Labour's Strategy for Industrial Success, Rebuilding the Economy*, 1994, *Britain Working Again*, 1994, *A New Economic Future for Britain*, 1995, *Agenda for Change*, 1995. The emphasis which is so similar in these publications to the discourse on the New Right includes the following: 'recovery without inflation', 'competition to improve performance', 'cost-effective production', 'commercially viable projects', 'high profits for investment', 'workplace flexibility', 'commercially viable projects'. Thompson concludes that supply side strategies are at the centre of New Labour's economic thinking and in Giles Radice's phrase 'as much competition as possible, government intervention where necessary'. And the latter is to be established primarily through a tighter regulatory framework than the Tories have achieved. The stakes remain with the capitalists.

Even the pledge emphasised again and again by Tony Blair on the creation of a stakeholder economy could have been made by Mr Major if he had thought of it first. Will Hutton has come to Tony Blair's rescue with a reference to the distinguished American economist Professor Kenneth Galbraith as an advocate of stakeholding, but the Tories could easily claim Anthony Eden, who fought the 1955 election on the call for a 'property owning democracy', as the true originator. And New Labour makes much of the fact that 60% of households are owner-occupiers. Much good this has done the million with negative equity in 1995 and a quarter of a million with mortgage arrears! True, some 25% now own some shares, if not very many.

Be that as it may, Will Hutton, originally one of the brains behind Tony Blair, has himself pointed out the central weakness of New Labour's concept of 'stakeholding'. This is that the only legal stake in a capitalist company in Britain is held by the owners of the capital. The best possible return to them, which as Hutton points out is seen in the market as a short-term return in annual dividends, is the one and absolutely binding requirement on managers. In the last resort, moreover, directors and managers are subject to take-over if profits fall, the bidder offering shareholders a better deal, whatever any one else including the workers may think. There is no provision in company law for other stakeholders, and although Tony Blair has since spoken in an interview with the *Times* newspaper (18.6.96) of a 'new Companies Act to allow two-tier boards to be set up in companies on a voluntary basis', he answered a direct question on the Frost Programme to the effect that he did not envisage making any change in company law — thus dissenting from Archbishop Temple and the Christian Socialists of the

Nineteenth Century. Mandelson and Liddle agree that 'the most radical step would be to amend the present statutory responsibilities of company directors', but they then confine themselves to proposing quite minor adjustments. Such caution seems to Hutton to fly in the face of all the evidence of low investment and asset stripping that marks the recent behaviour of British capitalist institutions.

> 'They are prepared', Hutton writes of Mandelson and Liddle, 'to advocate limits on take-overs, more powerful non-executive directors, more disclosure of pension fund activity and a new private bank specialising in providing medium loan finance to small and medium sized companies — but beyond that useful start they go no further.' (Hutton, *Prospect*, p.48)

But, Hutton complains, New Labour appears to believe that in the UK, 'by wiser macro-economic management, markets and companies can be allowed to get on with being dynamic — albeit with some prodding towards long termism.' He simply does not accept such naivety. He also points out that such soft treatment for capital is quite out of kilter with the stakeholder principles of rights and obligations. Such obligations to the wider community are to be rigorously applied in the cases of offenders, the young unemployed and public sector workers. Demanding duties will be imposed upon them in exchange for their meagre rights. In contrast, British business and finance will continue to have unqualified rights, pure and simple. Their only duty will remain to enrich themselves. Such a lack of evenhandedness does not bode well for a cohesive society. Hutton makes the same point about the contrasting attitudes of New Labour to the unions and the civil service.

> 'Top civil servants will be forgiven their complicity in the last 17 years, but Labour's long suffering trade union allies will be kept at arms' length. This lack of equity, along with the timidity over economic policy may appease the powers that be, but risks undermining the whole New Labour project.' (Hutton, *ibid.*. p.50)

Or does it just reveal the whole project to be a sham?

If it is, then it is a very dangerous sham. Appeasement of the transnational companies, while cold shouldering the unions not only breaks all the links to Old Labour, but pushes the boat of New Labour out into shark infested and stormy seas with no life-boats at hand. Joining the 'enterprise of the market and the rigours of competition', as the new clause IV has it, 'with the forces of partnership and cooperation' is one thing in an economy of small-scale competing companies. But the British economy isn't like that.

A study by Grazia letto-Gillies of London University, entitled *International Production*, published by Blackwells in 1992 demonstrates that the UK economy is, apart from the Netherlands, by far the most heavily dominated by transnational companies. In the various measures used by letto-Gillies, the domination is five times that of other European economies and three times that of the USA, and it has been increasing faster than elsewhere. This is the reality behind Tony Blair's claim that New Labour is firmly on the side of the 'wealth creators and entrepreneurs' and determined to build a Britain 'safe for foreign investors'. Peter Mandelson, not to be outdone by his leader, speaking at a business leaders' lunch at London's Savoy Hotel on May 13 1996, stressed that the UK needed to 'see healthy profits' and that in turn would 'inevitably lead to inequalities in incomes.' It is such statements which make the total absence of reference in Mandelson and Liddle to a transnational company so amazing. Some of their directors can hardly have been missing from the Savoy luncheon. Will Hutton suffers from the same inhibition, but he does understand the need for a more robust government interventionist policy from New Labour.

How Different is New Labour's Economic Policy from Tory Policy?

It may be that Hutton is carping. Is New Labour's economic policy so timid? In Tony Blair's Singapore speech we note the continuing preoccupation with the threat of inflation. 'Low inflation' heads the list of policy aims. This might be expected of a monetarist Thatcherite, like Norman Lamont, who justified unemployment as 'a price worth paying' to get inflation down. Of course, someone else picked up the bill, while our betters took the change. But for New Labour there are two questions to be asked. The first is why the fear? Inflation fell steadily from its post-war peak under Mrs Thatcher's measures in 1980 until the boom and bust of 1990, since when the rate has fallen again to a figure around three per cent a year. This is a world-wide phenomenon and not expected to change, barring 'shocks' like the oil price hike which hit Labour in the UK and many other governments in the 1970s. This could change if governments borrowed for current and not capital expenditure or spent beyond their revenue receipts. They are forbidden to do this under EMU, and there is no need for such action if taxation is increased in time. Given the globalisation of capital, it has, however, become necessary for increases in public borrowing and in taxing and spending to be done not on a national basis, but on an international basis — European and even wider.

The second question for New Labour follows the first. What is the result of this preoccupation with inflation? 'Running the economy to choke off inflation,' as Will Hutton wrote, 'may have the effect of choking off everything else.' We quoted earlier the judgement from the United Nations Conference on Trade and Development (UNCTAD) *Trade and Development Report for 1995*, which criticised 'the generally restrictive monetary policies' which had 'created a weak economic growth dynamic, and generated an increasing imbalance between labour force and the tools — i.e. capital — to employ labour productively.'

New Labour blames Conservative governments for incompetent and ideologically driven economic policies, but its spokesmen do not seem to be prepared to challenge the basic monetarist ideology, characterised by UNCTAD, as subordinating all other policies to the control of inflation. Mandelson and Liddle state that 'New Labour has made it clear that a growth objective should be set alongside an inflation target.' (M&L, p.79) They quote the authority of Professor James Meade for this proposal. Having been fairly dismissive of old Labour's pursuit of old Keynesian policies of demand management, they claim that Meade was a 'New Keynesian'. Governments must deflate as well as inflate. Old Keynes of course knew that very well and regarded it as a political problem of incomes policies, so long as it was remembered that prices can rise from working below capacity as well as from over-heating.

As Hutton reminds us, Meade himself always insisted that the 'golden rule' of public finance meant that fear of inflation should not be allowed to limit higher public borrowing so long as the borrowing was to finance investment. Meade meant investment that would bring a commercial return. Otherwise, if there were no resultant economic growth, such borrowing would simply add to the pressure on interest rates. Tony Blair's insistence on 'sustainable' public finances might or might not allow for investment in job creation. There is the usual ambiguity. Sustainability depends on the tax take from rising incomes as well as on the level of public spending.

'Sustainable public finances' have therefore to be taken with Tony Blair's next prescription, of 'internationally competitive tax rates'. It is suggested by Mandelson and Liddle that these are 'somewhat below those of our main European partners'. In fact, according to the Central Statistical Office's *Economic Trends* for January 1995, by 1993 they were *absolutely* below *all* our European partners and only just above Australia, Japan and the USA. As Will Hutton points out, the range of proposals in Mandelson and Liddle — for the needs of the NHS with an ageing population, for a seriously underfunded education system, for reestablishing public sector pay parity, infra-structure investment and improved welfare standards — must imply some extension to the tax base. But Gordon Brown has been adamant as shadow chancellor that there will have to be saving before there is any spending, 'reordering our priorities and making savings fom waste' — as he put it in what Victor Keegan called (*Guardian*, 30-4-96) 'one of the most cheese-paring speeches any would-be Labour chancellor has ever made.'

The fact is that New Labour has made so much of the Tories being the party of high taxation that it has left itself with little room for manoeuvre for the very necessary increases in public spending, if the needs of ordinary working people are to be met. Hutton suggests that at least there must be an increase in corporation tax, especially on the UK North Sea oil operators who are barely taxed at all, and on those with higher incomes who have been given so much by the Tories. For New Labour not to say anything about taxes except for a promise of some remission at the bottom end and a windfall tax on utilities (clothes which the Tories might borrow or pawn) only raises suspicions among the electorate and fails to persuade those in Middle England who need not to be kow-towed to, but on the contrary to be retaught the benefits of security for all and with it greater social cohesion.

What Will New Labour do about Unemployment?

The only reference to the labour market in Tony Blair's Singapore speech is a warning that 'minimum labour standards' should not be such as to 'lead to rigidity or inflexibility in the labour market.' Combined with the promise not to 'repeal the main parts of the 1980s [anti-] trade union legislation', this is not a very encouraging outlook for workers faced with low wages, long or unsocial hours and other poor working conditions. The words 'rigidity' and 'inflexibility' in this context always mean refusal to accept poorer conditions of work. The absence of any direct reference to employment, unemployment or full employment confirms the suspicion that the cure, if any, for the current disease of mass unemployment is expected to come from general growth in the economy plus a more flexible and better educated work force and some quite minor measures to help the young and the long term unemployed.

Recent experience, not only in the UK but elsewhere among developed countries, has shown that the rate of economic growth only at best creates employment at half the growth rate and is barely enough to begin to reduce unemployment. This is because of the labour saving effect of new productive investment, which has not recently been compensated for by extra employment in services. For growth to increase employment, it would be necessary for governments to encourage labour intensive growth or to do more to ensure the transfer of wealth from capital intensive industries to finance labour-intensive employment. Much of this would be public employment, in the caring social services, environmental conservation, urban renewal, energy-saving or in teaching and health care. This in effect means higher taxes on both profits and earnings in the capital-intensive sector, something that we have just seen New Labour is reluctant to attempt.

New Labour has also rejected the possibility of finding money for new employment by increased government borrowing. This is ruled out under the Maastricht Treaty criteria for entry to European Monetary Union, but left-wing economists like Andrew Glyn agree that borrowing to create jobs carries inflationary dangers. Markets will always react to the fear of inflationary effects from increased borrowing by government, even if this yields, as Professor Meade allowed for, a commercial return. In the case of investment in public, or private, industry, the return is direct. With investment in training and education it is only indirect. Glyn and others therefore believe that taxation, even of middle incomes, is the only way for governments to find the money to invest in jobs to end unemployment and the growth of inequality. The costs of raised taxation can be absorbed by faster growth, and the UK is among the least heavily taxed of all industrialised countries.

As far as concerns the effect on British labour costs, manufacturing industry's labour costs per hour in the UK in 1994 were already the lowest among the developed countries, barring only Spain and Portugal. They were in fact just one half of what they were in Germany. They could only be lowered still further with a subsidy from government, unless the whole social condition of the people were to be put in jeopardy. Such subsidies have already been introduced by Conservative Governments in the form of Family Credit, as a means-tested life-line for low paid workers, often single parents. New Labour has embraced a similar scheme in the cash tax rebate for employers taking on long term unemployed. This in effect is a gift to employers with no corresponding obligations. Much the same system was tried in the nineteenth century at Speenhamland, to make up farm labourers' wages from the local rates, and the result was that more and more farmers paid inadequate wages until the rates became overloaded, and collapsed under the strain.

Like all other schemes for helping low skilled labour into employment, two problems have to be overcome. The first is that any form of means-testing reduces the incentive to raise pay, as benefits are cut with each rise in pay. The second is that employers, as at Speenhamland, will commonly substitute subsidised labour for unsubsidised. Gordon Brown in proposing the recruitment subsidy to encourage private sector employers to take on the long-term unemployed, believes that such financial incentives could be used as part of the general aim of New Labour to encourage corporate social responsibility. The same approach is to be used in relation to the young unemployed. Both employer and employee will be expected to agree to an element of training where the state provides a subsidy to help employers to take on unemployed young people.

Once again, the obligation will be far heavier on the employee than on the employer. The unemployed youngster will lose some of his social security benefits if he refuses a job with training. This is virtually direction of labour as practised in war time. In Gordon Brown's scheme, the employer was originally to have been under compulsion to provide training. But New Labour has now backed off this and, instead, the sense of corporate social responsibility of the employer is to be relied upon. Alas, neither Christian love nor the dread of hellfire will prove strong enough to persuade most employers to modify their behaviour one iota. Such a lack of evenhandedness is not going to make it easy for New Labour to win very wide support for its policies among the millions of the unemployed.

New Labour's only offer to the unemployed in the event is to get trained for another job. But where will that job come from? Education and training to raise the general level of skills of the workforce, and particularly of the unemployed, are certainly an absolute necessity if structural unemployment is to be reduced. But the consensus among economists as expressed by the European Commission (Directorate of Economic and Financial Affairs) is that all such supply side measures require for their success a simultaneous expansion of demand. The fact is that, while some unemployment is only cyclical and should be ended as the economy recovers, some is what is called 'classical' and depends on new investment especially in labour-intensive activities.

It appears that New Labour is committed to skills training and to a system of grants for an 'individual learning account' as a form of tax privileged monthly savings. They are also committed to regulations for utilities requiring them to raise standards of conservation which would generate new low-skill job opportunities. Tony Blair in his Singapore speech spoke about partnership between the public and private sector to 'revitalise our infrastructure'. But the commitment to government intervention including public sector investment and social provision through local authorities, so necessary to ensure the actual switch of employment from labour saving industries to labour using services, is decidedly weak.

Yet all the evidence recently reviewed by economists suggests that the most important element in the long post-war era of full employment was not just reconstruction with US aid and US technology after war-time destruction but was the impact of government intervention. This is what the Clare group of economists had to say in the February 1995 issue of the National Institute *Economic Review*, from which we quoted earlier:

> 'It has become fashionable nowadays to think the unthinkable. Among the unthinkables of the 1980s which has recently been having some attention is the idea of full employment as an object of government policy. Generally accepted in the 1950s and 1960s, the idea became buried in the 1970s by the increasing concern of the public about inflation ...'

The group went on to suggest that the 'surge of investment was the significant influence on the high tide of full employment in the 1950s and 1960s' and to ask what were the conditions which induced it. This is where they make the statement we already quoted, which bears repetition:

> 'The first was the confidence engendered by the full employment policy itself. The knowledge that governments of all political parties were committed to full employment and would adjust their fiscal and/or monetary policies to offset any contraction of aggregate demand for goods and services must have downgraded one important element in the risks attached to spending money on capital projects.'

It may be true that the joint public-private ventures which Blair proposes could have the same effect particularly since the public element is likely to make it possible for private firms to borrow funds more cheaply — i.e. a form of subsidy from government — but it would be surprising if the appeal to 'corporate social responsibility' carried quite the same conviction to private businessmen that a firm commitment to full employment once carried.

New Labour has explicitly denied any such commitment. Quite contrary to Old Labour's special incentives of the 1950s and 60s and 1970s, the proposals that have come from New Labour for incentives to investment have all assumed that 'the venture capital should not be public' and the institutions involved should be 'totally at arms' length from Whitehall'. 'Only a modest injection of public money would be required', according to Mandelson and Liddle, 'to lever a much bigger amount of private capital . . .' All would depend, they conclude, on developing a 'stakeholder culture in industry and the City', which implies 'changing the nature of the relationship between the City of London and the British boardroom.' (M&L. p.89) How this is to be done is never made clear and remains no more than a pious hope. But we shall see later that it could not be done effectively today except by joint and common action with the other members of the European Union.

Equality of Opportunity or of Outcome? More 'Fat Cats'?

When Gordon Brown, as Labour's Shadow Chancellor, delivered the second John Smith Memorial lecture at Edinburgh University on April 19th, 1996 he chose as his theme New Labour and Equality. His castigation of the inequalities in our society — educational, social, cultural, economic and political — recognised a situation that is not only an immoral deprivation of a large part, perhaps a half, of the population, but is fatal for the economic progress and security of the whole people. In emphasising the need for New Labour to embrace and pursue equality of opportunity, he derided a supposed 'hankering of old Labour after an unrealisable equality of outcome.' He illustrated this by asking how even the most egalitarian Health Service could keep us all alive until the age of 90. No-one would of course expect such a thing, but they would expect free prostate operations, cancer treatment, hearing aids, dentures, spectacles and other action to meet the needs of the elderly. They would also expect co-ordinated action to correct the differences in infant mortality between different social classes, as documented in the *Black Report* and in *The Health Divide* by Peter Townsend. Action is also possible to diminish the gaps in life expectation between adult members of different social groups.

Gordon Brown's onslaught on 'equality of outcome' was too much for Roy Hattersley. Roy is not one of Old Labour's left wingers, but he has been complaining vigorously that Brown's argument was wholly incompatible with any true movement towards equality. He quoted one of Tony Blair's inspirers, R.H. Tawney, writing that

> 'it is only the presence of a large degree of practical equality which can diffuse the general opportunities to rise.' (*Guardian*, 25.07.96)

One does not need to search far for justification for equality of condition in the writings of the Christian Socialists, who are so warmly praised but as wholly ignored in the writings of New Labour. It can be found very clearly stated in the works of Adam Smith, who presumed that perfect markets would lead to complete equality. In this he was wrong. But he was not wrong in his moral commitment, which assumed that such equality was the natural goal of society.

Brown insisted in his lecture on the importance of 'reward for work, effort and contribution to the community'. So, of course, would 'Old Labour' socialists in order to maintain incentives and motivation, until we reach in any particular area of economic organisation that degree of abundance that enables the attainment of distribution 'according to needs'. Even then, needs are unequal, varying with age, size of family and, as Bernard Shaw reminded us, compensation for the unfulfilling nature of much work. All organisations including families have nasty and boring tasks to be performed, which should be shared equally or, if not, then rewarded especially for their performance.

Rewards for contribution to the community should not, however, mean continuing the obscene differentials that exist everywhere today between managers and workers — and certainly not agreeing with Tony Blair's 'desire to see hundreds of new millionaires'. Such 'rewards' are not 'incentives'; they are trophies recognising triumphs in the class war of greed against need. And the measurement of work and effort, despite all the pseudo-scientific jargon that surrounds it, remains a highly subjective affair, generally determined by management to strengthen their own power.

The trouble with Gordon Brown's proposal of 'equality of opportunity' is its ambiguity. Where and when does opportunity start? He chooses to start it with schooling, and especially post-16 schooling. But the main inequalities, as he recognises, start earlier with the level of skills and education of the parents. Are we to wait a whole generation to educate those who will be the next generation of parents, before we can correct existing inequalities? More seriously, how is it proposed to counteract the cumulative tendency to inequality that is inherent in capitalism? 'To him that hath shall be given, and from him that hath not shall be taken away even that which he hath.' That is the dynamic of the capitalist system. It looks suspiciously like the dynamic of New Labour.

— Gordon Brown understands that the market alone cannot be relied upon to correct inequalities. 'It is only government', he says, 'that can make equality real'. The market is only the instrument through which capital accumulation works. The fundamental issue is the private ownership of capital, which Brown no longer perceives as a problem. On the contrary, he says that the role of owners has been 'relegated' and furthermore that capital along with raw materials and inventions 'can be acquired from just about anywhere'.

> 'Only a quarter of capital', he went on, 'is tied up in physical capital and nearly three-quarters is intellectual capital. Hence the premium the company pays for extra skills, or years of education'. He has to add that 'the skills needed for the 21st century economy are also quite different'

This last *caveat* is necessary or he could not explain the existence of unemployment among skilled workers and graduates.

Brown's picture is in any case wholly unrealistic. Individual entrepreneurs and small companies, as we both know well from personal experience, encounter the greatest difficulty in raising capital, not just for physical assets, but to feed their intellectual capital while they are developing their businesses. Brown says that modern industrial policy means not only breaking up monopolies (does he propose to change Tory policy in doing this? and if so, how?), but also, he says, 'ensuring that small businesses have a real chance to compete with large: ensuring that access to capital is fair especially for the self-employed.' (Again, one wants to know, how?)

In What Does the Modern Economy Differ from the Old?

'In the modern economy,' Brown concludes, 'pro-competition and pro-equality go hand in hand'. But what kind of competition is he speaking of — Nestlé and General Foods, Unilever and Proctor & Gamble, Ford and General Motors, Shell and Esso, ICI and Du Pont? For that battle of the giants is the reality of dynamic market competition today. Finding a niche in such a world is an almost impossible task and, even if you succeed for a time, you are still very likely to be destroyed or taken over as a sub-sub-contractor.

What regulation does Brown propose, short of social ownership, that will challenge the power of ICI or Mr Hanson or the Sainsbury family to corner even more capital? But, of course, it is not intended that New Labour should do any such thing. In a volume of essays entitled *What Needs to Change: New Visions for Britain*, with a long introduction by Tony Blair, the chairman of J. Sainsbury plc, David Sainsbury, contributes an essay on 'A Competitive Economy'. which begins:

'In looking at economic and industrial policy, I start from two strong beliefs. Firstly, it is companies that create wealth. It is they who have to build and sustain a competitive advantage over their rivals in foreign countries . . .'

and he goes on:

'Government should not get directly involved in corporate decision making, but should seek to create an environment in which companies can build competitive advantage . . .

Secondly, building and maintaining competitive advantage in world markets is today a tough and demanding task. . . . If government seeks to put a break on economic change by protecting companies or giving them assistance, they will not make the necessary changes.'

This is pure Blair doctrine and it is based, of course, on the assumption that the interests of the company and of private capital are the same as the interests of the working people in any country. Investigation among the young wage-slaves in Sainsbury's stores will soon refute this bizarre assumption.

What has changed? What is at issue in the relation of capital and labour is the same as it always was — the monopoly of capital. No amount of small shareholders — thought to be 20% to 30% of all households in the UK today — or of institutional company holdings by pension funds can alter the inequality between those who have access to capital, whether from family holdings, like the Sainsburys, or other corporate funds and those — the great majority — who do not.

What is wrong with capitalism, as we saw in an earlier chapter, is not just the inequality in power as well as income between owners and non-owners. It is the requirement of the system, that owners and managers of capital shall accumulate or die. Competition means ever-increasing accumulations of capital in larger and larger concentrations. What Marx predicted over 100 years ago is evident now for all to see — a continuous process of centralisaton of capital. He has been derided for so long for seeing this process at one pole and at the other pole a continuous immiseration of people. But who can deny now the drastic impoverishment of the Third World, or the actual decline in living standards of the poorest quarter to a third of households in the industrialised countries themselves. For a time the polarisation process was halted by deliberate state action to redistribute from rich to poor world-wide and within each country. When under the rule of monetarism these actions ceased, the cumulative process of enrichment and impoverishment was resumed.

It is not difficult to understand why this still happens. Capital can only be accumulated through making profits. Profits are the difference between the value of what workers produce and what they are paid. By creating a reserve army of unemployed labour, as we have again today, wages and conditions of labour can be kept down and profits expanded. It does not need a Marxist to explain that this is, of course, a wholly self-destructive process. Lower wages mean reduced purchasing power to buy back the extra products generated with the new accumulations of capital. Only the taxation of capital to fund spending by governments, whether on armaments or on public services, can offset this contradiction. Private capital cannot be 'regulated' into socially acceptable behaviour. It has to be taxed and challenged by social ownership. Any other policy will only lead to short term gains for the rich, worsening poverty for the poor and in the long term economic breakdown and collapse of economic and political and social order. We have seen it in Peru, in Sudan and Somalia, in Yugoslavia and now in Russia and Eastern Europe. It is coming nearer and nearer home.

So, What can New Labour 'Deliver'?

The issue of New Labour's approach to membership of the European Union, especially in relation to common policies for tackling the environmental crisis and for eradicating the scourge of unemployment, will be examined in later chapters. In both cases New Labour has failed to seize opportunities for working together with social democratic and other parties of labour on the continent to develop joint and common approaches. Cooperation even within the family of parties adhering to the Socialist International has been rudimentary. Cooperation with other Left and Green parties has been non-existent. The tragedy of this failure is not only the lost opportunities for action but that no attempt has been made to instruct the electorate in the real causes of environmental degradation and of the unacceptable increase of unemployment. Neither has there been any action to explore or explain the real possibilities of joint action and common action in the European Union for creating the international movement that is necessary to stand up to international capitalism.

This is one example only, but a desperately serious one, of the total failure of New Labour to live up to the proud rhetoric of its claim to care for the community and establish principles of equality and cooperation in its practical policies. Nothing except the absolute depravity of the Conservative government will give New Labour a victory at the polls. If, as the political commentators are beginning to suggest, a last minute cut in income tax together with a recovery of movement in the housing market, gave the Conservatives renewed support, New Labour might try to join up with their natural allies in the Liberal Democratic Party. The main obstacle to such a fusion would come from the inherent radicalism and decency of parts of the Liberal Party itself. Lib-Lab unity is certainly the implication of Eric Hobsbawm's yearning for a new Popular Front.

The old Popular Front was initiated to prevent the spread of fascism. It failed then. But this new Front is more likely to give rise to fascism than to stop it, if it appears to exhaust the promises of democracy, bringing no comfort to those driven into misery. New Labour would not then need to realise the rhetoric which we have had to question in some of the more sensitive of the several parts of its programme that we have analysed.

If, however, New Labour should win outright at the next election, the answer to the question which Mandelson and Liddle pose in the sub-title of their book — 'Can New Labour Deliver?' — must be to recognise what they propose to 'deliver' and to whom? After the disastrous local election results for the Tories in May 1996, Tony Blair was telling disillusioned Tory voters that they should join Labour — there were no policy differences that should divide them. Mr Howarth has already crossed the floor of the House, as they call such defections. Will there be more? Will a One-Nation government, as Tony Blair likes to call his prospectus, have room in it not only for Liberal Democrats but for Tory 'wets' like Kenneth Clarke? What will he deliver to them?

For whom else will they deliver? We have to come back again to the question of constituency. Without the unions and without the participation of working people, who will a party of professional people be serving? There was always a tension in Old Labour between manual workers from the unions and the largely professional leadership of the PLP, but it was moderated by the unions in Conference and by MPs from the mines and factories. We have emphasised that nearly half the working population is still involved in manual, service and clerical labour. It is now impossible for New Labour to share the same profile.

And where are now the socialists among the ranks of New Labour? The new intake of Blairites from the media, law and business are not reassuringly socialist in their evident convictions. Many are not even liberal with a small 'l'. None are distinguished by their record of work for the poor, or the unemployed, or the excluded people. The socialists of Old Labour in Parliament are likely to be in a minority and all assigned to the back benches, with no Conference platform to speak from. Over one hundred MPs have already been recruited by Mr Blair for his government. The detail of who's who is immaterial, but that means more than a hundred Party members in Parliament tied to a Party policy determined from above, and held in place by the benefits of office. Complaints are coming from the right and the left of the party, from Austin Mitchell and Jeremy Corbyn.

What then will this New Labour actually seek to deliver? What they say they want to do does not seem to add up to very much. What they ought to deliver they don't want to deliver. There is little doubt about what the British people want. Among other things, they would like the basic social needs to be met, including first of all a job, then decent housing, better schooling for all, a universal health service and a solution to chaos on the roads. New Labour's programme, as far as we have been allowed to see it, does not at first sight look like filling much of this bill. We cannot just wait and see, however. If after looking more carefully at the programme, as we try to do in this book, we come to the conclusion that New Labour cannot offer what the people need, then we must all start thinking about alternative ways for people to meet their needs. That means an end to the politics of 'delivery' to respond to requests for benefits like so much packaged food from the supermarkets. It means beginning a new alliance, in which we can jointly shape policies of our own designing, and not as they are prepared for us by the spin doctors, so to work together to achieve our own objectives. We have now to consider what these must be.

CHAPTER 7

Rescuing the Welfare State

'The Welfare State is in need of a thoroughgoing shake-up'.
Mandelson & Liddle, op.cit., *p.142*

Does the welfare state need shaking up or rescuing? The answer will depend on who you are — unemployed, insecure at work, pensioner, disabled, sick? Or young, able, healthy with a guaranteed job and no thought for the morrow? But the first and most demanding requirement of any government concerned to protect and advance the interests of working people is to rescue what is left of the Welfare State in Britain, including new guarantees of employment after 17 years of intense activity by Conservative demolition squads. Tony Blair's speeches and New Labour policy proposals have made great play of their commitment to the community and the 'strengthening of the common bonds that tie the country together', as Mandelson and Liddle put it. In place of what we earlier saw them calling 'some 1945 New Jerusalem that never really was', they advance the following aims for New Labour in a 'changed and changing society' (M&L, p.143). This is a statement of even more than usual ambiguity and we have added in brackets what we believe the sentences might mean in practice:

'. . . a welfare state which is universal in its reach but no longer uniform in what it offers' (i.e. more private beds in public hospitals and a basic pension with private top-up)

'. . . a decent minimum quality of life and fair life chances while permitting greater individual freedom of choice' (i.e. a very small minimum wage and selective schools)

'. . . public and private finance and provision' (i.e. private profit from public transport and communications)

'. . . individual responsibility, not dependency' (i.e. support for private pension schemes)

'. . . services that offer people a hand-up, not just cash payments that give them a hand-out' (i.e. unemployment benefit conditional on accepting compulsory work or training)

'. . . in other words . . . opting in, not opting out' (i.e. a Singapore-type universal fund for all welfare services that can be topped up by those with higher incomes, but has no redistributive effect from rich to poor)

This certainly would be the 'shake-up' which Mandelson and Liddle promise, but what would be left of the principles of the Welfare State? Full employment is not even mentioned.

Paying for Welfare — from Gladstone to Blair

Nobody on the left is expecting any great change in the direction of the British economy in the event of a New Labour government being elected, because political initiative has already given place to the alleged dynamism of the market. This may prove illusory. Or the market may dynamically implode, leaving a big economic crisis and small credibility for those who have become its champions. But most people are hoping that at least something of the post-war welfare state will be rescued from the salami chopper of the Conservatives. It is not only that resources have been withdrawn from health and education, pensions and social services, but the whole structure of the welfare system has been distorted to give some appearance of equity while denying the reality. There is a fairly obvious indication in the pronouncements made by New Labour spokesmen on the relationship of taxes and expenditure and the balance of 'obligations and rights' that the same conjuring trick is being prepared by Mr Blair.

Conjuring with the tax system has a long history. If we look back a bit to an earlier Prime Minister, who believed that his policies were driven by deeply held Christian principles, it has to be noted what an apparently cynical view he took of the purposes of government and the aims of taxation. What Mr Gladstone established in the 1850s appears to have remained in place for at least a century. It was not what Will Hutton has taken from the school of historical revisionists to call 'domination by a City-Treasury-Bank nexus', but quite simply a centralisation of power in government to manage the economy with the aim of minimising expenditure while appearing to be fair.

Here is a recent summary by a British historian of the history of the UK tax system:

'W.E. Gladstone in his budget of 1853 laid down the main principles which were to be pursued for the rest of the century: the tax system was always to be carefully balanced . . . to ensure that the system had the appearance of being equitable. The tax system was to be a means of integration and not conflict, encapsulated in the annual ritual of the budget.'

'By 1924 . . . the British government was not simply following the wishes of the City and the Treasury . . . The concern, above all, was to restore a high degree of consent to taxation by stressing the equity of the fiscal system, and its apparent even-handedness between classes and interests.'

'The aim was to create an illusion that the tax system was 'neutral' between interests and classes, who were rigorously excluded from the formulation of fiscal policy, itself a matter for a handful of officials in the revenue departments and the Treasury in consultation with a few ministers. But . . . a simple emphasis upon the power of the Treasury and the City as the key to the structure of the British state obscures a much more complicated process of reallocation of responsibilities. The result by 1951 was the emergence of a welfare state which was funded to an unusual degree by national taxation, with a reduced role for voluntarism, the market and local government.'

M.J. Daunton in Past and Present, *February 1996*

The problem at issue is the political basis of the tax system supporting the welfare state in Britain. The view has steadily taken hold over the years that the particular development of the British state dominated by the so-called 'City-Bank-Treasury nexus' provides explanation enough of the constraints on taxation for welfare expenditure. Michael Daunton had already challenged this basic thesis in an earlier number of *Past and Present* (February 1989) as Michael Barratt Brown had done in two contributions to *New Left Review* in 1988 and 1989. In the article from which the passage above is quoted, Daunton went on to question the assertion that the share of GNP taken in taxation was 'noticeably lower in Britain than in other countries' and pointed to what he believed was its essential characteristic:

'The striking feature of the British fiscal system in the first half of the Twentieth Century is not so much the level of taxation as its structure, with a high reliance on direct taxation of personal income and profits, a narrow base of indirect taxes and a low level of social security contributions from employers and workers.'

This tax structure remains in place to this day, in spite of the Thatcher Government's successive increases in VAT and the tax concessions made to the profits of TNCs. Most recently it was reported that Mr Murdoch's companies had avoided £76 millions of tax liability.

What must surprise readers of the passage quoted above from Michael Daunton is the cynical view attributed to Gladstone and to subsequent Treasury ministers, that what mattered was the "appearance" of equity and the creation of an "illusion" that the tax system was "neutral" between classes and interests. The nation state had been supposed by historians to be a truly integrative force creating social cohesion, not a sham. It was Mrs Thatcher and Mr Major who believed that governments could abandon the illusion and still be voted into office by those who thought that they benefited from the open pursuit of inequality, without bothering about the effect on the rest. Tony Blair's popularity may well stem from the fact that he preaches equality for the rest, without frightening away any number of those who would suffer if his preaching became a reality. Gladstone would have been proud of him.

Some New Labour spokesmen have openly confessed that they cannot end selection in state schools or the tax concessions to private schools or reduce tax concessions on house mortgages without losing votes, even to make the quite limited changes they plan in the incidence of taxation in order to benefit income earners at the lower end of the range at the expense of those at the upper end. This is the reason for the extreme sensitivity about the choice of school for her children by shadow minister Harriet Harman and, on the other side, about the egalitarian sentiments on fair taxation expressed by shadow minister Claire Short. The next most sensitive issue is that of British sovereignty in relation to the European Union and the issues are closely linked. Not only must there be no suggestion that British taxpayers are subsidising foreign producers whether of lamb or fuel, but there must be no sense of loss of a common national interest that overrides class and local attachments.

Gladstone was immensely successful in establishing the myth of laissez-faire and what was called a 'nightwatchman' or minimal state, while in reality all the state support systems for the development of capitalism were put in place — a common market, single currency, standard measures, central bank, royal mail, company law, police force, state education, sanitary and other local government services, a colonial empire imposed upon a quarter of the world's people, not to mention an army and a navy that patrolled the seven seas — some nightwatchman! some state! British public expenditure per head of population by the end of the Nineteenth Century exceeded that of any other contemporary state. It was not surprising that Mr Gladstone was so concerned to achieve a 'balanced tax system', but without the tribute drawn from India after 1857 his task would have been impossible, as Mrs Thatcher's tax cuts in the 1980s would also have been without the North Sea oil bonanza.

The creation and development of the welfare state has always had a double aspect: on the one hand, it was a victory for the trade unions and the socialists who had for long struggled to win universal social provision of health, education and security in ill-health and old age; on the other hand, that it was based on some redistribution of wealth from the rich to the poor was accepted by the rich in the interests of social cohesion and for fear of revolution. The latter fear was particularly effective while the Soviet Union existed as an apparent challenge to capitalism. After this challenge disappeared, it has become more difficult to maintain the basis of the welfare state in the taxation of the better-off.

But by now the welfare state had become for a large majority of the population not just a support system but a badge of dignity that all are in certain crucial respects equal citizens — in the hospital queues and in the doctor's surgery. Getting the rich minority to go on paying when they were increasingly opting out of a deteriorating service was becoming a major issue in the 1980s and one that the Tories had decided to meet by reducing the service. New Labour has a real problem on its hands in seeking to make the system seem to be fair. Already, dependence on the more progressive direct forms of taxation has been reduced, so that tax payers at all income levels pay the same proportion of their income in tax. The rich, in other words, do not any longer pay a higher proportion; and the poor, who may not pay any direct taxes, still pay indirect taxes.

Workers and the State

New Labour claims that it is a One Nation party, which has abandoned Old Labour's concepts of class struggle and seeks to build a 'reunited kingdom'. It is never made clear when it was ever previously united except by force of arms as a nation-state. There is much argument on the left about the relationship of working people and their organisations to the state. Marx saw the state largely as a repressive force acting on behalf of the bourgeoisie. The liberal state was supposedly of very limited powers, but, as we have seen, created an essential framework for private capital and claimed to protect the liberty of the subject, both from internal and external attack. That was proclaimed to be its guarantee of the interest of all. At the same time, the state provided a forum for debate and arena for struggle between different interests and increasingly between capital and labour.

The institutional recognition of some of the interests of labour by the nation state was the chief victory of the unions a century ago. The alternative of a workers', democratic international which Marx had tried hard to drum up failed to outweigh the national state allegiance of more than a few workers, when the suffrage was extended to include the majority, or later all, of the employed population. The idea of international unity against the power of an increasingly international capital never died, although the idea of the international as an alternative to the state system did fade away.

Recognition, not just as organisations of labour but as full members of their own national society, was undoubtedly what the early trade unions were concerned to win. It was one thing for the 'gentlemen compositors' and other craft unions to achieve Gladstone's blessing in the mid Nineteenth Century. It was quite another for the state to recognise the dockers and carters and drivers who were being led by Ernest Bevin 'out of the abyss' at the end of the century. Looking ahead from the founding of the New Unionism in the 1890s, Ken Coates and Tony Topham, in their history of the Transport and General Workers' Union, wrote

'Recognition . . . is a powerful reinforcement of labour solidarity, since it compels employers to define the social world in the same terms as does the trade union . . . Even when he hates it the participating employer has sanctioned it. The organised working class . . . draws strength from its adversaries, even when it is under attack. Political reform involves a wider recognition.' (p.100)

The need of the owners and managers of capital to integrate and incorporate labour leaders into their capitalist system was not lost on the leaders. Some were happy to be assimilated; others used the opportunity to advance the status and interests of working people, especially to protect them against unemployment and casual employment. The elevation of the 'dock rats' from the status of casual labour is perhaps the most striking example of successful trade union struggle. Neil Kinnock's jibe in later years at decasualised dock workers indulging in the pleasures of the Benidorm beaches, while others less fortunate were in poverty, came ill from one who had enjoyed his Mediterranean holidays in gracious Tuscan villas. Today, after the heavy onslaught on port trade unionism, it is not so likely that many dockers will be found on the Spanish *costas*, even if politicians can still get away to the sun from time to time.

This may tell us nothing about the reasons for the failure of trade unions to raise the whole people to a decent standard of living, but it tells us much about the claim of the working class to be part of British society. However exploited, impoverished and marginalised a part of the British working population may be, very many of them, even if they are insecure today, feel that they have arrived. They have their own houses, motor cars, TVs, videos, a small garden and perhaps an annual holiday in Spain or Greece. Some sociologists like David Donnison believe that the old class consciousness of wage earners, even the social consciousness of manual as against non-manual workers, is not what matters now. The real division lies, they think, between the regularly and securely employed and the unemployed and insecurely employed . Will Hutton, as we saw earlier, believes that as many as 60% in our society fall into this last category, divided between 30% unemployed or retired unemployed and 30% insecure. Only 40% form those whom Professor Galbraith calls the 'comfortable and the contented.' The widening gap is in great part because the protective shield of the unions has been severely dented.

The End of Collectivism?

The problem we saw earlier for both Galbraith and a party of labour is that half of the larger two categories do not vote. New Labour has decided to appeal both to the insecure centre, which it is argued has become separated from the base, and to some of the contented. Although class differences are recognised by most people, what used to be called working class solidarity has undoubtedly been weakened in Britain today. Indeed the enfeeblement of this is what makes the plight of those at the very bottom with whom Donnison is concerned so particularly distressing. In the 1930s the unemployed still had the extended family of the street to support them. In the tower blocks of today they are often isolated and lost and depend as never before on costly support systems — a car to get to work or to the shops, central heating, a refrigerator, working lifts, protection against mugging and vandalism.

It is this mis-called 'under-class' who desperately need the welfare state and in the jargon of the day it is they who politicians think should be 'targetted' for welfare provision. But such specificity spells the end of the universalism of the welfare state, as it was originally established. And it is unemployment that has created the deepest fissure. At present, the long term unemployed do not form a special class of people since they still live in the same welfare system as all other welfare 'clients'. But the effect of Mr Blair's 'reforms' may well be to create a special marginalised class, beyond hope.

It is, however, not only the bottom end of the social spectrum that has been affected. The whole position of the class which depends for its livelihood on selling its labour has been weakened, and in many ways. The worst damage has come from unemployment and the threat of unemployment, but there are many other causes, to which John Hughes has drawn attention: the destruction of some 40% of full-time manual jobs since 1979, the abuse of private pension funds to 'assist' premature retirement, the much increased charges for health service prescriptions, dental and opthalmic treatment, the privatisation of the public sector, with consequent loss both of trade union protection and collective values and the vast spread of media advertising to encourage private spending.

All these factors have led, as they were intended to in Mrs Thatcher's radical right programme, to the decline of an organised and self-confident working class. Yet, this still existed two or three decades ago, in a Labour Movement with its trade unions, trades and labour councils, Working Men's Clubs, Clarion Cyclists and Ramblers, Woodcraft Folk, cooperatives and socialist societies. It is this decline that has made the Blair counter-revolution possible. But has it made it necessary?

The Protest against Centralisation

We have to ask, in particular, whether the Blair reforms in the welfare state are in effect to continue the steady process of dismantling which the Tories have begun? Strong support for reform, even for a 'thoroughgoing shake-up' comes from many who think of themselves still as socialists but have become genuinely disillusioned with the centralised management, bureaucratic style and insensitiveness, not only of the old Labour Party and the unions, but even more of certain local government offices, parts of the nationalised industries and the social services. Over years it came to seem to many concerned people that Labour councillors and the public service unions had become part of the problem not part of the solution. It was not just the social democrats who abandoned the Labour Party in the 1980s but many true socialists. Some like the DEMOS group have been responding positively to the apparently fresh and unbureaucratic image that New Labour has been presenting. The new journal *Soundings* best reflects this tendency. But they should recognise that it is not necessarily bureaucratic to be organised, and that the greater bureaucracy may have been created at the top of the Party.

David Donnison, who was himself chair of the Supplementary Benefits Commission under the last Labour governments, assigns the blame for the centralising trend in Labour thinking to the bureaucratic socialist ideas of what he calls 'mainly male, middle class, London based members of the Fabian society and other intellectual bodies' during the inter-war years. This not only ignores the large number of women in these groups — Virginia Woolf, Beatrice Webb, Barbara Wootton, Eva Hubback, Eleanor Rathbone, Marjorie Spring-Rice, Naomi Mitchison, Margaret Cole — but neglects the central place of Douglas Cole's Guild Socialist contribution to the New Fabian Research Bureau. Their whole emphasis was on local government, in Cole's words,

> 'resting upon small and manageable cells of neighbourhood organisation . . . with a constant and real contact between members of the neighbourhood group and those who represent it upon the larger civil authority.' (Coates & Topham, p.45)

The Socialist Medical Association in particular insisted that primary health care should be provided by health centres under the control of local authorities. Alongside their concern for decentralising the delivery of welfare, the Fabians did have a very real appreciation of the absolute necessity for central funding to ensure redistribution of resources from the rich, persons and areas, to the poor. But, while control should be central, they insisted that execution should be local.

In industry the argument against centralised bureaucracy had a long history which Ken Coates and Tony Topham traced in their *Readings and Witnesses for Workers' Control*. These go back to the ideas of Robert Owen, the Rochdale cooperators, the Christian Socialists and William Morris in the Nineteenth Century and were brought into the centre of the Labour Movement in the early years of the Twentieth not only by the Guild socialists but by trade union leaders, in particular Noah Ablett of the miners and Tom Mann of the dockers and engineers. When the TUC wrote its *Interim Report on Post-War Reconstruction* in 1944, its recommendations for future nationalised industries included

> 'nomination by workers' organisations of candidates from whom the Minister shall select a number of the board members' and added that 'execution of

policy . . . not only as a matter of right, but in the interests of efficiency of the industry be subject to the continuous influence of those whom it directly affects.'

Experience in industry of war-time joint production committees, consisting of managers and workers' representatives, had demonstrated the true worth of the workers' contribution to policy making as well as execution. Yet by 1953 the TUC in its *Interim Report on Public Ownership* had retreated completely from its 1944 position. The coalfield areas that corresponded to the area organisations of the Miners' Union were replaced by divisions and later by much more centralised management on the advice of a retired chairman of ICI, Lord Fleck. The railways, which had always been run as a uniformed service on military lines were given to retired generals to manage through a centralised hierarchical structure.

Central Control but Local Delivery

Despite all the projects of socialists between the wars, it is a fact that the Welfare State which the post-war Labour government presided over, was, in the words of one historian:

> 'one of the most uniform, centralised, bureaucratic and "public" welfare systems in Europe, and indeed in the modern world. Yet a social analyst of a hundred years ago would have predicted the exact opposite: that the provision of social welfare in Britain was and would continue to be highly localised, amateur, voluntaristic and intimate in scale by comparison with the more coercive and *étatist* schemes of her continental neighbours (in particular imperial Germany).' (Harris, p.116)

So, what had happened? The answer is important in seeking to unravel the forces at work influencing the future trajectory of New Labour's welfare policies. It was certainly not the Labour Party left nor the Stalinists of the 1940s, whom Viscount Mountbatten had brought into military planning as his scientific advisers. James Meade who was in the Treasury during the war joked about the 'gosplanners' (after the Soviet *Gosplan*) giving way as the war ended to 'liberal socialists' in the leadership like Sir Stafford Cripps, who gave 'two cheers for the market'. In the article about Gladstone and the Treasury, which we quoted from earlier, Michael Daunton tells the joke and seeks to give the answer to our question in terms of what he calls 'organisational configurations which encouraged certain kinds of collective political action.'

What then were these 'organisational configurations'? Daunton believes that they revolved very much around that 'illusion' generated in Britain over a long period of time of a 'neutral' central government tax system, which Gladstone had first created as a means of integrating the newly enfranchised population into the British nation-state. In later years, says Daunton, by contrast with Germany, where state and local income taxes financed the welfare policies at local level, in Britain

'the fiscal regime of the central state was seen to be a fair means of distributing resources between prosperous and declining areas, between rich and poor and between unearned and earned income.'

It was crucially necessary that the payment of taxes should not be called in question. At the same time, Daunton goes on,

'the allocation of responsibilities to the central state, local government or semi-autonomous bodies to which powers were delegated, was influenced by an assessment of which would be most "trustworthy" and amenable to influence.'

We know who Mrs Thatcher found untrustworthy and we should be warned, in accepting her designation of 'overspending local authorities', that Mandelson and Liddle express their own remarkably strong concern about the 'disastrous error of risking loss of control of public expenditure.' Daunton finds the same forces at work at the high tide of Labour's power. He takes the example of the National Health Service which emerged in 1948 from Aneurin Bevan's negotiations with the doctors, local authorities and voluntary hospitals as something very different from the Labour Party's original plans for a regional structure under democratic local control embracing general practitioners, community services and hospitals. The combination of central government desire to keep a tight hold on spending and of the resistance of the doctors and the voluntary hospitals to democratic control, resulted in the establishment of privately run general practices and regional hospital boards controlled by consultants. As Daunton quotes one authority, it was Bevan who thus helped 'to consolidate the undemocratic control of health care by a tiny elite.'

The pressure on governments to reduce public spending by centralising control has been evident throughout the Thatcher-Major years, and it seems that in this, as in other matters, New Labour's strategy is in Mandelson and Liddle's words 'to move forward from where Margaret Thatcher left off'. The shadow chancellor, Gordon Brown, has made that abundantly clear in one speech after another. Despite all the rhetoric about decentralisation and reducing the power of the state, the Thatcher regime accomplished the greatest centralisation of state power of any British administration — in the control of the police, in the finance of education, in managing the funding of the Health Service, in the provision of social security and generally in the destruction of some local authorities and the reduction of the powers of the rest. In the process some apparent devolution was introduced by the central appointment of several hundred Quangos, made up largely of Tory supporters and formally accountable to nobody. It does not appear clear, moreover, from announcements made so far, whether New Labour proposes to reverse these measures, or whether instead it might choose to change some part of the membership of the Quangos with its own placemen and even women.

Side by side with centralisation a process of privatisation has been carried through by Tory governments. This has gone far beyond anything attempted in other industrial countries. While it has given an impression of decentralisation and competition, the reality has been to concentrate power in the hands of a small number of very large companies, some previously existing, some newly created for the purpose, several subsequently merging their interests, subject only to arbitrary regulation by centrally appointed regulators or Quangos. So far, with the possible exception of Railtrack, not even then with the whole railway system and not even certainly with a reversion to public ownership, New Labour has made no proposals for ending privatisation. All it has offered is a once and for all Utilities Tax to try to claw back some of the taxpayers' money that went into sweeteners for the sale of the 'family silver'.

The State Pension at Risk

In no area of welfare provision is the issue between state and private control of such importance as in that of the provision of pensions. Peter Townsend and Alan Walker, two highly respected experts on social policy, have issued the most sombre warning:

'The outcome of the current policy process [of New Labour] on pensions will determine the whole character of the next Labour government's social policy, as well as the future of the welfare state in the UK . . . a policy on pensions will affect policies on the sick and disabled people, the unemployed, the low paid and lone parents, because retirement pensions are an integral part of a National Insurance scheme which affects everyone as beneficiaries and dependents.' (Townsend & Walker, p.3)

Townsend and Walker fear that New Labour is 'on the brink of adopting the wrong policy', because it is said that revitalising the old scheme would be 'extremely costly' — a truly Gladstonian judgement! Peter Townsend has since confirmed these fears in a pamphlet he has written with Barbara Castle.

The old National Insurance scheme established in 1946 by the Labour Party on the basis of the Beveridge Report was for universal contributory insurance to cover pensions, sickness and unemployment. It redistributed income across the years of a lifetime *and* across the range of incomes from rich to poor. Payments were not means tested and its universality made it cheap to administer. It treated all contributors equally in benefit. Means-tested benefits were seen by Beveridge as a 'last resort in time of trouble'. They have unfortunately steadily grown. They have many disadvantages. They reduce the household incentive to find employment, they are humiliating, they divide families; and, moreover, the present means-tested income support payments are not taken up by nearly a million older people who are entitled to them. Professor Atkinson, an authority on the history of poverty, estimated that this is the same number who failed to benefit under the 1930s' schemes of means-tested national assistance and supplementary benefit. (Townsend & Walker, p.17)

The reason for the reintroduction of means testing twenty years after the Beveridge Report was that the pension and benefit rates failed over the years to keep up with inflation and rising wage incomes. In 1966 the then Labour government proposed a minimum income guarantee without means testing, but in the event assessment of average household earnings and average housing costs proved impossible. Yet New Labour is again talking about a minimum pension guarantee as if it could be introduced without a means test. It may sound better, but it will inevitably repeat the supplementary benefits provision introduced on a means tested basis in 1966. The next Labour government in 1975 made a real step forward introducing — at the time with all-Party support — a State Earnings Related Pension Scheme (SERPS), which would year by year have added new contributions to build up a bigger pension in the future. At the same time, pensions were linked not only to inflation but to rising average earnings.

Tragically, the Thatcher and Major governments cut the earnings link and scaled down SERPS, while encouraging people to move to private and occupational pension schemes to supplement their dwindling state pension. Such schemes have very serious disadvantages. They are much more expensive to administer, they are liable to the kind of villainous abuse, as we saw in the cases of Maxwell and Barlow Clowes, they reduce the pool available for the state pension, they are difficult to transfer from one job to another and to maintain during unemployment, they have no redistributive effect from rich to poor and they build up large sums in the hands of private financial institutions which are, of course, profit making bodies. Moreover, it is these sums in private rather than in state hands which strengthen the City's preoccupation with the largest possible quick returns: the 'short-termism' of which Will Hutton complains. This is because the private institutions need to meet regular claims from pensioners and they are unable, like the state, to take a long-term and wider social view of their investment policies.

What New Labour is evidently proposing has been packaged with the appearance of fairness and of continuing SERPs, and also with the attraction of choice of something extra for those who can afford to choose. A minimum pension guarantee is proposed so that the linking of pensions and earnings need not be reestablished but so the poorest pensioners would be protected. The minimum was said by Donald Dewar, New Labour's spokesman in September 1995 to operate 'automatically', but Labour's experience in 1966 showed that such a scheme was unworkable without means testing. Townsend and Walker quote actuarial studies to show that a revived SERPS could rescue a universal state pension by extending contributions from the highest income earners and by ending mortgage interest tax relief. But this is anathema to New Labour given its faith in winning the votes of the contented middle class.

Since Tony Blair's visit to Singapore, where his stakeholding vision was unveiled, rumours have abounded concerning new forms of compulsory saving for sickness, unemployment and old age. With or without help from the spin-doctors, the Blair-friendly tabloids have broadcast these thoughts. All such forms of saving involve the private financial institutions; which must make them more costly, more risky and more unequal than state schemes, and will once again only encourage the short-termism of such private finance. The Singapore Central Provident Fund, which was singled out for praise by Blair's social service adviser, is, according to an IMF report non-redistributive', provides a 'low level of pension and the absence of indexation' (i.e. to movements in prices or earnings) and according to a World Bank report, is in effect 'a hidden tax on workers to finance general government expenditure'.

The *Sun* newspaper (Jan 9, 1996), with possible inside information after the Singapore visit, leaked the notion that, as part of New Labour's innovative plans, all individuals at birth should have £10,000 put into a savings account to be drawn on in the event of sickness, unemployment and in old age. It has a wonderful appearance of equality, but hardly alters the real inequalities of birth.

Assuming, moreover, a 5% per annum real return over a life time — with no drawings for illness or unemployment — the cumulative result would be at the age of 64 a lump sum of £80,000 at present values. For the next 20 or so years of life this individual could have £4000 p.a., or about £80 a week, by leaving the capital intact, or on average £120 a week if he or she sold off the capital year by year. The current single person's pension is about £60 a week, but has to be supplemented by at least as much again from private sources or from Social Security. So the net result would be a very similar income in the end without a means test. That would be a great gain, but this is all on the assumption of a lifetime with no illnesses and no periods of unemployment and no maternity/paternity leave, the expenses of which would run down the initial capital endowment. And all the evidence suggests that periods of illness and unemployment in the lives of most people are increasing rather than diminishing. Such a scheme would offer a bonanza for the financial institutions who would in effect be replacing national insurance as well as offering top-up schemes of contributory insurance for the better paid. But it could not benefit the great mass of pensioners.

Redistributing Income through Social Spending

All these subterfuges result from one single problem — the grotesque inequalities of income distribution among those who socialists and Christians alike believe to be of equal value. No one, of course, supposes that everyone's work is of equal value but Bernard Shaw once explained the implications of that fact in the Preface to *Androcles and the Lion*:

> 'Nothing, therefore, is really in question, or ever has been, but the differences between class incomes. Already there is economic equality between captains, and economic equality between cabin boys. What is at issue still is whether

there shall be economic equality between captains and cabin boys. What would Jesus have said? Presumably he would have said that if your only object is to produce a captain and a cabin boy for the purpose of transferring you from Liverpool to New York, or to manoeuvre a fleet and carry powder for the magazine of guns, then you need give no more than a shilling to the cabin boy for every pound you give to the more expensively trained captain. But if in addition to this you desire to allow to human souls which are inseparable from the captain and the cabin boy and which alone differentiate them from the donkey-engine, to develop all their possibilities, then you may find the cabin boy costing rather more than the captain, because the cabin boy's work does not do so much for the soul as captain's work. Consequently you will have to give him at least as much as the captain unless you definitely wish him to be a lower creature, in which case the sooner you are hanged as an abortionist the better.'

Christian or not, New Labour is very far removed from Shaw in this parable, but nearly everyone else who leans to the left would wish to see the inequalities of inheritance, education and opportunity reduced, so that income differences were not so wide. This is not just our view but one confirmed by UK opinion polls over the years, which are quoted by Townsend and Walker. Three-quarters of respondents in 1987 thought that 'income differences were too large'. Two-thirds in 1991 would be willing to see 'higher taxes to pay for more social spending' (up from one-third in 1983). 78% in 1994 said that more should be spent by government on pensions, and 57% agreed 'even if this means raising taxes', so that the pension was 'nearer the average wage'.

What then are Tony Blair and his advisers worried about? We have already agreed that a large proportion of the respondents favouring more taxation for more social services either don't pay direct taxes or don't vote. Another proportion may place their cross in the voting booth in a manner opposite to the way they answered that nice lady who asked their opinion earlier, especially if there has been a virulent newspaper campaign against Labour in the run-up to an election.

So, Mr Blair assumes that his only hope of becoming Britain's Prime Minister is to suck up to Mr Murdoch and plan to do nothing which will upset him or the other owners of capital whose power and wealth would be challenged by any actual steps towards socialism. Well, that is his business, but let him in that case cease to call himself either a democratic socialist or a Christian. After all, did he not tell the Tories that they couldn't be Christians if they followed 'their narrow self interest'? It may be, however, that his assumptions are incorrect. It might be possible that those who already say they would like to see more taxation for more social spending should be encouraged and educated to vote for new ways of taxing and spending.

Mr Blair and his advisers may have been looking at an earlier pamphlet produced by the DEMOS group, that by Robin Murray and Geoff Mulgan on *Reconnecting Taxation*. It is Murray and Mulgan's view that the trouble with the UK tax system — and it is widely prevalent elsewhere — is that taxes whether on incomes or on purchases are all collected by government and just go into a common pool. Governments then decide how to allocate from the pool to different lines of expenditure in proportions that are not even discussed in advance in Parliament, let alone in the wider forum of public opinion. The nonsensical charade of the Chancellor opening his little red box to reveal the secrets inside is reenacted every budget day. Much of the detail is quite unintelligible to the non-expert and some of the criteria for allocating funds to different local authorities, for education, for example, are not understood even by the experts themselves. Why Kent receives most and Derbyshire least in the per capita allocation of funds for schools is said no longer to be known in the Department for Education. Three people did know, but one has died, one has left the country and the third can't remember.

Murray and Mulgan suggest that we should look at two main new ways of taxing and spending. The first is to involve the public through referenda and the second, which follows from the first, is to earmark taxes for specific purposes. *Universal contributory* insurance against sickness, unemployment and old age was deliberately chosen by Beveridge as the most popular as well as the most cost-effective method of raising the money as well as of spending it. Road tolls and the original road tax are other examples of purpose specific taxation, which Murray and Mulgan suggest should be extended to a public transport fee, similar to the BBC fee. The fee would be managed by a public transport agency which would have to reveal its plans for discussion, and not just carry out government instructions, with or without subsidy.

Higher taxes on the rich could, they suggest, be allocated to not-for-profit agencies to finance housing and home care for those on lower incomes. Pollution taxes or carbon taxes could be used to fund environmental programmes, taxes on inventions and patents to finance universities. Mulgan and Murray included here a graduate tax to fund higher education. A fairer arrangement would be a similar tax on those who employ graduates, since the actual rewards available to many graduates themselves are not at all munificent. Certainly this would be an improvement on New Labour's latest proposal that state loans should replace the present mix of state grants and private loans. Any system of individual loans means that all students pay the same. Mulgan and Murray suggest that their graduate tax would need to be progressive, i.e. a higher rate levied on higher incomes. So would the other taxes; or we should be back to the present regressive tax structure (i.e. the same rate for all income ranges or sometimes a higher rate on the poor).

Even if the graduate tax were progressive, however, there is a stronger objection to it from a socialist viewpoint. Whatever is being said by leaders of the 'reformed' National Union of Students, who have hitched themselves to the Blairite band-wagon, more and more young men and women will be put off university education by the prospect of the burden of loan repayments or extra taxes in the very years of maximum expenditure when they may be setting out to have a family. The attack on free education is an attack on the socialist principle of distribution: 'to each according to his need'. At a time when education and re-education are becoming lifelong needs, free access becomes the test of a civilised society. The only argument for levying charges on common goods is that people sometimes waste them if they come free. But people don't waste education. If they can't use it to improve their circumstances at work, it might come in useful to help them to get rid of dishonest politicians! And maybe there's the rub?

We have already accepted Townsend and Walker's arguments for a purpose specific payment in for contributory National Insurance, where everyone receives the same payment out. And we did so because contributions in are at least proportional to income, or would be if the top rate was raised; and they have a progressive element in the employers' contribution. The objection to road tolls and fees is that even if they were related to the size of the car this would not ensure much income redistribution. The same objection can be made to car parking fees as a means of restricting cars in city centres. The rich can easily afford to pay them and the poor do not necessarily get a better and cheaper public transport system. Discrimination in taxation against heavy lorries might put more freight back onto the railways. Dr Beeching once proposed that taxation of lorries should be according to the cube of the weight, and not the square, because that better reflected the damage done to the road.

Decentralising Public Spending

A major criticism of increased taxation is the lack of popular control over taxes that are pooled and then allocated according to central government decision. There is widespread agreement on the need to decentralise to local and regional authorities the delivery of services. The powers of regional government would then need to be strengthened, not only in Scotland, Wales and Ireland, but more widely, and the local authorities would need to have their own taxing powers returned to them, with necessary support from the centre for poorer regions. By the end of her time in government Mrs Thatcher had reduced the proportion of income raised locally for local government from 55% to 20%. It has always been seen as a socialist principle that funds for local expenditure, although determined centrally, should be spent locally for services managed by local representatives subject to local election. In this respect, as well as others, New Labour's prevarication over the grant of financial powers to a Scottish Parliament does not bode well for its future popularity.

That the centralisation of government by the Tories needs to be reversed is widely recognised. This should not, however, be at the expense of agreed central policies for redistribution of income. Tony Blair has made noises implying that he recognises this, but there is at the same time a 'centralist tone', as Will Hutton describes New Labour's plans for government. It would be disastrous for any advance in democratic socialism if the decentralisation consisted, as it did under Thatcher, in the transfer of powers from democratically elected government to unaccountable private financial institutions and business dominated Quangos. According to a report from *Democratic Audit*, members of Britain's unaccountable quangos outnumber elected Council members by nearly three to one.

All powers to spend public monies need not, however, be held by government bodies. There are advantages for democratic participation in providing funds for non-governmental organisations. These could follow the almost defunct system of allocating funds to 'responsible bodies', subject to regular inspection. Examples were the Workers' Educational Association, University Extramural Departments and Women's Institutes. Such voluntary bodies do not appear in the New Labour manifestos. They would need to do so, if the hours that we all have free from work for voluntary activity were to grow in the near future in the way that many of the experts in these matters expect them to.

CHAPTER 8

Unemployment and the Future of Work

'There is, of course, nothing difficult in principle about creating jobs which the least skilled could fill . . . But the costs of such deliberate job creation would need to be met either by consumers through higher prices or by citizens through higher taxes. If, as a result of these extra burdens, there is pressure for higher wages, and employers agree to pay them, then costs will rise, competitiveness will suffer, and the net gain in employment in the long run may be small. Roughly the same logic applies to schemes for compulsory work sharing and, in particular, for reductions in working hours which some European socialists espouse. Unless the planned fall in hours results in a compensating reduction in pay, then costs will rise and competitiveness will suffer. Only if pay willingly falls in line with shorter working time can the number of jobs be increased without risk.'

Mandelson and Liddle, op.cit. from the chapter on 'Delivering Prosperity', pp.99-100

With these dismissive words the spokesmen for New Labour reject any answer but cheaper labour to the whole question of the future of employment and the nature of work. Yet, there is no other question that a truly radical party of labour would have more cause to examine most seriously, in advance of finding itself in power, than that of the meaning of work for the great majority of the people, as the new technology is introduced more and more widely and more and more rapidly. It is not just the fact that in 1996 there are in the UK three to four million men and women who would like to have paid work and cannot find it. Nor is it the fact that most of them will never find paid work. It is the much bigger fact that on calculations of the impact of new technology, given the present ordering of the relationship between capital and labour, there never will be paid work for more than a half perhaps of those who will be seeking it. Such futuristic calculations are ridiculed by those whose economic models are based upon past movements of productive investment. The question is raised because the new investment is very much more labour-saving than any in the past since the Industrial Revolution two hundred years ago.

The Destruction of Jobs in the UK and Elsewhere

Figures for those who are unemployed can be massaged, and have been continuously massaged by Conservative governments over the last 17 years, to conceal the continuing gap between those in employment and those who would like to find paid work. What cannot be massaged are the figures of those in employment, full-time and part-time. John Hughes in a study in 1994 of changes in employment in Great Britain between June 1978 and June 1993 showed that there had been a loss over those years of nearly three million full time jobs. At the same time, there had been an increase of 1.4 million part-time jobs, one million of them for women. At first sight it appears therefore that the net loss was only about 1.5 million, but each part-time job is only equivalent to half a full-time job. The net loss in full-time equivalent jobs was thus 2.2 million. And this is out of a labour force of 20 million in 1993.

Within these figures the loss of jobs over the 1980s in manual occupations and the loss of jobs in production and construction industries was even greater. Manual jobs went down by 3 million for men and half a million for women between 1979 and 1993. More non-manual jobs made up for these to some extent — 400,000 more jobs for men and 780,000 for women, although many of these were part-time. Over the same years there was a fall of employment in manufacturing industries of three million and another 700,000 in other production and construction industries. Since 1993, when Hughes's study terminated, although there has been a fall in the official figures for the unemployed, there has been practically no increase in the level of actual employment.

This picture of declining employment has not been confined to the UK, but has recently been experienced throughout Europe. While employment grew in the European Union between 1981 and 1991 by 7 million, 4.5 million jobs were lost in 1991-3 and one million regained in 1995 until a new recession occurred affecting Germany in particular. The important point to notice is that while some growth took place in output in 1994-5 and some new jobs were created then, these were not enough to reduce the rate of unemployment except marginally and by 1996 the growth was halted. The fact that Germany then suffered the highest rate of unemployment since the war has not only raised questions about the German bankers' safekeeping of the whole European

126

economy but also about the efficacy of the German economic model which Will Hutton and others have been recommending to New Labour.

While economic growth in Europe has not been rising faster than labour productivity, so that employment has stagnated, employment has continued to rise in the United States and also in Japan and even more markedly in South East Asia. One explanation for the loss of jobs in Europe, especially in manufacturing, has been that competition from Japan and from new industries in East Asia and cheap labour everywhere, including the USA and Mexico and most recently Eastern Europe, has been increasingly penetrating European markets. This is the basis for Sir James Goldsmith's argument for protectionism both for the UK and for Europe against what he sees as the threat from cheap labour in the East. This should not be taken too seriously. According to studies referred to in the latest European Commission *Annual Economic Report*, that for 1996,

> 'available evidence has concluded that competition from low wage economies has had a negative effect on employment in some sectors, but that it is not particularly large, and may well be set off by rising employment in other sectors.'

It is very easy to blame cheap labour elsewhere for Europe's recent decline, but there are other factors to take into account. First, as we have emphasised before there is the much neglected demand side. The United States has been able, from its dominating political, economic and military position, to go on borrowing for many years, chiefly from Japan, to maintain demand in its economy, running a trade and government deficit such as no other country could conceive of. Japan has persistently taken measures to maintain home demand when growth faltered. Contrary to much advice from the World Bank and the IMF, the governments of the advancing South East Asian countries have continuously supported their industries with finance and even export subsidies to maintain demand at a time that European governments were following monetarist policies of fiscal moderation.

We showed earlier that economists were increasingly arguing that monetarism had gone too far and were looking back wistfully to the 1950s and 60s when governments made full employment a primary policy objective. What could be done by a new Labour Government to move back towards full employment would depend very much on cooperative action in Europe, which is the subject of another chapter of this book. But we have already indicated the lines along which a serious policy of job creation might be pursued.

The New Technology and Job Losses

The second answer to the cheap labour argument is that the new technology rather than cheap labour is the main cause of job losses in industry. The threat to jobs lies not in our fellow workers, but in the way the new technology is being introduced. One important finding in the European studies was that job losses in small and medium-sized enterprises (SMEs) had been less than in large enterprises. The employment policies of the large transnational companies are global. This is what we saw earlier in looking at the latest stages of globalisation, in which not just movements of capital are global but the organisation of production processes by the transnational companies. Their synergies will comprise cheap and semi-skilled labour in one place, special skills in another, raw materials in a third, markets in a fourth. When governments seek to compete for inward investment, they are divided and conquered or reduced by the giant accumulators of capital to supplying the least remunerative factor — cheap labour or raw materials. But the jobs are being destroyed not just by competition but by the new productive processes using less labour, *even when it is cheap labour*.

What has been happening in the UK and throughout Europe is that right up until 1995 productivity — output per person employed — in industry has been growing at between 2% and 3% a year, but since in recent years demand has not been growing any faster than productivity, there has been no room for new employment. The facts are already becoming clear and the idea that the problem can be solved by greater competitiveness is being steadily invalidated not only for the British economy but also for other European economies. The figures for productivity increases are misleading. They are national averages. When they are disaggregated we find that some companies and sectors have productivity gains on a phenomenal scale: two or three *hundred* percent in one or two years. These reflect not only new techniques but also new management systems. The result is that national figures for productivity conceal very uneven growth, If some companies have over a hundred percent growth, others must have practically no growth at all. Some will be competitive, others will not. Raising productivity as a whole implies an expansion of demand. Yet the main thrust of European governments, which New Labour are apparently to follow, is still to improve the supply side of the labour market, through training and infrastructure investment, as if the main problem was competition in labour intensive industries coming from the East and from the USA, where cheap labour is abundant, and not in raising the productivity of labour.

The success of the United States not only in keeping down the unemployment rate — at about half European levels — but also in maintaining a steady growth of employment is cited as evidence that an unregulated economy based on cheap labour can work. It has failed, however, to maintain the number of skilled jobs and the survival of industry and employment is very uneven, the areas of highest unemployment being also areas of lowest wages. That may sound obvious, but it denies the argument for labour market flexibility, i.e. low wages for unskilled work to solve unemployment. The future prospects for employment in the United States are not, moreover, expected to be any better than they are already presenting themselves in Europe.

Future Employment Prospects

Recent statistical studies such as those of Christopher Freeman and Luc Soete (*Work for all or Mass Unemployment*) show declining rates of increase in employment in the United States and Japan corresponding to the actual declines of employment in Europe in the 1990s; and others have suggested (UNCTAD, 1995) that growth in China and even in South East Asia may begin to abate. There must be some question about this because the countries in this region have a long way to go to catch up with consumer demand and productivity levels in the more advanced industrialised countries. The Pacific rim running down from Japan has moreover become a region of self-reinforcing growth in sharp contrast to the set-backs in the neighbouring regions of Western Europe (Eastern Europe and Africa) or of North America (Central and Southern America).

Certainly, the United States is not expected to be immune from the world-wide declining tends in employment in the fairly near future. Jeremy Rifkin, in his authoritative study, *The End of Work: The Decline of the Global Labour Force and the Dawn of the Post-Market Era* has spelled out what he sees as the implications of the new technology for anything like full employment as we have seen it in the past. He envisages a rapid decline in the demand for labour in the next two decades, not only in the USA but world-wide. There could, he believes, be a loss in the USA of some 25 million jobs out of 120 million, to add to the number of unemployed, which in 1995 was about 8 million. He assumes the same kind of figures not only in the older industrialised countries but also in the new ones as labour-saving investment takes place, even within existing known technologies, to affect service industries as well as production.

His most chilling prediction is of the supplanting of all small-scale farming, both for food crops and for export commodities, throughout the Third World, as the result of the introduction of bio-technology.

We will look at bio-technology in the next chapter, but the implications for an advanced industrial country like the UK of this and other new developments in technology in industry and agriculture are likely to go far beyond anything envisaged in the manifestos of the political parties. They should have been warned more than a decade ago in a Report to the Club of Rome on *Micro-electronics and Society*. The authors then envisaged a permanent rise in the number of unemployed and the need to consider new forms of occupation in place of long hours of what we call work, these to include continuing education.

Longer Hours of Work: Fewer in Work

The most testing problem for a government with a commitment however modest to working people — those presently in secure employment, those feeling insecure or those actually unemployed — is that, although those without work steadily increase in number (whatever the statistics say), more of those in full-time employment work longer hours. While this lengthening of the hours of the full-time employees is taking place, there is also much more part-time employment. The part-timers in fact work shorter hours in the UK because employers do not have to pay national insurance and other employer's costs for those earning less than £61 a week. In some cases the state even subsidises such part-time employment if the wage is particularly low. Yet, for many full-time, mainly male, employees the working of overtime is a requirement of the employment contract. The UK has the highest proportion of its labour force working over 48 hours a week and also nearly the highest proportion of part-time workers of any industrialised country. But the trend is similar in other such countries — towards a two-part work force — full-time men working overtime and part-time women working undertime. It is not quite so simple as that, but things are moving in that direction.

The reasons are clear — labour costs are reduced for employers in both ways. Overtime rates never fully compensate the worker for the advantage to the employer of not paying so much in wages, even at overtime rates, in relation to the extra value added by the worker, using the same capital equipment for longer hours. In both cases, of using overtime work and part-time work, moreover, the employer does not have to pay the employers' costs — national insurance and other charges — for extra full-time employees. John Hughes has shown that not only were there more full-time workers working over 48 hours a week in 1991, for example, compared with 1984 — 20% of the total (24% for men) compared with 15% — but that the actual hours over 48 had greatly increased. A later TUC study in 1994 showed that a third of full-time male employees were working 48 hours a week or more and 27% were working over 50 hours. This compared with 26% and 20% respectively in 1984.

The effect on employment of these long hours can be calculated. A 48 hour week is regarded as 'excessive', a 44 hour week as 'usual' and a 39 hour week as 'basic'. John Hughes has shown that all the extra hours worked by those working more than 48 hours in 1991 amounted to one and a quarter million 'basic' working weeks. The hours of those working over a 'usual' 44 hour week add up to two million 'basic' working weeks. So, there would have been work for two million more people on 'basic' hours had the 'excessive' hours came down to 'usual' hours. If the TUC results for 1994 were similarly calculated, it would be found that by 1994 even more of the unemployed could in principle have been employed.

John Hughes has further pointed out that the UK accounts for half of all the hours over 48 worked per week in the whole European Union. The 20%-30% who work such excessive hours in the UK compares with about 5%-6% in Germany, France and Italy. Most European countries have laws regulating maximum hours and the Maastricht Social Chapter and European Directive on Working Time require the acceptance by Member States of a maximum 48 hour week. The average in the UK for full-time male employees is about 45 hours, but about a half work longer hours. The British government has refused to agree to any such maximum. What about New Labour? Are these the 'rigid, costly rules . . . and inefficient practices which will harm our competitiveness and deter inward investment' according to Mandelson and Liddle if imported to Britain under the Social Chapter, which Tony Blair has been seeking to distance himself from? One can see how many jobs would be destroyed in Europe if the British deregulation of working hours became universal. At the same time one can see how many jobs would be created by an agreed reduction of working hours.

Any such proposal seems to be ruled out for New Labour by Mandelson and Liddle, who appear to have accepted *in toto* the Tory government's pursuit of competitiveness through lengthening full-time work and increasing the numbers of uninsured part-timers. It is safe to say that there has never been a more revisionary and inhuman commitment by a Labour leadership team in the entire history of the Party. Massive productivity gains make possible shorter hours and *higher* wages at the same time. To cut wages would be to cut demand and increase unemployment. But the argument of Mandelson and Liddle is precisely that deployed against the regulation of hours for women and children in the struggles for the ten-hour day and on throughout the Nineteenth Century. New Labour has not only crossed over to the other side; it appears to have lined up with the worst zealots of the Victorian millocracy.

Does Low Pay Increase Employment?

We noted earlier that low pay in the United States had not greatly affected levels of employment. Areas of high unemployment were still also areas of low pay. John Hughes has revealed the same phenomenon in the UK, comparing regions, sectors and categories of workers. In the years from 1990 to 1995 the greatest falls in employment coincided with a fall or slow growth in real earnings, whether he looked at regions, manufacturing industry compared with services, manual compared with non-manual workers, men compared with women. Where unemployment rose fastest, among manual workers working full-time in manufacturing, the earnings of the lowest decile actually fell in the five years. In every category and in either gender earnings rose faster in the highest than in the lowest earnings deciles. The worst experience was that of young workers and non-manual women workers where chances of *full-time* work decreased as well as real earnings. 'Deregulated markets', as Hughes summed up, 'have proved hostile to young workers, not least to those seeking full-time work.'

Hughes's studies covered the most recent period, the early 1990s, but the poor had already been getting poorer throughout the 1980s, as Peter Townsend showed in a 1990 study, *The Poor are Poorer*. Between 1979 and 1989 the poorest 20% of the population actually saw their incomes fall in real terms. We are talking about 11 million people in the UK. Most of these would be pensioners and unemployed, but increasing numbers would be workers on very low pay. According to the European Commission's European Poverty Programme, comparing 1985 with 1975, there were more people in the European Union living in poverty (defined as under 50% of average expenditure), some 50 millions more in fact. In particular, the Programme found that 'the proportion of low income persons . . . increased above all in the United Kingdom'.

Doubts have been raised about the UK poverty figures because housing costs are sometimes excluded in calculating expenditure. But Townsend has responded that some of the poorest households are excluded because their poverty is so extreme that to include them would distort the sample figures. A similar exclusion is applied at the top of the scale, where the highest incomes are not included in the sample. So in Jan Pen's march past of income earners the ants scurrying along at the front would be even smaller and the giants at the end with their heads miles high in the clouds would be even taller. David Donnison has, moreover, pointed out that the real costs of living have been steadily rising more rapidly than the statistics reveal, because poor households are increasingly having to pay more for the only available goods and services, as central heating, refrigerators, transport to shops and to work become necessities and not luxuries.

Quite apart from the inequity of cheap labour policies, said to be justified to attract foreign investment, there are many good reasons why these are mistaken and can be shown, as in the United States, not to work. But even if they did work they would be wrong.

We can test this. The most exhaustive studies of policies of wage moderation and general labour market 'flexibility' have been carried out at the Free University of Amsterdam. During the 1980s governments in the Netherlands pursued policies of wage moderation, to the extent that, while real wages in the European Union during the years 1984-90 rose by 1.8% a year, the corresponding figure in the Netherlands was 0.4%. The result was that the Netherlands had no better growth record nor increase in employment (allowing extra part-time employment to be counted as full-time equivalents) than the average for the European Union. An ever more important discovery from these studies was that wage moderation had impaired increases in productivity and entrepreneurial quality and had discouraged product innovation. The overall result was no increase in Dutch exports or decrease in imports and a particularly poor performance of small and medium sized enterprises relative to their counterparts in other countries where wage increases were stronger.

The Real Effect of Low Pay

It appears that none of the arguments for labour market flexibility and wide wage differentials stands up in practice. Higher wages limited to companies enjoying monopoly positions diminish the incentive to take innovative risks. Lower wages in SMEs give an extra competitive option to non-innovating firms. Flexibility in wage formation thus works against innovation; greater ease in firing workers gives a competitive advantage to non-innovators; a highly mobile labour market discourages employers from investing in the training and education of their workforce; while parents' low pay discourages children from continuing education; environmental and resource use laxity reduces the incentive to develop a competitive advantage in energy-saving technology.

The so-called 'dynamic competitive market', which New Labour wishes to free from 'old fashioned' restraints, including those protective powers of the trade unions and a minimum wage above the poverty level, is not so dynamic after all. It is the same story that has been revealed throughout the history of the British economy. It has not been the strength of British trade unions but their internal divisions and failure to take positive, as opposed to purely defensive actions, that have aided Britain's industrial decline. Again and again the British economy has been saved by external factors — imperial expansion, tribute from India, war-time expenditure, Lend-Lease and Marshall Aid, North Sea oil. The list is running out, and support from the European Union will not be the next external factor unless true cooperation in joint and common actions of Britain in Europe can be developed.

Low pay, slow growth and unemployment make up a syndrome of decline. Low pay means low purchasing power and a reduced multiplier effect from injections of investment. It is the central contradiction of capitalist development. Exploitation of workers generates profits for capital accumulation to be invested in new production. But low pay reduces the capacity of workers to buy the extra products. John Hughes's studies showed that in the years 1992-5 there was a redistribution of around £24 billion each year from British wages and salaries to gross profits, but these were not translated into increased productive investment in the UK. Nor has there been any corresponding increase in economic growth which averaged 2.5% a year, while purchasing power from wages and salaries rose by less than 1% a year. It was not to be wondered at that this kind of a 'boom' fizzled out after 1994.

What is then the response of New Labour to this return of a capitalist economy to its old ways? The rhetoric says that they have the 'ambition to conquer unemployment', but there are three ominous sentences about pay and employment in Mandelson and Liddle (M&L, p.101), repeated in similar words in the Manifesto.

'The government can help tip the balance in favour of the labour market outsider [i.e the unemployed] against the insiders [the employed] and thereby increase general pressure for responsible pay.'

'Policy should address the barriers in the existing social security system which hold people back from taking low-paid work or undertaking training.'

'Recruitment subsidies such as Gordon Brown has already proposed to encourage private sector employees to take on long-term unemployed . . . should be part of a concerted drive to encourage companies to extend their corporate social responsibilities . . .'

This reflects all the one-sided bigotry of Conservative idealogues. On the one side it favours subsidies for business (how much is needed to encourage 'corporate responsibility'?) and on the other reduced social security to get the unemployed to work for lower pay (sorry! for 'responsible pay'). What kind of 'fairness' is that?

We have dealt elsewhere with the Speenhamland type subsidy to employers who will pay less than a living wage. But New Labour's rejection of increased taxes on the rich to fund new employment means that no serious attempt will be made to fulfil 'the ambition to conquer unemployment'. Mandelson and Liddle doubt whether the poor couple they describe would be helped by 'levelling down' their rich couple's privileges. More than this, they now propose measures of redistribution, not between families — rich and poor — but within families. Older people, in their fifties and sixties, in so-called 'empty nests', should, they say, sell their houses, if they own them, and 'mobilise the capital to spread wealth between a family's generations — to pay for long term care for the very elderly, to invest in their children's or grandchildren's education and training, to give young people a better start in married life.' It is not explained where the 'empty nesters' then would live or how much would be realised if they moved into smaller accommodation. But we may apply Kant's principle and ask if Messrs. Mandelson and Liddle, or for that matter Messrs Blair and Brown, will do this when they are in their late fifties? We fear that Mrs Be-Done-By-As-You-Did will, in the end, brick all these worthies into the next chimney to that occupied by Mr Grimes.

New Patterns of Work

There is no doubt, of course, about the need for spreading earnings over a lifetime, given the future likelihood of greatly reduced working time, but we have argued that this is best done through state schemes. Current levels of unemployment are still relatively low compared with the prospects of job destruction in the future envisaged by Jeremy Rifkin. Such a scenario could hardly be contemplated by individuals or by governments without major changes following in work patterns and in the distribution of paid work. But the view of economists of a Keynesian or Marxist persuasion is that the market on its own cannot be relied upon to make such changes.

In one of the best chapters in his book, *The State We're In*, the chapter entitled 'Why Keynesian Economics is Best', Will Hutton derides the classical economic theory of work as a commodity which is offered on the market for whatever price will overcome the 'disutility' of working, it being presumed that leisure is naturally preferred. But nobody prefers to be unemployed unless it makes them actually financially better off, as in the case of the partner of an unemployed person. Work is a necessity not just to earn a living, but to achieve human dignity and solidarity. And paid work in our society is essential to that achievement.

We have seen that employers prefer longer hours from full time workers and shorter hours from part-timers, but the workers themselves have sometimes connived with their employers. Longer full-time hours are worked by men to raise their wages for many reasons — because of housing costs, travel to work costs, holidays abroad, even modest luxuries: but, more simply, very often because they start with an impossibly low basic wage. This is itself very much the result of weakening trade union power. Part-time work is sought by women because most of them still have a part-time or nearly full-time job at home, but want more independence and need a second income in the household. People are increasingly divided into 'work-rich' households with both partners earning and 'work-poor' households with neither. All this is partly the result of employer cost cutting and a means-tested social security system, but partly the result of the 'free' choices of the workers within the given very unfree market framework with weakened trade unions.

It is becoming increasingly clear to many workers, however, that accidents at work and individual ill-health are associated with long hours of work and the shedding of labour. There is now evidence for this from surveys that have been made. One example is the TUC report published in 1995, *Hard Labour: Britain's Longer Working Week*, which not only reveals the health and safety risks involved in long hours of work but also many examples of employer pressure being put on workers, both better paid white collar workers and manual workers, to extend their hours of work. The Tory government's proposals that the 48 hour week maximum should be a voluntary decision for each worker is one of the silliest proposals to come even from this government. Who gets the job in an interview — the one who will work long hours or the one who prefers not to? Much overtime has been shown to be involuntary. What will New Labour do about this in their pursuit of a flexible market? There is an even more sinister fact about institutional overtime. Almost half of it is unpaid, which tells us everything about the generous instincts of businessmen when freed from trade union constraints. What will New Labour do about this?

It is not only the workers but the general public who suffer from cost cutting by downsizing. There have been examples on the railways and at sea of accidents due not only to human failure through long hours of work but directly as the result of manning reductions. The worst example of this was in the loss of nearly 200 lives on the roll-on-roll-off ferry *Herald of Free Enterprise* (an ironic name!) at Zeebrugge. The inquiry revealed that as a result of reduced staffing the chief mate had two tasks to perform on departure, requiring him to be at the same moment in different positions on the ship — one on the bridge to oversee the ship's movement away from the quayside and the other at the stern to see that the entry-exit doors were closed (see RA Cahill, *Disasters at Sea*). Christopher Gifford, a retired mining inspector, has given other examples, ending up with the BSE disaster, of the results of government deregulation on the health and safety of workers and of the public at large, in his pamphlet, *Deregulation, Disasters and BSE* (Socialist Renewal, Spokesman, 1996).

Mandelson and Liddle see an important role for the trade unions in protecting workers' conditions at work, but the unions are warned off from 'trying to get their own way by dominating the party structures to which they are linked'. There is certainly plenty of work for the unions to do, especially in extending their reach to home work and smaller work places, where union membership is weak, but where increasing numbers of people and especially women are employed. One of the groups hit hardest by the pressure to lengthen hours is that of the full-time women workers who also have a family to care for. A survey by the charity *Parents at Work* of white-collar working mothers found two thirds working longer hours than contracted for and one in five working more than 60 hours a week. Most complained that the quality of their family life was suffering and some felt that the children and the marriage itself were at risk.

The Link between Hours of Work and Unemployment

The struggle for a shorter working week has been a historic issue for trade unions, but the link to full employment has always been recognised as necessarily involving state intervention. The association between hours of work and the level of unemployment has a long history but has recently reappeared as an important issue. In Europe in 1880 people worked about 3,200 hours a year. From then until 1970 the hours of work were steadily reduced to about 1,700 a year, while at the same time incomes grew and unemployment rose and fell with booms and slumps, but did not disappear. After 1970 the hours of work stabilised and mass unemployment occurred, comparable only to the 1930s. In a few European countries — Belgium, Denmark, Germany and the Netherlands — there has been a deliberate attempt to reduce hours of work to cushion the increase in unemployment. With this experience in mind, the European Parliament in 1995 commissioned a report from its Committee on Social Affairs and Employment on *A Reduction in Working Hours* and appointed Michel Rocard, a previous Socialist Prime Minister of France, to act as rapporteur.

The Rocard Report found that in most European countries and in the European Union, both in the Commission and among the social partners — employers, workers' representatives and governments — all had shied away from tackling this question. The Report, nonetheless, made proposals that, Rocard believed, could solve the problem. He found that many companies had in fact greatly reduced working hours and yet had not only maintained the number of their employees but had gone on to recruit new workers. However, in most cases workers' pay had suffered, so that extending such initiatives had not proved acceptable. Since neither employers nor workers were able to agree on the pay implications of reduced hours, governments would have to take action.

The Rocard Report therefore proposed a system of compensation from the resources currently spent by governments on maintenance of the unemployed, to ease the process of reducing hours and thus to generate a demand for new employment. He recognised that productivity increases made possible a reduction of hours but the initial payment of the same wages for shorter hours created problems. The key to the solution was that machinery should be kept operating for longer hours, even though individual workers' hours were reduced. This concept of decoupling capital hours from labour hours was taken up by the European Commission directorate general of Economic and Financial Affairs as a major recommendation for encouraging employment-intensive growth. There remained several different ways of proceeding with a reduction in hours of work and for compensating employers and employees for the initial losses involved, bearing in mind that many workers working overtime are among the less well paid for basic hours.

Rocard systematically explored five not necessarily mutually exclusive alternatives: gradual early retirement working part-time and taking a part of a state pension; voluntary part-time working with full employment rights; reduced overtime working down to a 'usual' level of hours; a reduced working week, perhaps to a four day week within ten years; increased time devoted to education and training within the working life-time. Rocard took the view that all these methods could be pursued but all would need an element of state subsidy in the initial period, which could very possibly be financed from resources released by the subsequent reduction in state payments to the unemployed, as the dole queue shortened. He proposed a simple form of compensation — by reducing the contribution of employers and employees to national insurance funds for each hour of work reduced.

The idea in particular of a whole extra day free each week or of much longer periods of holidays to bring down the annual hours of work replicated a proposal made to Ken Coates by Frank Cousins, the one-time general secretary of the Transport and General Workers Union, that the aim should be a one thousand hour year of work. The rest of present work time in different amounts could be given up to recreation, serious sport, education and active involvement in the life of the community, even including, no doubt, political activity. The same idea was advanced in France during the 1970s by Andre Gorz, and taken up by the then general secretary of the German Social Democrats, Peter Glotz. There is no sign of it in the Blair Revolution, which, as the epigraph to this chapter from Mandelson and Liddle indicates, does not apparently include anything so radical as support for a proposal from any of the fellow socialists in Europe with whom Tony Blair has said that he hopes to create a radical new agenda.

Moving Towards a New Relation of Paid and Unpaid Work

If the scenario painted for the Club of Rome and by Jeremy Rifkin is even half correct, then there is a major crisis for governments to face in the next decades. Since these projections have been given the authority of a retired US State Department Adviser, as we have already seen, writing in the official US publication *Foreign Affairs*, they cannot be lightly dismissed. A doubling of the present levels of unemployment would create problems of social breakdown and disruption of law and order beyond even the worst experiences of the 1930s. It should hardly be necessary to recall that these led to fascism and world war.

There is some recognition of the scale of the economic and technological changes throughout the world in Mandelson and Liddle's exposition of New Labour's approach to what they see as a wholly new situation for a British government. In this situation they dismiss both the New Right and Old Labour, the first for their abandonment of the regulatory role of government and the second for allegedly believing that government can do everything. New Labour's position quoted earlier from Mandelson and Liddle was that

> 'they do not seek to limit markets, but — crucially — recognise that they need to operate within a fair framework of rules that upholds the public interest and that public action needs to complement the weaknesses of the market place.'

The use of the word 'complement' is peculiar; it would imply similar weaknesses in public action. Perhaps they meant 'counteract', but when they get down to detail, the public action proposed is nearly always of a regulatory nature. The difficulties with such limited intervention have already been discussed, but they are very obvious in the case of reducing hours of work. Rocard's Report at once grasped the need to involve the financial resources of the state. By contrast, the emphasis placed on 'competition in a dynamic market' in all New Labour pronouncements leaves rather little room for the Rocard type of intervention. It would be rendered almost impossible if national insurance were to be made less than universal, in the manner that was discussed in the last chapter. A change in the hours of work such as Jeremy Rifkin foresees will go far beyond what can be dealt with by a regulation of the market. If British unions want legislative action against long hours of work, such as was pioneered in Victorian Britain, they will have to lobby others, as well as New Labour, to get it. That the unions should continue to give financial support to a party which seems determined to act against their vital interests in many areas is an interesting example of the law of inertia at work on the political plane.

Rifkin envisages nothing less than a major switch of state resources to finance not only the transition to shorter hours of work but the support for education and training and what he calls the 'third sector' of voluntary work. Rifkin working in the American political scene is not looking for funds from the very limited resources of national insurance. He looks to cutting the massive tax concessions that he reveals are being received by transnational companies operating from the USA and particularly by agribusiness. These concessions together amounted in 1993 to $130 billions, that is over 10% of federal government revenues in that year. Much the same could be done in the UK, taking into account the subsidies granted in privatising state companies, export credit guarantees for arms sales abroad and the softest tax regime in the world for the oil companies operating in the North Sea. Rifkin's main proposal for raising finance is the same as we saw coming from Professor Galbraith — to tax the rich. He makes a list of spending on goods, concentrated in the hands of a few, of money that should be available to all. Cut back some of this obscene conspicuous consumption and how much there would be for the people, here in the UK as in the USA.

We can now take into consideration another insight in Will Hutton's chapter on 'Why Keynesian Economics is Best', where he quotes from Paul Ormerod's book *The Death of Economics*. Classical economic theory tells us that there are rising costs as supply is increased and diminishing returns as demand is increased. Neither of these effects is borne out in the actual operations in our economy for a wide range of the products of modern industry. Far from costs rising as supply increases, they fall from economies of scale. On the demand side, the taste grows by what it feeds on, or, as Ormerod puts it, 'The more one has, the more one wants and the greater the satisfaction obtained from having it' — not one car for the family but one for each member, not one TV and video, but one for each room. So, there are no forces in the market to restore equilibrium. Adding regulations is like Ptolemy adding epicycles to his model of the sun moving round the earth, when all the time it was the earth moving round the sun. Putting the market at the centre and not the human being commits an identical error. Individuals operate in markets but as such, as purchasers, they are not expressing their full personality, as we have noted earlier, when they are merely buying something. There is vastly more to people than can be expressed in purely market or monetary terms. 'Bring out number, weight and measure,' said William Blake, 'in a year of dearth.'

Rifkin believes that we are in effect moving into a post-market era. The exploitation of labour will decline as less and less labour is used in production of goods, and caring services are increasingly supplied on a voluntary basis. Government decision on resource allocation will become more and not less widespread, even though governments do not own the means of production. Such decisions will in part be decentralised and in part agreed at an intergovernmental level subject to tele-referenda. If all this is coming, it is ironical that New Labour should be just now turning away from systems of common ownership and management towards the market and private enterprise. Given the continuing power of large scale capital ownership, Rifkin's optimism seems somewhat naive, but his insistence on the need for mechanisms of redistribution against the market's allocations should provide a stimulus for any true socialist.

There is an alternative in the growth of self-employment in nearly all advanced industrialised countries which suggests one way of filling the gap between the number of potential workers and the number needed by the big owners of capital for their operations. This is the alternative promoted by the UK business school gurus, who have become hitched to the Blairite wagon (see Charles Handy, 'People and Change' in Giles Radice (ed.) *What Needs to Change* with the introduction by Tony Blair, Harper Collins 1996, pp.22ff.): develop your own portfolio, go out there and do your own thing as a self-employed professional or a small business man, become one of Tony Blair's hundreds of new millionaires. That is their message and that is the meaning of the individual in the market, to which New Labour's advocates are appealing. So much for all the windy rhetoric about community. Yet, the brutal fact is that nearly all the self-employed and a very large proportion of small businesses live by sub-contracts or sub-sub-contracts from the big companies.

The main emphasis of Rifkin's book which must concern us is on the switch from paid to unpaid work, which he believes could be encouraged by tax deductions for hours of registered voluntary work. As paid work occupies less and less of our time, the third sector of voluntary work comes into its own. If financial assistance could be given for education and training, use could then be made not just of the free time available but of the natural human desire to help fellow humans. This could be of special value for older people both as givers and receivers, now that we live so much longer and are required to retire so much earlier. For most people there are at least twenty years between retirement and death, and with earlier retirement this period will be longer. Mandelson and Liddle put much emphasis on mutual help inside the extended family. But there are great dangers of exploitation in such arrangements, not to mention family ill-will, which a properly registered system of third sector working could avoid.

There is here a litmus test for all the talk coming from New Labour about community and a strong society. Unless practical measures are taken to strengthen social action against the corrosion of market competition, all such talk will remain windy rhetoric. Above all it is space and time that people need for their development and at least minimal financial resources to expand all the voluntary activity that already exists. It is a striking fact about the Mandelson/Liddle manifesto that the only references to the voluntary sector are in relation to partnerships with local authorities in bidding for job creation grants and what they see as the most 'cost-effective' development of public services. The role of adult educators and the Open Colleges and the huge range of caring associations and campaigning groups particularly for conserving the environment gets no mention. Yet a party of labour should above all things provide an umbrella for people's own voluntary initiatives. That should be the meaning of community. At one point Mandelson and Liddle mention the 'social entrepreneur', a concept of David Donnison's, but without any apparent inkling of Donnison's understanding of the role of voluntary bodies. This involves the mobilisation of the millions of 'carers' and concerned people whose contribution to society goes largely unrecognised and unrewarded. But this does not mean that they should replace the professional social and health services as a sort of cheap substitute. That may well be in the minds of Mandelson and Liddle when they refer to them as 'cost effective'. Their role must be supplementary and complementary to the professional services, and they deserve to be rewarded.

At the very heart of our humanity is the work we do and the pride and satisfaction we get from work, whether paid or unpaid. This satisfaction reflects our contribution to society. In this the market and the community must always be at odds. In the last resort, as was made plain in Christ's Sermon on the Mount, 'No man can serve two masters . . . Ye cannot serve God and Mammon.' All the words the New Labour speakers write and utter seeking to make the market social by regulation, and to tack 'Old Labour values of community and responsibility' onto competition in the market, are in vain. Community must in the end mean working and owning in common. And the more we make space for voluntary work in place of exploited labour, the more fulfilled we shall be in our common humanity.

CHAPTER 9

Responding to the Ecological Crisis

'There is tremendous concern, particularly among young people, about the environmental challenges facing the globe . . .'

Mandelson and Liddle, op.cit, *p.164*

This sentence which we have already quoted is the sole reference in the Mandelson Liddle book to the ecological crisis affecting the whole planet, which involves all the issues of resource conservation and the possibility of 'sustainable' growth as well as the environmental challenges. The young people are, of course, absolutely right to be concerned, but what is New Labour's response? According to Mandelson and Liddle in the second half of the sentence at the head of this chapter

'. . . but many of the issues can be addressed only on a continental scale — a purely national approach would be damaging for competitiveness and jobs.'

There is some truth in this — that the environment is not just the UK's environment, but this is not what the authors mean. What they are saying is that avoiding pollution and conserving energy is costly and would reduce UK industry's competitive position, if it was not done in agreement with Britain's competitors.

The fact is that the reputation of the UK in the matter of environmental damage and waste of resources, especially of energy resources, is among the lowest of all industrialised countries. This can readily be discovered by looking at the number of environmental issues in which the UK is in breach of European regulations. These range from power station emissions to dirty beaches. There is even wider international concern about the THORP and Sellafield nuclear waste disposal plants, not to mention the Shell Oil Company's devastation of the Ogon River estuary in Nigeria.

This is not just a British problem. The industrialised countries, as a whole, and their corporations are the world's chief polluters and chief users (and wasters) of irreplaceable resources. They account for a quarter of the world's population and consume three-quarters of the world's energy fuels and other resources. This is a degree of inequality that offends our humanity and should offend Mr Blair's Christianity.

There is one particular environmental disaster that naturally concerns us, which follows from the abandonment of deep mined coal production in favour of opencast mining in parts of England, Scotland and Wales. There are two results affecting the environment, quite aside from the destruction of the livelihood of whole mining communities. The first is that minewater pollution of water courses in the neighbourhood of closed pits takes place if pumping and treatment of this water are not continued. The European Commission has been asked to investigate whether European legislation protecting the water environment is being followed. The second is the effect of opencast mining not only on the look of the land, but on the health of surrounding populations, first from the dust, noise and traffic pollution and secondly from the voids created which have attracted the attention of waste disposal companies. Once again European law on the environment is being invoked. It is clear that this needs stringently tightening.

Together with unemployment the ecological crisis should surely head the agenda not only of young people, but of all political parties, not least of New Labour. With the deepening crisis of resources, all talk of economic growth based on a dynamic competitive economy has to be questioned. Since the Mandelson Liddle book was published, Tony Blair has made a major speech on the environment (27.2.1996). In it he states how he assumes that environmental problems will be dealt with by New Labour:

'by balancing the interests of all, not just the producer but the consumer, not just economic growth but the environment . . . That is what the concept of stakeholding is all about . . .'

What Blair did not say was who is to do the balancing and with what instruments. His only practical proposal was for a Parliamentary audit committee to have this responsibility. But with what powers? And with what stakeholding in the companies being audited?

Labour Saving and Energy Wasting

'Balancing' the needs of the environment against economic growth is not just a small matter of monitoring and adjustment. It is the central crisis of our times, which is at the centre both of growing unemployment and of environmental degradation. The two are intimately connected, as Jacques Delors put it in a Working Document to the Party of European Socialists Working Group on *A New Model of Development* (dated 27.3.1996):

> 'Our model of growth, which emerged from an industrial economy based on assembly line techniques, is beginning to break down. By failing to take sufficient account of environmental costs and by the disproportionate emphasis of technological research on replacing labour input by a combination of capital and energy, we are locked into a pattern of wasting both human and natural resources.'

It is not only that every enterprise seeks to increase productivity, that is labour productivity, which means reducing labour input per unit of output, but the economic growth of nations is measured in output per person. These increases result, as Delors makes clear, from the substitution of capital, and chiefly of energy, for labour. Unemployment rises and at the same time irreplaceable sources of energy are used up and the incomplete burning of these leaves behind a trail of pollution and environmental devastation. Ironically, the costs of environmental protection are included in the measure of economic growth in national output. Delors gives a figure of 1.5 million people in the European Union alone engaged in environmental measures. But the actual loss in resource waste and environmental damage is far more than the value of these people's work. The problem is that it is not so easy to measure in money terms.

It is possible to measure the cost of hospital treatment, and other medical attention and of days of work lost as a result of environmentally associated illness. It is possible to measure the cost of energy which is used up in less than the most energy efficient systems — the motor car is a prime example — and of raw materials used up because of low levels of recycling. But the costs in human discomfort and distress are incalculable today. How could we measure the lost resources that will not be available to our children and grandchildren? Or to those in countries not yet industrialised? We know the money cost of what we buy, we increasingly know the energy value and other food values of what we eat, but we do not know the energy cost of what we buy. We talk of productivity always in terms of labour productivity. We have no energy accounts to compare with the national income and expenditure accounts and labour statistics. We could know this, and a start has been made on a framework for an energy accounting system (National Institute *Economic Review*, August 1996), but it will not enter the politicians' calculations until it is pushed higher up their agenda. If that happened, then we could have widely available energy accounts to show economic growth, calculated not only in terms of output per unit of labour input but in terms of output per unit of energy input. David Pearce, Edward Barbier and Anil Markandya have proposed a system for pricing all use of environmental capital. Michael Barratt Brown has summarised this elsewhere (*Models in Political Economy*, p.175) as follows:

> 'Not only would energy use and the depletion of other non-renewable resources be priced, but so would the saturation of the soil, seas, rivers and air with waste products, and the irreversible destruction or degradation of the environment in global warming, ozone-layer destruction and reduction in bio-diversity and seed types. In this new economics, money values can be placed on the loss of production, on the cost of correction to damage to human health, and to the land, seas and rivers, and also on property prices and costs of travel to work when these are affected by environmental nuisance like road traffic and aircraft noise.'

The next problem after knowing the facts is deciding what to do about them. There are many ways we could reduce energy and material consumption by restricting certain kinds of consumption like packaging and using energy more productively; and we can consider how this could be encouraged. But the scale of the task is forbidding. Here are the conclusions of a discussion in October 1995 on *Ecological Restructuring* by a group of twenty distinguished European economists interested in an Alternative Economic Policy for Europe:

> 'If the world-wide environmental space, i.e. the total of bearable uses of resources and emissions into nature — were to be preserved, the use of resources would have to diminish by fifty per cent until the year 2050. If additionally the principle of egalitarian per capita distribution of this environmental space were to be enforced, this would mean for Europe a reduction of resources by eighty per cent (and an increase for the third world of seventy per cent). If during the same time a modest economic growth of two per cent were to be maintained this would require an increase of the productivity in resource utilisation by a factor of 45 — which is very unrealistic. Even a zero growth would require an increase of resource productivity by a factor of ten.'

Nothing less than a total change in lifestyles in the industrialised countries could allow for such reductions in energy use. And the trend of present growth in these countries is, as we have seen, towards less use of labour and more application of capital and energy. Jacques Delors quotes a figure for growth in the European Community from 1970 to 1992 in real terms of 73 per cent, while employment increased only by 7 per cent over the same period. Even

> 'zero growth without any fundamental changes in the relations between production, the input of materials and energy and the output of wastes would', according to the European economists quoted above, 'only extend the process of environmental destruction rather than halt it.'

Capital owners, as they make clear, would introduce further measures to increase labour productivity.

How to Reduce the Waste of Resources

The motivation to take the ecological crisis seriously must lie in the widening realisation of the costs of inaction.

> 'Annual losses suffered by the industrial countries due to environmental damage are higher than the annual growth of the GDP, i.e. there is a tendency of a negative balance in the growth rate which is prone to increase with the continuation of the growth process.'

This comes from one of the contributors to the workshop already referred to. The group of economists in discussion confirmed the judgement of Jacques Delors that

> 'one reason for the under use of labour and the increasing use of capital and energy is, of course, the differential tax burden placed upon the two factors of production represented by labour and natural resources. The former is taxed excessively highly, while the latter are neither assessed at their true value nor protected against exploitation.'

But the group of economists felt forced to conclude their discussion with the following warning:

> 'If ecological stability is in the long run incompatible with permanent economic growth' [and several members of the group had suggested that it was] 'the pressure for maximum accumulation of private capital has to be ended which is linked to the control of the capitalist systems via the maximum profit imperative for the individual firms. This means that growing parts of profit income have to go into luxury consumption or are taxed away and spent for government expenditure or that wages have to rise substantially. The first would create the parasite society, the second and third way will

encounter — although reasonable in the economic and social sense — considerable resistance from the side of the capital owners.'

They can say that again and no doubt Tony Blair, like Professor Galbraith, is well aware of this resistance. The question is whether a party of labour should not be educating the population in the facts of the planet's ecology rather than kowtowing to the capital owners.

There is no doubt, however, that some capital owners are responding to growing public concern about the threat to natural resources and to the environment. Several large retail companies in the UK have joined up with the World Wide Fund for Nature to lay down criteria for a sustainable forest programme for timber production. Other companies have realised that they can benefit from taking the ecological crisis seriously, as indeed would some countries, and indeed the European Union itself. According to Jacques Delors

> 'We must avoid the false argument that environmental protection and job creation are incompatible. Both experience and research have shown that the two are linked in the medium term and inseparable in the long term. For example, if we were to fail to develop 'lean technologies' now, we should forfeit our lead in a market which is set to grow by 50 per cent by the year 2000.'

Delors proposes several types of actions which European Governments could take preferably in agreement, and insists that this means planning — joint planning — and cannot be left to the market. His proposed measures include changing relative pricing structures to give a premium to clean technology, introducing a fuel tax — total environmental taxation in OECD countries, he says, amounts to less than 1 per cent of GNP — penalising pollution, by identifying taxes or subsidies which have become 'incentives to pollute' and promoting technological research into those processes which are the most economical of natural resources.

> 'Social democrats', he adds, 'should in particular reconsider the concept of a tax on carbon dioxide emissions the proceeds of which would make it possible to reduce the statutory contributions payable in respect of low paid workers.'

He calls this 'the "double dividend" approach: less pollution and more employment'. And adds 'And if not all the States of the European Union are ready to embark upon it, there is nothing to stop those who wish to from setting an example for others.'

It would be nice to think that he had New Labour in mind, but if he did, we have heard only carefully crafted banalities from that quarter.

One other possible method of environmental protection has been proposed by Professor Pearce and his colleagues. This is that the costings they recommend should be supplemented by surveys of what a sample population would pay for environmental improvements. Instead of government relying on command, and controls and prohibitions, they would require that polluters and wasters pay compensation to society and that the prices for goods and services should include the costs of the bads and *dis*-services now and in the future. It should not be impossible for governments to devise a 'green' market akin to the 'social market' which Tony Blair advocates. As with the social market the implications need to be spelled out.

The Real World

Such an explication of a 'green' programme has recently come from UK environmentalists, in the launching of a new coalition of 32 campaigning organisations representing millions of people, called *Real World*. In a remarkable statement published in the *Guardian* (April 3, 1996), they say that they are agreed on the causes of the problems they are severally engaged with. They are, they say

'a failure to appreciate the costs (as well as the benefits) of today's global economy, a failure to halt the abuse of the earth's life support systems, a failure to reform our antediluvian democracy; and politicians' outright refusal to tell the people that yesterday's received wisdom (based on full employment, no holds-barred economic growth and international security through military muscle) is dangerously redundant.'

And they are all agreed on the answers:

'putting the task of meeting human needs and respecting our international obligations above today's unthinking obeisance to short-term unaccountable market forces, and about putting solidarity, social cohesion and a concern for future generations above today's mean-minded individualism . . . there can be no long term protection for the environment without reducing and finally eradicating poverty.'

Real World does not put itself forward as a political party, and will not endorse parties or candidates, but insists that they must influence the *content* rather than the outcome of the next British election. Before the last election, they say, 'there seemed to be a growing determination to address the chronic problems of unemployment and 'social exclusion'. But come the election all this disappeared.' One important contribution that *Real World* is making is to the process of political education, which we believe is being seriously neglected by New Labour both in the presentation of its policies and in the manner of its electioneering.

In the particular matter of developing environmental awareness there is no sign of any initiative at all coming from New Labour. The whole approach to economic development through increased market competitiveness and attracting inward capital investment tells against conservation and environmental concerns. The good suggestion of Mandelson and Liddle that these must be dealt with on a continental scale is not followed up with even the most rudimentary hint of proposals for continent-wide action. And official Labour has exercised continuous vigilance in the European Parliament to try to block any support for the proposed carbon tax.

The inevitable fear remains that New Labour will follow the Tories in their search for 'opt-outs' from all forms of European social legislation. What has been established at a European level in the promotion of ecological measures following upon the World Commission for Environment and Development (Brundtland Report of 1987) and the UN Conference on Environment is little enough. But shortly after the Maastricht Conference the European Union did set some ecological goals: the reduction of CO^2 emissions, the restriction on waste exports (the Basle Agreement), the obligations of ecological aid in the course of implementing the 'global environment facility' (GEF), the 'pilot programme' in Brazil.

The most important issue in the protection of the environment, in Europe's towns and cities, and world-wide, remains the emission of climate-relevant gases. The proposed reduction of 25 per cent to 30 per cent in the 1987 level of emissions would require major structural changes in transport, energy production and distribution, waste management, urban planning and agricultural policies. Such changes would themselves imply social, political and economic changes which at least one of the Alternative Economic Policy Group we have been quoting, regards as 'not very likely to occur without heavy social and political conflicts'. This is Professor Elmar Altvater of the Free University of Berlin.

Professor Altvater notes that in the White Paper of the Commission of the European Union the question of sustainability is postponed to the last chapter, after earlier chapters have proposed schemes for the modernisation of Europe's energy and telecommunications networks and transport facilities which he believes to be 'absolutely not sustainable'. He has no expectation of an 'efficiency revolution' in the capitalist mode of production, such as have occurred before, leading to a more sustainable growth path. The only sustainable revolution would have to be one that reversed the whole movement from the use of fossil energies to the use of living labour but he regards this as a total reversal of a deep tendency in capitalist societies. New norms of human behaviour — self-sufficiency, recycling, greening of the market, small is beautiful etc. — would be required, which seem to Altvater to be 'inconsistent with the institutional system of modern societies'.

Perhaps, it is understandable that New Labour's leaders should not wish to become involved in such a difficult issue, but what sort of cowardice is that? Jonathan Porritt, a key founding member of 'Real World', describing the difficulties involved in bringing together the 33 voluntary organisations that form the coalition, emphasises the common view that was arrived at, that it is impossible to 'divorce our concerns for the environment from our concern for a more just and equitable economy'. The proliferation of motor cars used almost entirely by the higher two-thirds of income earners at the expense of the lower two-thirds is a case in point. The UK in the last twenty years has failed to reduce the consumption of fuel in relation to national income at all, let alone per head of the population. Yet the idea of a fuel tax has not passed the lips of any of New Labour's spokesmen. Will they ever learn?

CHAPTER 10

The European Dimension

'After fifteen years of full membership of the European Community and a resultant total shift in British trade — from a quarter of our trade conducted with the European Common Market to well over a half — there is no possibility now of withdrawing. Our old trading partners in the Commonwealth have gone elsewhere or fallen back from lack of development. The only two options are either the half-way house of an economic community of sovereign states, or full federation in a United States of Europe.'

Michael Barratt Brown, European Union: Fortress or Democracy? Towards a Democratic Market and a New Economic Order, *Spokesman, 1991*

'The unemployed are the excluded people . . . excluded, by successive degrees, from one human linkage after another. To will a cure for this plague of adversities, we must of course choose rational forms of political action. In modern Europe, this implies joint action, by all the states of the European Community, coordinated and urged forward by their common institutions. But how can we set such action free? That is the overpowering question of the day. There are millions of unemployed workers, and their families bring further millions to the legions of those who suffer. But there are millions of others, still at work, still aware of their common humanity, still unwilling to accept the division of Europe, entailed in the creation of a tormented underclass, in, but not of, our own community.'

Ken Coates, 'An Afterword' in A European Recovery Programme, *edited by Ken Coates and Michael Barratt Brown, Spokesman, 1993*

The question of Britain's membership of the European Community has always divided the left as well as the right; and in both cases positions have changed over time. Tony Benn who was once in favour moved steadily against. We who were once opposed moved as steadily in favour. We would argue that circumstances had changed, as the quotation above indicates. Many on the left, like Stuart Holland, saw the whole of Old Labour's economic planning as part of joint action to treat with the European company. But the most compelling argument today is that the crisis of European mass unemployment absolutely demands a response of European-wide action. How, then 'to set such action free'?

When these words were written some years ago, it seemed possible that action would be taken to realise the proposals put forward in 1993 by the European Commission President, Jacques Delors, in a White Paper on *Growth, Competitiveness and Employment*. We have to recognise three years later that this has not happened. Today, it seems to us more than ever necessary, as unemployment continues to rise. But the reasons for action at the European level need to be made clear. In the long run it is our belief that the future happiness of the British people, and in particular the recovery of hope by the men and women who are unemployed, lies in the creation of a socialist federation of the European peoples committed to building a world-wide commonwealth. We do not believe that the nation-state is any longer on its own a vehicle for socialist advance, because the national framework no longer gives expression to genuine democracy, maintaining some of the forms, but not disposing of effective powers. The recuperation of these powers is a task to be jointly tackled in several advanced countries at once, in a common democratic programme.

Social Protection

Before we look at the much more intractable problem of unemployment, it is important to notice the many forms of social protection which have been advanced through the European Community. These have been introduced over a long period of time and well before the Social Chapter was included in the Maastricht Treaty. The British Conservative government opt-out from this Chapter was entirely in line with a studied reluctance over many years to fulfil the requirements of European regulations for social protection. New Labour's apparent readiness to accept the Social Chapter would be encouraging, were it not for the recurrent reassurances given to the business lobby that this will be quite painless for them and in effect that some verses in the Chapter will be omitted. There is an alarming absence of references in Mandelson and Liddle to any advantages for the British people from the Chapter's social requirements. On the contrary, they are distinctly cool about what they call

'introducing rigid costly rules and importing to Britain inefficient practices which will harm our competitiveness and deter inward investment.' (M&L, p.171)

Their main concern is that Britain should be 'at the negotiating table when proposals for legislation to implement the Social Chapter are being made.'

That is to say that New Labour can be relied upon to restrain the profligate continentals from any urge to protect working people. The emphasis on 'our competitiveness' reveals an assumption about the common interest of capital and labour which we do not accept.

The British TUC, not the most radical of labour organisations, is not so reticent about the interests of labour. In a policy statement for the 1996 Trades Union Congress, *The European Union: Trade Union Goals*, the TUC General Council described the very great advantages for employment protection already achieved through European legislation and the further advantages to be gained through the Social Chapter if the opt-out were ended. The statement listed the following measures which the Tory government had blocked:

● equal rights for part-time workers;
● obligations on employers to inform and consult workers' representatives;
● a safe limit to the numbers of hours worked;
● provision for three weeks' annual holiday, rising to four weeks;
● proper rest periods at work;
● time off for new parents and family emergencies;
● proper consultation over redundancies;
● proper consultation when a new business is transferred to a new employer.

It seems a pretty minimal list of decent employment practices and it will be an important test of New Labour's ethical claims whether they are prepared to reverse the Tories' blocking strategy and go on to support the European Commission's Social Action Programme of 1995. This goes much further in requiring consultation in national undertakings with more than 50 workers, health and safety rights, maternity leave and special rights to protect young workers and part-time workers, continued vocational training, legal guarantees for trade union freedom and collective bargaining, a minimum income right, legislation on poverty, social exclusion and housing and measures to combat racism. This official list of areas for improved protection gives some indication of the advantages for labour of working together throughout Europe to level up working conditions instead of allowing them to be levelled down by the power of international capital to divide and conquer each national group of workers.

Federalism and Socialism

We have at several points in this book had to make it clear that many of the assumptions of Labour Party policies in the past for maintaining full employment and protecting the needs of working people are no longer valid. The change results from the limitations placed upon individual nation-state actions by the integrated international operations of the big transnational companies, and we have already noted that no industrialised country is more affected by these companies than Britain. Short of world-wide agreement to replace or at least to regulate such companies' operations, the best hope for the British economy lies in countervailing action at the European level. The most urgent requirements of action, which we have identified, are in relation to unemployment, the degradation of the environment and excessive exploitation of natural resources. In all these fields there are now in existence European Union programmes which are soft-pedalled, if not actually in abeyance. They could without doubt have been activated by a strong initiative from Labour in the UK working with Social Democratic and other groups in Europe, if New Labour had not put a stop to any such thoughts in its overwhelming lurch to the right. We do not suppose that such initiatives would resolve the problems presented by global capitalism, but they would ameliorate them and help to generate the appetite for a wider challenge.

A very wide cross-section of British politicians has given support to the idea that Britain should play an active and positive role in the European Community. Over and over again, we hear the claim that 'we should be at the very heart of Europe.' The Labour leaders have in recent years been very active indeed in support of this idea. It is true that Michael Foot and Neil Kinnock like many others in the Party were initially opposed strongly to British membership, but Kinnock underwent one of his serial conversions, and he was succeeded by John Smith, who had long been a partisan of Britain's role in the European Union.

Nevertheless, the majority of the Labour Party has remained extremely agnostic about membership of the Union, fearing the idea of development towards federalism. But this fear is partly the result of misinformation and lack of proper explanation of the meaning of the term. Frequently, British politicians of all parties speak about federalism as if it meant the emergence of a strong and centralised European state. The truth is the exact opposite. A federal state is, by definition, decentralised, consisting of a group of units whose governments have agreed to pool certain specified powers for effective joint action, while reserving others to be determined separately.

In all federations there is a problem of agreeing what belongs at which level of government: in the European Union, the problem is supposed to be decided by the principle of 'subsidiarity'. The idea is that powers should be exercised at the level which is best equipped to wield them, so that joint powers should cover matters that inevitably require cooperation between all concerned, and separate powers should govern those issues which do not have major joint implications. There is an extended literature on all this, but most of it has been no more interesting to leaders of the Labour Party than it is to the public at large.

The debate on Europe has been conducted very largely as if it were a matter of foreign policy, and not of our internal governance. Indeed, the supremo in the Labour Party who deals with European affairs holds the title of Shadow Foreign Secretary, and the Foreign Secretary he shadows has responsibility for Europe in his brief. But Europe has for some time ceased to be a branch of foreign affairs. Today it needs to be seen as an extension of our domestic arena, whether in the business of trade and economic development or in the growing area of social and environmental cooperation. More and more of our legislation, and of our action, is already shared. And when it is not, the result can be seen in the confused response to the human implications of BSE.

One good reason for doubts among socialists and other progressively minded people about our European involvement is the so-called 'democratic deficit' in European decision-making. This starts at the top. Europe's governing body, the Council of Ministers, by meeting in secret, challenges every tenet of open government. It has also well understood that such closet negotiations give none of the national electorates, nor even their parliaments, any direct influence on the course of decisions. What information filters out about Council meetings is distorted by anonymity, screened through leaks which may or may not be accurate. Briefings are unattributable. Reports are full of speculation, which is not commonly wrong, but is no substitute for open decision-making.

The European Commission which supplies the Council of Ministers with drafts for decision is appointed by the governments of the Member States, and its members have since 1994 been subject to ratification by the European Parliament. In fact, the Commission is far more open than the Council of Ministers, and often betrays the wish to consult more closely with the Parliament. But the powers of the Parliament are sadly incomplete, and in Britain it has been the fashion among Tories and Labour spokesmen to oppose their extension, as 'creeping federalism'. It would be more correct to speak of 'creeping democracy'. Labour shadow ministers who claim their determination to place themselves at the heart of Europe have still maintained full-scale opposition to this kind of democracy. They like the Tories have sought to preserve national 'sovereignty', even in areas where no effective separate national sovereign power exists. Sovereign today are the global corporations, and democratic institutions of all kinds lag far behind in their effort to match them.

A very important recognition by Labour of the realities of the present position would be to separate European business from Foreign Affairs, and to conduct this business through the appropriate ministries and offices. Labour could have done this, while in Opposition, and in this way could have unravelled the confusions which exist within the present Foreign Office. A Blair administration does not promise to be any more audacious in this sphere than elsewhere. It will be dominated by Mr Powell, who, as an old Establishment man, has been hand-reared in the Foreign Office. He probably knows that aliens begin at Calais.

The argument for federation was very carefully rehearsed by the Cambridge economist, and one of the Tory Chancellor's 'wise men', Professor Wynne Godley. When he analysed the proposals of the Maastricht Treaty for an Economic and Monetary Union, he found them to be seriously defective. The treaty, he argued, had been framed within an overall view which saw economies as self-righting organisms, 'which never under any circumstances, need management at all.' Within this view, all that could then be done was to control the money supply and balance the budget, and he went on:

'It took a group, largely composed of bankers (the Delors Committee) to reach the conclusion that an independent Central Bank was the only supra-national institution necessary to run an integrated, supra-national Europe. But there is much more to it all. It needs to be emphasised . . . that the establishment of a single currency in the European Community would indeed bring to an end the sovereignty of its component nations, and their power to take independent action on major issues. . . . The prospect is grave indeed unless federal budgeting arrangements are made that fulfil a redistributive role . . . to stop it [a country or region failing to compete successfully in world markets] suffering a process of cumulative and terminal decline . . .'

Without a federal government, in other words, economic and monetary union on the limited basis of the Maastricht Treaty will simply abolish the powers that were hitherto exercised by nation-states, and put nothing in their place. Money will not only talk, it will be the only voice we are allowed to hear.

The Necessity for Redistribution

That voice is already deafening. The irresistible fact is that there is now a very real danger not only of missing an opportunity for generating common programmes to protect and advance the interests of the peoples of Europe but, more, of a total breakdown of relations. The whole European project is in the balance. The requirements of the Maastricht Treaty for convergence on ultra-conservative fiscal policies in each state, without complementary countervailing all-European borrowing for joint investment plans, have already led to a serious check to economic recovery in the Union and to rising unemployment. If these trends persist, if indeed, as seems likely, the situation worsens, popular protests such as have already been seen in the strikes in France and the demonstrations in Germany will spread. But, unless these protests join up behind a demand for changes to be made in European governments' policies, and for the democratisation of European decision-making, the danger is that they will generate nothing but national exceptionalism, secessional pressures and xenophobia. The 'restoration of national sovereignty' may give someone the power to persecute minorities, but it will not restore democratic influence over economic life.

Instead of acting in common, European governments under pressure from the right, even the emergent far right, could begin to take separate protective measures. We could see a return to the protectionist beggar-my-neighbour policies of the 1930s and we all know what they led to — fascism and war. The rise of unemployment in Europe is not just an unfortunate, temporary and necessary side-effect of measures that can guarantee future prosperity for all. It strikes at the very foundations of the post-war welfare settlement. This judgement is not some personal quirk we share, but a view that is now being expressed in establishment circles by those with the most inside knowledge and experience.

No less an authority than the Director of Studies at the Council on Foreign Relations in the United States, Ethan B. Kapstein, writing in the semi-official State Department journal *Foreign Affairs* (May-June issue for 1996), has issued a grave warning not only to leaders in the United

States, but to those in all industrialised countries. He ends an article entitled 'Workers and the World Economy' with the following words:

'Like the German elite in Weimar, they [the economic advisers of governments] dismiss mounting worker dissatisfaction, fringe political movements, and the plight of the unemployed and working poor as marginal concerns compared with the unquestioned importance of a sound currency and balanced budget. Leaders need to recognise the policy failures of the last 20 years and respond accordingly. If they do not, there are others waiting in the wings who will, perhaps on less pleasant terms.'

Yet Mr Kapstein insists that measures can be taken by governments to create jobs, to reduce inequalities of incomes, to protect the sick and the elderly. But they require economic policy coordination between the industrial powers. This was of course achieved at the end of the Second World War, but he points out that there is a more recent precedent. At the Bonn summit in 1978 in the wake of the oil crisis, the OECD called on governments to stimulate their economies. Member countries agreed on a package of national measures. These had considerable success until undermined by the second oil crisis caused by the Iranian revolution. Economic recovery in Europe, the US and Japan is not threatened today by such external shocks. The breakdown is internal — in the combination of selfishness and monetary dogma which pervades the thinking of political leaders and their economic advisers. The times cry out for imaginative leadership, in Europe in particular where the European Union already offers a potential framework for common action.

New Labour's Response

As the trend of Tory pronouncements shifts steadily to the right, to the delight of the Tory Euro-sceptics, the stance of New Labour becomes ever more ambiguous. Every positive statement of commitment to cooperation in Europe is immediately qualified by negative appeals to national sentiment and the defence of British sovereignty. In his Singapore speech Tony Blair promised that New Labour would take an active role in Europe, including participation in the Social Chapter. By July he was arguing in a letter to ten thousand British businessmen and women (July 16, 1996) that 'he would use the national veto to prevent Brussels imposing backdoor social security burdens on British industry.' New Labour spokesmen have opted for Economic and Monetary Union, but with heavy qualifications about conditions and timing. Robin Cook criticises the Tories for their incompetence and neglect of European regulations over BSE, but supports the Tory stance on British beef exports and similarly on environmental issues.

It is the same with Mandelson and Liddle. They apply their 'modern' sense of Britain being a part of Europe to the need for European partnership to fulfil many of their objectives. They make the claim for

> 'the new agenda for the left in Britain which has now embodied in New Labour what social democratic parties throughout Europe are doing, establishing a fresh identity in the wake of their failure to present a coherent intellectual alternative to the spread of right-wing thinking.' (M&L p.169)

We must recognise that the enthusiasm of New Labour in working with their social democratic partners in Europe on the key issue of unemployment has been at best luke-warm. It has to be seen that the 'fresh identity' of social democracy in Europe is hardly prepossessing. Original thinking has not been its hallmark. There is more thought going on among the mix of greens, feminists, leftists and independent socialists in Europe about alternatives to current failed policies, especially on unemployment, more indeed among some Christian Democrats, than there is to be found among many of the leaders of the Social Democratic parties in Europe. To put it mildly, in European socialist politics the pursuit of power has become more fashionable than the pursuit of truth; it shows, and the fashion has been spreading across the channel. However, if the truth does not yield to this approach, neither, it seems, does power.

Yet, old Social Democracy in Europe did once, and relatively recently, embrace the federal argument without flinching. It insisted on a European Parliament with effective powers, not only of control, but of initiation of important areas of legislation. It even sought actively to create a European Socialist Party, with individual membership directly registered and involved in decision taking. This was a development out of the Confederation of the Socialist Parties of the European Community which had been formed in 1974. The Confederation left with the national parties the determination of joint policies decided at conferences and other meetings. But the idea of creating a Socialist Party on this basis went beyond this, since it would have become a supra-national party.

This proposal was, however, strongly opposed by Neil Kinnock for the British Labour Party and less strongly by the Danish Socialist Party, the Dutch, French, German, Italian and Spanish Socialist leaders all having given the idea their support. The pressure for the idea came primarily from the realities of the European Parliament, where the Christian Democratic Parties maintain something of an international party organisation, with which the British Conservative Party works in an uneasy association. In Brussels and Strasbourg, united responses were increasingly required from the Socialist grouping. Any movement towards a true Economic and Monetary Union would at once demand joint decision-making by Socialists on a democratically organised basis.

But, whether monetary union is stalling or not, for the time being the project of a European Socialist party is in abeyance. The membership cards which were actually printed for issue following the foundation conference in the Netherlands have been withdrawn from circulation and locked away in a filing cabinet somewhere in the miles of corridors in the European Parliament in Brussels. If there were to be a European Parliament with effective powers, there would need to be a framework of political organisations, and among them a European Socialist Party. If this were then to be truly representative, it would need to be based on all the multilateral networks of contacts necessary to maintain an active democracy at local, regional and European levels, with support groups, exchanges of information and means for the generation of ideas.

The failure of the European socialist parties to generate new ideas for European unification after the initial impulse towards European Union, in no small part, arises from the reluctance to create functioning international networks for grassroots exchanges — among trade unionists, women's organisations, pensioners' associations, ecological societies, Third World solidarity groups and so on — to organise a truly European debate, creating a truly European focus, for joint and common activity.

No individual party can bear all the blame for this failure, although the British Party must bear a heavy responsibility. Nationalism remains for all the besetting sin, and in the British Party the spin doctors have tended to resist any moves that could arouse the antagonism of a chauvinist press and media. Mandelson and Liddle's world view is quite sufficiently chauvinistic, they might think. Their criticisms of the memories of empire and the 'myth of Britain's world power status, reawakened by the Falklands War' are followed immediately by a harking back to the past in talk about '*our* world class industries'.

In the matter of flag wagging, the spin-men have been foreshadowing Eric Hobsbawm's advice (*New Statesman*, 3.5.96), which followed Stalin's recommendation to the pre-war Popular Fronts in Europe and to the post-war British Communist Party. This was to speak up for 'the country', 'Great Britain', 'the Nation', 'patriotism', 'the People' — 'in the pre-election rhetoric of those who hope to form the next government of the United Kingdom'. If Labour does not raise the Union Jack, Hobsbawm warns, the Tories will, 'and in doing so will catch us off balance', like Thatcher with her promise of 'putting the "Great" back into Great Britain'. Of all the unexpected sights offered by New Labour, the vision of Professor Eric Hobsbawm, distinguished co-editor of the *Collected Works of Karl Marx and Friedrich Engels,* published in Moscow in fifty scholarly volumes, striding purposefully in front of Lord (Roy) Jenkins, the non-commissioned officers of the SDP, and Tony Blair's army of admen, spin doctors and novice pornographers, bearing a giant flag of the Union, could only be properly captured in a cartoon by Steve Bell, to give pleasure to the unreconstructed partisans of Old Labour.

So, on New Labour Party packaging, red, white and blue labels appear around the Party's programme slogans and the new leaders may feel that they have to do more if the Tories with Sir James Goldsmith at their heels fight the election on the issue of 'Britain against Europe'. Already we have seen Emily's children, tastefully deployed at the front of the Labour Party Conference, keeping time with a jazzed up version of the Red Flag by waving snazzy little Red Ensigns. Was it Mr Mandelson who discovered how to incorporate patriotism into the people's emblem?

What Sort of Europe?

In fact the issue should be about what sort of Europe it is intended to construct. If we take Mandelson and Liddle's word for it, New Labour appears to have made some decisions, although there is always room for 'U' turns, if Scottish devolution is the precedent we can trust. It appears to be agreed that the European Union should be expanded, but social and economic cooperation deepened and reinforced with binding rules. Common policies should be agreed on foreign affairs, overseas aid, the environment and defence — in association with the United States — and home affairs and justice made subject to 'pragmatic intergovernmental working'.

According to New Labour, the single currency in an EMU should be regarded as an option, but only when 'there is real economic convergence in the main countries' (M&L, p.170). Although Gordon Brown has sounded more positive about this option, moves towards federalism are to be resisted. Majority voting, according to Mandelson and Liddle, should be limited in the Council of Ministers to the smallest possible number of issues, but there will be need for some leadership from the five larger states, under what is called by Mandelson and Liddle 'a new London-Paris-Bonn axis'. The historic relationship of the UK with the United States is not to be abandoned. This was after all what Bill Rodgers and his social democratic friends fought so long and so loyally to retain against the arguments of the Labour left, in all the engagements on nuclear disarmament, neutralism and pacifism.

The general principle, laid down for the development of the European Union, that nothing should be done which would 'threaten the identity of Europe's nation states' is firmly stated by Mandelson and Liddle:

> '. . . the EU is an organisation of freely associating independent nation states, and its democratic centre lies not with a European-wide Parliament linked to the Commission and assuming the status of a federal executive but with its member states' elected national governments and national parliaments whose representatives are on the Council of Ministers, exerting control over the Commission.' (M&L, p.176)

This view would be challenged by those who see the democratic centre in the smaller bodies of people, the nations and regions which form the existing nation-states, and who are seeking measures of self-government at that level. Mandelson and Liddle argue enthusiastically for devolution not only for Scotland, Wales and Northern Ireland but for English regions. The implications of this for the UK nation-state in Europe seem not to have been recognised. It is a common problem. It is not only in the UK but in many other European nation-states, which are composed of several nations and regions with strong local identities, where these would like to have direct access to the European Commission and particularly to European funding. The exercise of democratic rights seems so much more real in communities of limited size and some sense of homogeneity. Scottish people, Basques and Catalonians and the Northerners in Italy are not alone in sharing this feeling to a greater or lesser extent.

The implications for democratic accountability of greater decision-making powers for the European Council do, however, concern Mandelson and Liddle. This is the Council of national government ministers meeting either at summits of prime ministers or as opposite numbers in departmental ministries — finance, agriculture, trade etc. They accept that, in the event of qualified majority voting being extended in the Council's decisions, it would be necessary, to ensure democratic accountability, to involve the European Parliament or, they would evidently prefer, either a system of joint committees of the national parliaments or an upper house of the European Parliament elected from national parliaments. This kind of delegated accountability can in no way make up for the 'democratic deficit' in the current system of decision making in Brussels. The general view in Europe outside of Britain is that the powers of the European Parliament should be increased. Its members do directly represent their separate peoples and the Parliament does provide an opportunity for those of like mind to get together and form resolutions for problems that are common throughout Europe.

The Crisis of European Unemployment

Nowhere is the need for fresh thinking greater than in the matter of unemployment in Europe. This has reached quite unbearable and unacceptable levels. At least 20 million men and women in the European Union are seeking work and cannot find it. That is over 10% of the population of working age, and in some regions and among the young people the proportion is as high as 30%. Yet there is not a word in Tony Blair's present day speeches about what Archbishop Temple called 'the mark of a diseased society' and the absolute need for remedies to be applied on a European-wide basis, as well as at national and regional levels. Mr Blair was at one time more forthcoming, as may be seen in his maiden speech in the House of Commons which we quoted earlier.

We have already shown that measures taken from the supply side in the labour market cannot solve the problem. A major pull on the demand side, such as is recommended by Mr Kapstein, is required from governments. But this cannot be done by each separate nation-state, as he recognised, so closely integrated is the network of the transnational companies' production facilities and capital movements. Common action in Europe could be effective. It has, moreover, become an absolute necessity as a result of the agreement at Maastricht that all Member States should seek to reach certain convergence criteria in order to enter an Economic and Monetary Union. To achieve these goals, governments have had to cut back their public spending debts and deficits to a fixed proportion of their national incomes. The effect of such a mass deflationary exercise has been to check the economic recovery that had begun in 1995. Warnings we had given in the European Parliament went unheeded. The monetarists who are still in the ascendancy in some of the chancelleries of Europe and in part of the European Commission have faith that private investment will come 'crowding in', as they call it, when public demands on finance are reduced and interest rates fall.

This happy event had not transpired by the middle of 1996 and had not been expected by M. Jacques Delors to transpire, when, as President of the European Commission, he put forward for adoption a specially designed plan for counteracting the deflationary effect of movements towards fiscal convergence at a low level of borrowing. The plan involved the issue of federal bonds through the existing European Investment Fund to finance a number of trans-European transport and communication networks (TENs), research and development projects, regional development schemes for the environment and for urban renewal and support for small and medium sized enterprises (SMEs). The European Union would then have created something like the United States federal government borrowing facility on top of the borrowing by individual states and localities. The individual member states could reduce their own borrowing to achieve the Maastricht criteria without the otherwise untoward deflationary effects, and a major financial lever would be introduced to raise employment and reduce unemployment.

To their disgrace, the European governments, on the advice of their Treasuries, had failed by mid-1996 to meet more than the warm words of the Delors Plan. Even the TENs programme had been cut back from 26 original to 14 'priority' projects and had been started with a few million ecus instead of several billion. Under strong pressure from some Euro MPs, M. Jacques Santer, who succeeded M. Delors, began to press for a 'common plan', especially to use some of the money that had not been spent on the Common Agricultural Policy. But this money became earmarked for compensation to UK beef farmers forced to slaughter their cows as the result of the BSE scare. Leave aside the fact that some farmers are exceedingly well-off, and even if we recognise real areas of distress, a grant to farmers is still just a one-off payment. The advantage of the proposed bond issue is that an initial sum subscribed could be levered up to have a real impact on the employment problem.

Finance for SMEs is a particularly effective way of creating jobs, since SMEs are responsible for some 60% of European employment. There are 15 million SMEs in Europe and if, on average, each created just one extra job with the extra funding, that would create the 15 million jobs which was the original target of the Delors Plan (see Coates &

Holland, 1995). Creating one new job costs around 20,000 ecus, so that an initial sum of 300 billion ecus would appear to be required. But such frightening figures do not represent the real cost. In the first place, the *net* cost would be much less, because of the tax take from the newly employed men and women, including those employed as a result of the multiplier effect of the new employment. Secondly, a much smaller sum injected could be levered up, possibly according to the British Treasury minister, Kenneth Clarke, by as much as eight times, through borrowing against subscribed reserves. Thus, Clarke argued that 7.5 billion ecus, levered up, would allow 60 billion ecus of projects to be underpinned.

This figure of 60 billions of ecus was estimated, in the European Commission's 1993 plans, to be sufficient, over the two years to 1995, to start the Delors Programme off. Even a 40 becu subscription which, levered up eightfold, could raise the 300 becu needed to promote a large part of the Delors Programme, would represent less than 1% of combined national incomes, and at least a half of that sum would be returned in the tax take. The calculations of cost per job have all been confirmed by similar studies of the means for an expansion of public spending in the UK by a group of Cambridge economists, Michael Kitson, Jonathan Michie and Holly Sutherland, reported by Larry Elliott in the *Guardian* of May 20 1996. French Prime Minister, Michel Rocard, in 1993 proposed a European fund of 50 billion ecus, which President Mitterrand later said should be raised to 100 billion. No such borrowing has ever been approved by the EU Council of Ministers and far smaller sums proposed have also remained unsanctioned.

Has New Labour been pressing for the Delors Plan to be realised? Has New Labour been rallying the Social Democratic parties in Europe for a 'coherent intellectual alternative to right-wing thinking' — where it mattered most, in finding employment for millions of men and women and young people deprived of the capacity to be a part of society? Has New Labour's Christian leader been working with other Christian leaders in Britain and throughout Europe to answer before God for the failure of governments to cure a disease for which they were themselves in part responsible? If so, we have not met them on their way. Officially New Labour's leaders, reversing the policy of the late John Smith, gave no support to their own Party members and others in the European Parliament who were pressing upon the Commission to act and to encourage the European governments to act.

The pressure to do something about unemployment in Europe through support for the Delors Plan and through other measures reached a crescendo in the summer of 1996, when a European Appeal for Full Employment was instigated by Ken Coates and a group of MEPs from different parties. It was launched in the European Parliament with the signatures of over 150 MEPs from 36 different parties and from all the countries of the European Union. It had received the endorsement of several hundred members of national Parliaments and of the European TUC and world wide ICFTU and the individual signatures of academics, writers and church leaders from right across the continent.

The significance of the wide ranging support for the Appeal was not only the importance that its supporters attached to the issue of unemployment, but the way in which it attracted support from so many different organisations in Europe — political parties of the left and centre, greens, women's organisations, churches, trade unions and minority groups suffering either unemployment or severe exploitation. Actions that follow will depend partly on national reactions, but also on the possibilities of joint and common initiatives through the European Union structures, to reduce working time, promote job creation measures and offset the public spending cuts inherent in the convergence criteria of the Maastricht Treaty. The support for the Appeal was an indication of the type of international campaign that could emerge from efforts to take issues of common interest out of the narrow confines of the nation-state.

Alternative Scenarios for Britain in Europe

By the middle of 1996 it had to be accepted that the Delors Plan was moribund. New Labour did not take it up and the Tories had never any intention of doing so, while the Finance Ministers of Christian Democrat, Centre-Left and Centre-Right coalitions and even Social Democrat governments persisted in their belief that their economies would turn up as private investment crowded in to fill the space left by cuts in public spending. As this failed to happen and unemployment rose, governments did not turn to common action. Increasingly there was talk from both far right and other xenophobes about an escape into individual nationalist forms of protection.

Three scenarios presented themselves as 1996 proceeded:

1. The whole project of an Economic and Monetary Union might be abandoned. The German mark, which has become much overvalued, undermining the competitiveness of German manufactured exports, will then have to be devalued. It would in

any case have been revalued inside EMU, but as part of a general revaluation of all currencies. The £ sterling which has also become overvalued would be further devalued. Beggar-my-neighbour devaluations would follow with increasing examples of export dumping. The whole complex structure of the Single European Act would begin to unwind and the European Union would disintegrate to the delight of the protectionists of the far right, who would greatly increase their electoral appeal. Such a disaster might provoke important counteractions, but it would be dangerous to count on things getting worse in order to get better. It was not the left but the far right that benefited from economic collapse in the 1930s.

2. A limited two-tier or even three-tier Economic and Monetary Union might emerge. The mark would still have to be devalued, but this might be concealed within the revaluations which would accompany the launch of the new inner-currency union. A small group of countries, possibly including France, might thus tie their currencies to the mark. Outsiders would in effect be controlled by the dominant group and depending on their competitiveness in various industries, benefiting as free riders (as Norway does) or losing out from their inability to protect themselves from free movements of capital. Considerable tension would be created between the several concentric circles revolving in such a project.

3. All social protection under the Maastricht Treaty might be abandoned in cutting back costs in Western Europe and admitting to the Union the Eastern European, 'Visegrad Four' — Poland, Hungary, the Czech Republic, Slovakia — and possibly even Slovenia and the Baltic republics. It is already widely canvassed that cuts are envisaged in current European Union regional and other funds, so as to free resources for the East by switches from the poorer parts of the West. This would be in effect a declaration of war on Western Europe's organised workers in a deliberate movement of capital to take advantage of cheap skilled labour in the East. This would accelerate the rise in unemployment and consequent social dislocation in the West, and possibly coincide with further military and security cooperation. Stronger forces would be needed because there would be much police-work to be done in suppressing the resultant unrest.

Of these scenarios, it would appear that the Tory government and, probably, large-scale British based capital prefer the last. The attack on them by the 'Euro-sceptics' comes from small-scale capital on the protectionist right-wing of the Tory party, led and financed by Sir James Goldsmith. Mr Blair's Singapore speech seemed to be closely in line with the thinking of the Tory government and big business.

The real way to 'widen' the Union is on the basis of a planned convergence, based on aid to the east for development, up to an optional level calculated also to create optimum employment gains in the west. Bridges cannot be built without planning them in advance. Nor do they come cheap. The resources of the European Union will have to be increased by taxing or borrowing, in order to accomplish anything worthwhile. The alternative is not to follow the right into protectionism, but to unify the left in Europe. This would need to be approached through developing a real campaign for a 'Social Europe', East and West, built around the demand for full employment, protection of the welfare state and recuperation of the environment. These are classic demands which have been used in the past by socialists in challenging the hegemony of large-scale private capital.

There remain the realities of New Labour's foreign policy perspective in relation to the power of international capital in the wider world arena outside of the European Union. The possibilities of building alliances against this power will be so much easier as part of a common European initiative than anything which a small country like Britain can do on its own. It is a very serious matter that New Labour appears to have abandoned even what remained of Labour's internationalist traditions and to be tied still more unquestioningly by the apron strings of the Atlantic Alliance, which has won the Cold War but lost any sense of direction. So the blind will be leading the blind.

CHAPTER 11

Labour and Internationalism

'. . . the new international economy has greatly reduced the ability of any single government to use the traditional levers of economic policy in order to maintain high employment . . . The days of simple home-based Keynesianism will not return, and national economies have to recognise their interdependence.'

Mandelson & Liddle, The Blair Revolution, *p.6*

New Labour is right to make it a continuing theme that the world has changed. Old Labour's policies of national economic planning and a national welfare state based on high national levels of taxation, we agree, simply cannot any longer work in a world of global capital flows. But New Labour has not got the implications right. We have just seen that they have got them wrong in relation to our new home in the European Union. They are just as wrong in relation to the wider world, if we take note of what Hugo Radice has to say in his contribution to the Socialist Renewal series, on *Globalisation and the UK Economy*. He has demonstrated that there are serious misunderstandings in much of the writing, including that of Mandelson and Liddle, about the nature of capitalist globalisation.

Capital has always been global, moving internationally from bases in the developed industrialised countries. What has changed is not that capital is more mobile — it can be moved quicker by electronic means, of course — but that the national bases are less important as markets and production centres. In other words, the big transnational companies are not only bigger but more free standing. Most importantly, their whole production and distribution operations are much more globally integrated. There is a further development peculiar to the UK, which we noted earlier, that such transnational companies have become more dominant here than elsewhere, both in terms of British based companies operating transnationally and foreign based companies operating in the UK.

The conclusion that Radice draws from his analysis is that the neo-liberal right view is wrong in arguing that nothing can be done except to open up markets and abandon all idea of national controls on capital. But at the same time, parts of the left, and also the extreme right, are wrong in propounding a national protectionist response to capital globalisation. Sir James Goldsmith and Professor Tim Lang may seem odd bed-fellows, but that is what they are in their advocacy of protectionism. The nation-state has not lost all importance, but it has become an instrument of international and not of national capital.

We have already seen that even the European Union, far from offering a lead and a challenge to the nation-states of Europe, reinforces their status as clients of the transnational companies. Indeed, this clientism applies not only to companies based in Europe, but also to those which originate in the USA or Japan or Korea. The present aim of the European Commission can be characterised as providing a better organised clientele for the transnationals. That is what the European states' governments now increasingly require of the Commission, because the big companies are requiring it of them. But the Commission could be given other, better orders.

Labour Responses to Global Capital

New Labour's response to the new globalisation is ambiguous — not for the first time. On the one hand, there is, as we saw in the plans for dealing with unemployment and also in their attitude to the environment, an emphasis on supply side improvements in infrastructure and in British labour's skills and flexibility, so as to sharpen the competitive position of the UK in attracting foreign capital investment. Tony Blair made much of this in his Singapore speech. On the other hand, there is talk of the 'partnership' of government with '*our* [emphasis added] world class companies' and agreement with Will Hutton's criticism of the short-termism of the City in failing to make long-term investments in British companies.

There is a contradiction here in New Labour thinking, which Hugo Radice has explained. Mr Blair shows a strong desire to entice foreign companies to invest in Britain, while Mandelson and Liddle evince a preference for *our* 'good' companies as against the 'bad' foreign companies, as well as laying blame onto the City for aiding and abetting the foreigners. This, as Radice points out, is to fail to understand that both 'good' and 'bad', 'ours' and 'theirs', will behave quite

173

opportunistically in choosing where they invest and will treat labour as equally subject to exploitation wherever they go. UK owned firms like any others have to compete in world markets and to integrate UK economic activity into their corporate planning. The flag may occasionally improve their sales, but never their behaviour. If the flag ever gets in the way of trade, it will be the first thing to go.

All this means that there is, indeed, no place for the historic social-democratic compromise of joint planning between national government and national industrial capital within a national plan and against the tendencies of the City's internationalism. A much earlier historic position has to be adopted by labour of challenging the power of international capital *per se*. We have long argued that all the talk of a distinction between the City and industry was mythical. While it is true that a national capitalism is no longer possible in a globalised economy, it is not true that national governments — and by extension the European Union — are totally lacking in powers to employ against the arbitrary actions of transnational capital. There is much that governments can do in bargaining — in making or withholding tax concessions for example, or in rendering measures of infrastructural support conditional on health and safety standards and environmental protection. But such bargaining has to have an international dimension or the transnational companies can simply continue to divide and conquer. There is room here for the European Union to take more account of labour interests in dealing with the multinationals, but a much wider framework of control would be more effective.

We noted in the last chapter that New Labour appears to have abandoned what remained of Labour's internationalist traditions. There is simply no sign in Tony Blair's speeches or in Mandelson and Liddle's book of any recognition of a need for international labour solidarity. Not only the trade unions at home but the international trade unions and the Socialist International have all been swept aside to present an unencumbered centre party. Little attention is given to the working of the International, and more often than not, Labour's leaders absent themselves from its meetings. Yet, the ICFTU, the European TUC and the Geneva trade groups all offer potential allies for strengthening the response of British labour to international capital.

Mandelson and Liddle feel able to describe New Labour's 'radical new agenda' being 'what social democratic parties throughout Europe are doing', but the Socialist International is not mentioned and in their chapter on Europe, which is rhetorically entitled 'Peoples' Europe' there is no mention of the Party of European Socialists. We saw earlier that they say nothing about associating with sympathetic parties in Europe, let alone with European trade unions. There is only talk of the danger for Britain of following the Tories in 'not being present at the negotiating table' when they should be there to deal with any threat of 'rigid costly rules' being introduced and thus, in their view,

'importing to Britain inefficient practices which will harm our competitiveness and deter inward investment'.

For 'inefficient practices' read protection of wages and working conditions. No wonder the unions are not mentioned! This is straight beggar-my-neighbour and it will lead to the re-emergence of all the strains which have riven the administration of John Major. On this matter there is no recorded difference between the attitudes of the two parties.

Mandelson and Liddle are most concerned with balancing membership of the European Union with NATO and 'the defence and security partnership with America' and with emphasising the benefits of 'Britain's historic links with America . . . in shared intelligence and nuclear capacity.' These goals will surely be well served since Tony Blair's *chef du cabinet* comes to him direct from the British Embassy in Washington, where dark rumours speak of him liaising between British and American intelligence.*

In line with their support for the Atlantic Alliance, Mandelson and Liddle see a 'real danger' that 'a core of European nations will finally

---

*Jonathan Powell, aged 38, according to the *Guardian*, was 'one of the leading indicators that we are going to win the next election. You are not likely to give up as our man in foreign climes unless you think Labour is going to win.' The *Guardian* went on to inform us that Jonathan's brother, Charles, had been a senior adviser to Mrs Thatcher.

Today, Jonathan Powell is the head of Blair's cabinet. Manifestly, he is a high flyer. The Diplomatic Service List shows his posting in Washington was very senior indeed. Since July 1991 he had been First Secretary (Chancery). Did this archaic designation serve to conceal the function of top level coordinator between the British and American Intelligence Services? Certainly this is a sensitive post for a young man, as well as an indication that there could have been juicier jobs in store within the diplomatic service. Jonathan's brother, Sir Charles, had been appointed Private Secretary to Prime Minister Thatcher in 1984, and he had remained in the Prime Minister's office until 1991. Had his influence played any part in the meteoric rise of Jonathan in Washington? And what was Jonathan actually doing when young Tony Blair tempted him to put diplomacy behind him? What are we to make of the First Secretary's real role? How was it possible that so senior a member of so sensitive a service could put everything behind him in order to take on the role of Chief of Staff of Mr Blair's office? And why would the leader want such an expensive right-hand man?

agree to cement their own military and monetary cooperation — with Britain, unable to make up its mind, excluded. This', they add, 'would do nothing for our world role and nothing to boost our influence . . .' What that role and influence might be is not specified, but enough has been said to make clear that it would have nothing to do with the control of global capital.

Even short of helping to strengthen international trade union links, there are a number of measures which European governments could take to make the taxation of international companies more effective. Murray and Mulgan made proposals in their DEMOS pamphlet for limiting the power of transnational companies to divide and conquer separate nations' company taxation systems. Since a global tax regime seems unlikely to be realisable, at least the European Union might agree on a policy of unitary taxation without requiring federal powers to do so. Murray and Mulgan suggest the method of 'apportionment' applied by the State of California to the companies operating within its borders. The tax authorities calculate the share of a company's business taking place in California and impose their tax on that proportion of the company's global profits. If enough states do this world-wide, transnational companies cannot so easily evade taxation by moving the location of their business or by using transfer pricing to avoid paying taxes where the tax rates are highest.

Murray and Mulgan have other suggestions for taxing what are called by economists 'rents', i.e. monopoly profits. Such taxation has been imposed in the UK on development gains in land values, on ITV licences and on North Sea oil franchises. They suggest that this could be greatly extended and the rates increased, especially in the field of telecommunications. They propose also to combine this with the sort of links, which we discussed earlier, between the activity taxed and specific state expenditure, e.g. between oil franchises and environmental protection. It is, however, far from certain that this would make the big companies more amenable to taxation. But judging by the public outcry at the decision of the Shell Oil Company to dispose of one of its gigantic oil rigs in the mid-Atlantic, it could be possible to generate a supportive public opinion for such taxation.

Non-Governmental Organisations and Networking

One of the public responses to the global reach of capital has been the world-wide proliferation of voluntary organisations. These include the environmental campaign bodies, which we looked at in an earlier chapter. They include Greenpeace who chased Shell over the threat to sink the *Brent Spar* oil rig and President Chirac of France over his nuclear tests in the Pacific. But also they include Friends of the Earth, Conservation International, the World-Wide Fund for Nature and all the Third World aid agencies like Oxfam, Comic Relief, Christian Aid and the Catholic Institute for International Relations. Then there are the Alternative Trade Organisations and Fair Trade initiatives and a host of campaigning bodies on debt relief, world development, Save the Children, and world-wide women's organisations and solidarity and friendship associations with particular disadvantaged peoples. Hugo Radice saw these new social movements as essential allies for parties of the left to encourage and unite with in developing radical internationalist programmes in response to global capitalism.

The question remains whether New Labour wants to develop such programmes. While there is some mention in Mandelson and Liddle of the role of voluntary agencies in job creation and in public services, such bodies do not figure in any of their international policies. The same is true more surprisingly in the DEMOS report on taxation. It is sometimes argued rather dismissively that the place of NGOs is quite marginal to government policies. This is a mistaken view on several counts: in the first place, the educational work of NGOs should not be underestimated and can be harnessed to winning support for programmes of increased public spending, to improve the lot of the underprivileged at home and abroad; in the second place, even the most market-oriented of the world organisations, the World Bank, has come to the conclusion that NGOs, both national and international, are the most cost-effective agencies for the delivery of services in many fields of development. There is a third reason for recognising the international importance of NGOs, which is less well-known and understood, but is worth discussing at some length.

Some NGOs, but not all, have developed in their international relations what Professor Diane Elson, the Manchester economist, has called, the 'economy of trust'. Most commercial organisations spend much time and energy on controlling, monitoring, checking and counter-checking their business transactions. In a highly competitive market they simply do not trust their suppliers or customers not to take advantage of them. There is an alternative — to build up a relationship of trust. It happens in some families and even in family businesses. It happens, as we saw earlier, among workers whose lives depend upon each other, as those did who worked in the coal mines. Such trust can take place on a wider scale. This is one of the lessons learnt by some NGOs working in the Third World, where for long there was a colonial relationship of domination and exploitation, which worked down from the European rulers into the behaviour of the colonial elite which inherited from them. In these conditions, nothing less than total openness and mutual respect could build up a new relationship. But out of this a sense of trust has been established and has proved an extremely effective alternative to normal commercial practice.

The 'economy of trust' is at work not just in the relationships between some European and Third World NGOs. It is working also between and among Third World NGOs themselves. Indeed, it was often from an older pre-colonial tradition of mutuality and cooperation that it was generated and nourished. There are many examples given from Africa in Michael Barratt Brown's recent book *Africa's Choices*. Examples were found in unions of cocoa farmers collecting for delivery to the state export marketing company, in women's credit unions, in artisans' cooperatives and in many forms of rural association for sharing seasonal work.

The economy of trust is often associated with networking — that is, the forging of links in commerce and in information exchange which do not depend on hierarchy and orders down the line from above. Some big companies have discovered the advantages of such networking and of the delegation of responsibility to profit makers at each level, but they use this as a conduit of profit to the centre, and for establishing exclusive arrangements, not for developing relationships of equality. A much more open networking has become the basic method of work of the international alternative trade movement, which has no private profit motivation.

If all the words in New Labour's pronouncements about partnership and social markets, cooperation and not confrontation were to be taken seriously, the economy of trust would surely have a special appeal. Instead, we find that 'the enterprise of the market and the rigour of competition' are always put before 'partnership and cooperation.' Even in relation to 'the goal of economic integration in Europe', Mr Blair insists that 'competitiveness is the essential pre-condition of a social market.' Of course, any enterprise in the market has to survive, but the point that is being missed all the time by New Labour's leaders is that competition is not the only or even the best motor of survival. The Japanese have learnt that competition has to take place within a framework of cooperation, as we have written elsewhere. But the limits of Japanese thought end at national survival. They do not extend to encompassing as an aim the survival of the human race. Yet, in the crisis we described earlier, it is this and nothing less that is at stake.

Reforming the International Institutions

Hugo Radice's analysis of the present system of global capital accumulation led him to the conclusion that it could neither be resisted within the shell of the nation-state, nor allowed to continue unchallenged, if the interests of working people were to be protected and advanced. What he called a form of *'radical internationalisation'* was required which would build upon the NGO experience we have just described. The 50th anniversary of the international financial institutions founded at Bretton Woods towards the end of the Second World War was celebrated with a massive protest from hundreds of NGOs world-wide that '50 Years Is Enough!' The protest was made in opposition to the utterly destructive policies pursued by the World Bank and the IMF in requiring all Third World countries to open their economies to the world market and to repay their debts by increasing their exports of raw materials. The result was the collapse of raw material prices as stocks built up, followed by economic disaster, when the foreign debts grew ever larger rather than receding. One after another the countries with the largest debts were plunged into economic disorder and civil war — Sudan, Somalia, Peru, Rwanda, Yugoslavia, Algeria and parts of the old Soviet Union.

The original aim of the Bretton Woods Institutions was the Keynesian one of redistribution: correcting inadequate demand so as to maintain full employment. The Fund and the Bank were created to ensure that governments did not cut back spending when they met balance of payment problems, thus starting a vicious spiral of beggar-my-neighbour actions such as had intensified the 1930s crisis. The full employment objective was written into the GATT articles of association and repeated in the Charter of the World Trade Organisation. It is worth quoting in full this statement which forms the first paragraph of the Final Act embodying the Results of the Uruguay Round of GATT, agreed to at the very end of 1993. The parties to that agreement recognised that:

'their relations in the field of trade and economic endeavour should be conducted with a view to raising standards of living, *ensuring full employment* [emphasis added] and a large and steadily growing volume of real income and effective demand, and expanding the production and trade in goods

179

and services, while allowing for the optimal use of the world's resources in accordance with the objective of sustainable development, seeking both to protect and to preserve the environment and enhance the means for doing so in a manner consistent with their respective needs and concerns at different levels of economic development.'

It is hard to have to accept that all this is pure rhetoric which enters not at all into the policies of governments. But certainly the principles enunciated in this statement have remained entirely unheeded in relation to the falling purchasing power of the indebted Third World countries or of the unemployed in the First World. Inequalities of income have widened in both worlds and between them. Those who lent money through the Fund and the Bank have called for early repayment, so that far from serving to ease the foreign debt problems of the poorer Third World countries, the international institutions have exacerbated them. The result is that the expansion of world trade has slowed down and become increasingly confined to exchanges between the already industrialised countries. But now the poor countries have begun to pull down the rich countries as unemployment has spread from the Third to the First World.

As Stuart Holland has pointed out, 'The Bretton Woods agreements were not just about liberalisation . . . Growth was to be "trade pulled" by liberalisation, just as it was "demand pulled" by rising public spending and higher incomes.' (*Global New Deal: An Agenda for the G7 plus*). The financial institutions and the original concept of an International Trade Organisation were designed by Keynes to intervene to encourage the growth of trade of the weak economies as well as of the strong and in particular to protect primary commodity producers against falling world prices for their products. This had been their fate in the 1930s and was to be their fate again in the 1980s. The GATT that replaced an International Trade Organisation became an instrument only of liberalisation without any element of positive intervention.

It is no better with the new World Trade Organisation that has now replaced GATT. It has even less positive intent than GATT, despite the first paragraph of its constitution. It is, in effect, a policing organisation to ensure that GATT rules of liberalisation are everywhere applied, and now not only to trade in goods but in services also, and in the freeing of capital movements too. The one freedom that is restricted is, of course, the freedom of labour to move from poor to rich countries and freedom does not extend to the opening up of markets from the control of a few giant transnational companies. Liberalisation is understood as freedom from state control, not from the control of global capital.

The Bretton Woods institutions need to be reformed, therefore, if they are to respond to the real needs of the world's peoples and not to the purposes of American and British finance capital. 'The 50 Years is Enough!' campaign had the effect of shaking up the World Bank into recognition that many of its programmes were useless if not harmful and that more attention should be paid to what people in the Third World countries themselves had to say. It did nothing to change the structure of dependence of these institutions on United States finance and United States foreign policy objectives. But a pressure of steam was built up, both outside and inside the financial institutions, which could be directed to a major reconstruction of the World Bank and the IMF. This would be greatly facilitated if the leading politicians of the European Union could be brought to recognise that competition with Japan and the USA will only lead to beggar-my-neighbour economic policies with similar results in fascism and war that they spawned in the 1930s. Only a framework for international economic cooperation can prevent a repetition of that tragedy today.

New Labour is Following Tory Foreign Policies

The Conservative government has done nothing to recognise the danger of beggar-my-neighbour competition for a small industrial country on the edge of Europe, that is more than usually dominated by opportunistic transnational companies. In these circumstances there would be an unprecedented opportunity for a Labour Party to take the lead first in Europe, and then world-wide, in rallying other similarly placed countries to promote the reform of the Bretton Woods agreements, which the Party played such an important role in establishing. The actual response of New Labour has been uniformly cool about any such initiative. The whole discussion of Britain in Europe by Mandelson and Liddle concerns the internal structure of the Union and its relationship to the United States. Wider responsibilities are barely mentioned. A reader arriving from Mars would have little idea that three-quarters of the planet's people live outside of Europe and North America and a group of small East Asian countries.

The only brief reference to this world comes in a passage relating the 'concern of young people' at the 'environmental challenges facing the globe' and about 'world poverty and the problem of sustainable development'. Is New, Young, Labour also concerned? The single proposal made by Mandelson and Liddle is that

> 'Britain can and should make its own contribution through bilateral aid and other policies, but the scale of this pales into insignificance by comparison with the influence a United Europe can wield, for example in trade negotiations and through the new World Trade Organisation'.

The reference to working through the new and liberalisation-oriented World Trade Organisation is ominous enough, but the examples of international cooperation that follow in the Mandelson-Liddle text are concerned mainly with Britain's role in NATO and the benefits accruing therefrom to 'Britain's world-class defence manufacturing firms'. They mean arms manufacturing and sales, which of course prosper best, not from successful economic development, but where a succession of wars and threats of wars can be stoked up and kept going.

Reliance on the World Trade Organisation implies reliance on world markets unfettered by the control of public authorities. The new WTO emerged at the end of the latest, so-called 'Uruguay Round' of GATT negotiations. Its outcome was typical of its whole history. According to World Bank calculations it was likely to give two-thirds of the benefits of the tariff reductions negotiated to the one-quarter of the world's people in already developed counties and one-third to the other three-quarters. Yes, we have got the figures the right way round. But for the peoples of the North the marginalisation of the South means declining levels of world trade and lost markets for Northern as well as Southern products — and that means lost jobs all round. On top of this the powers of the WTO were extended to liberalisation of services and foreign investment as well as the movement of goods from state controls, thus reducing still further the defences of individual countries' governments against the spreading tentacles of the giant international companies.

New Labour's leaders, in their enthusiasm for what they call 'the enterprise of markets' — although, of course, markets do not supply enterprise: transnational companies supply that — fail to recognise the corrosive effects of markets on the position of those whose bargaining power is already weak. They recognise that some regulation of national markets is needed to prevent the more obvious exploitation of monopoly positions and some collaboration with other nations in Europe in what they call the 'social market'. But there is not a word uttered about any form of international regulation which would begin to challenge the international power of the giant transnational corporations. Could it be that they are looking over their shoulders all the time at Mr Murdoch? In any case, regulation appears to be their only policy prescription, not that the weaker parties in the market should be strengthened.

There are in New Labour-Speak no words even of comfort for the poorest countries in the world which were once British colonies and suffer under a burden of mounting foreign debts, incurred originally at the proposal of international financiers including some British bankers, which these countries do not now have the means to repay. Their poverty is not only the result of their weak bargaining position in world markets, and the World Bank's demands upon them to export or die, thus reducing the world price of their primary commodities. In great measure the reason for their weakness is that the industrially developed countries continue to use protectionist devices, which the World Bank does not permit to the unindustrialised countries, to exclude any imports other than primary commodities such as could compete with their own manufactures. This kind of protectionism is a Tory policy, but New Labour shows no signs of distancing itself from such nationalist, and incidentally short-sighted, posturing.

It may be that one day we shall hear a speech from Tony Blair on the needs of the world's poor and, if not on the demands of Christian charity, at least some recognition of the common interests of poor people everywhere. But the omens are not good. At a recent conference organised at Church House, Westminster, by a group of Christian and other aid agencies on the urgent need for debt relief for the world's poorest countries, New Labour was not represented. It was not a minor event. Speakers included the Bishop of Southern Africa, the ex-President of Zambia, Kenneth Kaunda, the recently retired deputy UN Secretary General and Executive Secretary of the UN Economic Commission for Africa, a director of Chartered Bank, an IMF representative and a Conservative government Overseas Development Minister. But no-one came from New Labour's shadow cabinet. Old Labour was there in the presence of Jeremy Corbyn and Bernie Grant and others including one of the present authors, Michael Barratt Brown.

New Labour's abandonment of its internationalist traditions was seen in its worst aspect in the half-hearted commitment to the European Union which we had to recognise in an earlier chapter. As in the case of unity with European socialists, social democrats and other progressive groups on the continent, so it is with the wider socialist movement, New Labour has followed in the wake of the narrowest nationalist sentiment of the tabloid press. No effort has been made to educate and lead the British people to see their interests as being linked to those of other peoples. It is a tragedy of historic proportions, when even Mandelson and Liddle recognise that the young people are ready for a more internationalist stance and when wide groups of voluntary agencies have come together in the 'Real World', that New Labour should remain stuck in the most backward reaches of chauvinism.

CHAPTER 12

Why Socialist Renewal?

.

'The Labour Party stands essentially for revolt against the inequality of
circumstance that degrades and brutalises and disgraces our civilisation. It
abhors and repudiates the unscientific and immoral doctrine that the
competitive struggle for the means of life is, in human society, either
inevitable or requisite for the survival of the fittest; it declares, indeed, in full
accord with science, that competition produces degradation and death,
whilst it is conscious and deliberate cooperation which is productive of life
and progress.'
  Sidney Webb, introducing the proposal to reorganise the Labour Party, including Clause
  IV.4 of its constitution, in an article in The Observer *in 1917*

'New Labour believes in the market and in efficiency and in the need to
compete . . . a strong society and an efficient economy . . . That is the
essence of our belief in One Nation policies and the principles of the
stakeholder economy.'
  Mandelson & Liddle, op.cit., p.30, under the cross-heading, 'Is this Socialism?' in the
  chapter on 'New Labour'

Here we have the contrast in its clearest form between New Labour and
Old: competition takes the place of cooperation; efficiency replaces
equality; one nation in place of human society; a stakeholder economy
to substitute for life and progress. How do Tony Blair and his
accomplices have the gall to speak of 'rescuing the party's traditional
values' to 'respond to the challenges . . . [of] . . . the new century'?
They say that the circumstances which brought Old Labour's
constitution into being have past. But we have had to note throughout
this book that capitalism has not fundamentally changed. True, it has
got richer, perfected its production techniques and labour productivity,
and extended its reach to compass the globe. But morally it has matched
all these glossy successes by continuous retrogression. More poverty,
more inequality, more arbitrary power, more ferocious dissolution of
human solidarity: these are its deepest achievements. The Labour Party

was not founded to meet a passing crisis, but to overturn a world in which 'things are in the saddle and ride mankind' (Ralph Waldo Emerson *Ode to W.H. Channing*).

Royden Harrison has reminded us that the Labour Party's 1918 constitution, including clause IV.4., was not a response to the success of wartime controls on the one hand and to the Bolshevik revolution on the other. It was rather the outcome of 45 years of argument and advocacy of common ownership. It was furthermore the end result of a much longer history of socialist thought, which reaches back to the Greek poet, Aristophanes, the early Christians and their medieval and Nineteenth Century followers and to the writings of Marx and Engels. It does not, therefore, cease to be relevant because we are no longer at war or at risk from any Bolsheviks. Nor does it have to be abandoned to make accommodations once more with a revived Liberal Party, which had collapsed in 1916. The Liberal Democrats of today are not seen by New Labour as necessary allies against the Tories to win elections, but they may be necessary allies against the old Labour left if, as seems all too likely, New Labour in government advances conservative policies in place of democratic socialism. The only fly in this ointment is that many Liberals may prove too principled and radical to go along with this.

Going back on Democratic Socialism

Royden Harrison describes the origins of Old Labour as follows:

> 'Independently of each other, Friedrich Engels and Keir Hardie had concluded that what was wanted was an Independent Labour Party, which would be impartial in its dismissal of Liberals and Tories. They believed that a party, which put the interests of working people ahead of all understandings and arrangements with established parties, was bound to become socialist.'

Clause IV was designed to clinch the matter, but it was the foundation of the Party in the trade unions that ensured the representation of working people. In the long run, but not necessarily very soon, they would find their freedom through common ownership and systems of popular administration. Sidney Webb warned that the words of the Clause should not become a 'shibboleth'. There could be many forms of common ownership and popular administration, but just one firm repudiation of the individualism which characterised all the other political parties. What Webb meant by individualism was the claim, once the households and clans had ceased to be organising structures of life and work, that the state should treat only with individuals, offering them protection — against harassment by other states and against any interference with their individual transactions in the market. Trade unions and cooperatives were seen as the working people's alternative, but they should also be seeking a framework of state support for their activities.

Mr Blair and his associates have taken two major steps to change the nature of the Labour Party, apart from their policy changes. The first was to excise Clause IV.4 of the constitution and to replace its basis for organising the economy in a commitment to social ownership and popular administration with some sentences which any Liberal and most Tories would agree to. The second was to restrict severely the role of the trade unions from the basic democratic structure of the Party. It is reasonable to ask after that what is left of Old Labour. Mr Blair insists that what is left are its 'core values', appropriately polished up for the modern world. This means, with the change from cooperation through common ownership to competitive stakeholding, that liberty becomes 'a balance of rights and duties', equality becomes 'fairness and social justice' and fraternity become 'a strong society'. What does this mean for the whole socialist project? Can New Labour be called 'socialist'?

Gerry Cohen has asked whether there can be socialism without common ownership, since New Labour still claims to be a democratic *socialist* party. Cohen assumes that by socialism we mean not just state ownership and regulation of the economy such as was practised in the Soviet Union and Eastern Europe, but a true equality of circumstance for all. This simply cannot exist, he argues, where ownership and control of wealth are in a few private hands and the great majority create that wealth by their labour but cannot exercise any control over the process or its outcome. The only alternative to such a division of capital and labour as exists in capitalist society, is common ownership of the means of production, distribution and exchange. Without that, socialism is impossible and, if Mr Blair wants to lead a party without the basic aim of common ownership, that is one thing: but he must not call it a socialist party.

Royden Harrison has asked further whether New Labour can even still be called a party of labour. And is it any longer important, if the distinction between capital and labour has become blurred as a result of the flexibility of the new technology? Is the working class no longer a reality, with the breaking up of work into fragments, including a huge extension of self-employment and home work? Have home ownership and home entertainment simply eroded all community life? Is there no longer a role for trade unions and a party based on the unions to give a voice to working people as a class? Harrison's answer is that there have of course been changes but not in the great division in society 'between those who give orders and those who must obey them.' What then would it mean to renew our faith in socialism? What would have to be the role of the unions and of social action?

Labour and the Unions

We know what it would not be. Mrs Thatcher has told us:

> 'What would please me immensely would be if the TUC was not, and the trade unions were not, a part of the Labour Party, and the Labour Party part of the trade union movement.' (quoted in *The Observer*, 1.5.83)

She must surely now be 'immensely pleased'! Of course, she would be, because she would know well enough that without the unions Labour would have lost the heart of its constituency. Her comment is not disinterested, although it seeks to appeal to a wider prejudice. We have to come back once more to the centrality of organised labour in any party of labour. The tabloid press may still employ the old fear of the unions among those with property, however little it may be, that they believe they might lose from socialism.

But for socialists, especially in the UK, renewal is intimately bound up with the relationship of the party of labour with the trade unions. New Labour has sought to end the historic integration. It was, in Lewis Minkin's phrase, always a 'contentious alliance', but Minkin asks us how far the factors that caused the founding by the unions in 1900 of a Labour Representation Committee have now disappeared; and he lists those that then influenced the unions:

> '— an unsympathetic and dominant Conservative government, a middle class resistant to working class candidates and their priorities, and a judiciary constantly finding resources of constraint in the individualistic orientation of English common law traditions . . . a climate of scape-goatism built up by a systematic press campaign against the unions as the obstacles to economic efficiency.' (Minkin, p.647)

What has changed? These all seem to be good reasons which still apply for the unions to need a political party. But Minkin's reasons for the Labour Party continuing to gain advantage from the attachment to the unions appeared to be less convincing in 1990 when he was writing, and have been disregarded by New Labour. They, nonetheless, bear repeating:

— union financial support (though this could be changed by a state funding system for contending parties in elections);

— what Minkin calls 'ballast', the solidity, despite all contentions, that held the Labour Party together when other parties, Liberals and Social Democrats, have split;

— not least important, the mutual interaction of committees and consultations which bring into the Party a broad social and industrial experience from the unions and particularly the actual day-by-day experience of low pay and poverty.

These would all be important arguments for a party of labour, but the leaders of New Labour wish to escape all that. They claim that two-thirds of their newly recruited members live in what are called 'the electorally crucial areas of the Midlands and the South' and 47% describe themselves as professional, 9% as students and 25% as retired. That leaves just 10% manual workers and 9% unemployed. Lists of wealthy business tycoons and media stars who support Mr Blair have been published in the press to reveal New Labour's new constituency, so that none of Minkin's arguments for links with the unions need now apply. With the aid of the media and the non-voters, it is evidently believed that 'Middle England' and the new professionals might win an election for Blair, provided that the old Labour constituents remained blindfolded by their ancient loyalties.

It only needs one-third of the electorate (42% of voters on a turn out of 78%) to win an election, as Mrs Thatcher recognised, so long as there are enough in the 'electorally crucial areas', where majorities on the first past the post voting system are slim. But who then is to look after those, nearly half of the population, who do not now call themselves 'professional' or 'retired' professional? We can assume that far fewer of the non-manual workers gave themselves this title in the past. Today, half of the men and a quarter of the women employed are still in manual occupations and a large proportion of the self-employed and of the women in non-manual work are not professional workers. There are still the unions to care for them. The great industrial unions have been broken by the decline of mining and manufacturing. These industries used to account for over a half of the workforce: today they employ only a fifth. The big service unions have done something to fill the gap by recruitment in health and education, but, as we showed earlier, this leaves the proportion of workers organised in unions at a level of a third of the workforce and not a half as it was in the 1970s. This is still eight million people, nearly a half of them women. It only needs 13 million votes to win an election. If all trade unionists could be persuaded and could persuade their partners and adult families to vote the same way, they would never lose.

The first task of socialists must then be to help to create the conditions in which the unions can recruit among those, especially women, who are most isolated and unprotected against exploitation. The second must be to involve the unions in every way possible in the demand that must be made of a New Labour government that it should put full employment at the top of its agenda. Full employment is not what Tony Blair has called a 'favour', but an essential precondition of all 'core values' of those who have only their labour to sell in the market. After that the unions have to insist that they be involved in the policy decisions that affect their members' livelihood. They will need themselves to put the interests of all working people, both nationally and in their own localities, ahead of any narrow special interests. That must be the lesson to be learned from the Tory government's capacity to divide workers and conquer them — mineworkers in Nottinghamshire from other miners, skilled from unskilled, men from women, south from north, white from black, young from old. It has been an essential role of the Labour Movement to generate and maintain the unity of labour. For unity is strength.

Unity cannot be achieved by talk about partnership and stakeholding, but only by action to defend the weak against the strong, to give support to groups who are resisting oppression and exploitation, everywhere to strengthen the power in the market of the many who own nothing but their labour against the few who own and control all the means of employment.

Tony Blair has stated on behalf of New Labour that his programme includes acceptance of the European Union's Social Chapter in the Maastricht Treaty. And this requires workers' representatives being elected to the Works Councils for companies over a certain size. This provision has been bitterly resisted by the British government, although some British employers have already learned to live with it. In fact it is a very tame measure of involvement, which can be used to separate union representation from the workers on these consultative bodies. Nonetheless, it will be of crucial importance for British workers joining those from other countries on the boards of transnational operating companies to be able to work out joint policies to put to management. For this it is essential that the unions themselves build up their own international links through the European TUC and the trade groups and directly with opposite numbers in the same firms, with the aim of establishing more open, more accountable, more democratic management.

The major problem for the unions in developing such international cooperation is the cost of travel and accommodation away from home. Financial assistance for this, such as the GLC was able to give when it was in existence, would be one way for New Labour to show that stakeholding was not simply a fig-leaf for the employers' interests. In view of what we said earlier about the exceptionally dominant position of transnational companies in the UK economy, the regulation of their activities with the support of the unions might be supposed to have a high priority for a reforming Labour government. But Mandelson tells us that New Labour will see that they are left alone to get on with the creation of wealth. We now know from the experience of PowerGen and the other privatised utilities who gains from that wealth creation. It is the private shareholders.

We have already noted the failure of New Labour to recognise and support the efforts of its own MEPs to develop with European opposite numbers the employment opportunities which are so desperately needed in face of the high and rising levels of unemployment and the threat of a further rise as the Maastricht Treaty convergence measures begin to bite. Tony Blair's commitment of New Labour to the Social Chapter and to playing a role in Europe could only be made a reality by discussion in advance with many different groups in Europe — trade unions, Green and Left parties, women's groups, independent socialists as well as Social Democrats.

There is much that could be done in Europe, jointly and in common — not only to put full employment at the top of the political agenda, but to share ideas about social welfare, family allowances, pensions, protection of the environment, health and safety at work, shared work, shorter hours, and paid educational leave. All of these are matters in which employers hope to exploit the differences between different groups of workers. But workers will see possibilities of levelling conditions up, instead of simply accepting the unilateral levelling down on which the Tories have been engaged. For working people must still look to governments to protect them against exploitation by the owners of capital, not only on a local and national but on a European and a world scale.

What has Changed?

New Labour speakers complain that to talk in this way in Britain today is to look back on a country that has gone for ever. Labour's new recruitment shows that we are all middle class now and living in Middle England. We have shown reasons to suppose that this might be at most the 40% at the top of Will Hutton's 40:30:30 division of British society — the secure, the insecure and those in despair. The disappearance of 'class voting' is not, moreover, confirmed by the opinion polls. Studies at the end of the 1980s, published in *The Observer* (31.12.89) showed 'class and class identity to be no less salient today than during earlier periods commonly acknowledged to be characterised by class voting.' In answer to Harrison's questions, we can note that 65% of Labour Party members surveyed in 1989 thought 'class struggle' to be a 'central issue in politics' and two-thirds in a MORI poll at the same time thought voters were more divided by social class than before. Of course, all that was before Tony Blair got to work recruiting in Middle England and spreading the gospel of self-denial to working class people. But seven years later not all the Labour voters of 1989 will have died or changed their views.

New Labour's argument is not only that people have changed but that circumstances have changed. The 1918 Clause IV was said by New Labour publicists to be

> 'the product of revulsion at the failures of Nineteenth Century free market capitalism . . . pauperism, unemployment, mass poverty and exploitation . . . The prevailing view was that because unregulated markets had failed, they had to be replaced.'

The Labour Party's founders were certainly right then, although they would not have hedged 'capitalism' round with references to unregulated markets, which leaves it open to New Labour to try regulation. But what has changed?

— Poverty? One-fifth of the UK population today live in poverty and one-third of the children, according to the Department of Social Security;

— Pauperism? 13 million have pay that is below half the national average. Half a million are homeless. 21 million can't afford a holiday or a treat out.

— Unemployment? 4 million are seeking work and are unable to find it. One million have been looking for over a year. That is 12.5% of the workforce and among young people and in some regions the proportion is 20%.

— Exploitation? 3 million part-time women employees have no national insurance protection. A quarter of male manual workers work more than 48 hours in a week.

— Unregulated markets? Besides the regulators of the privatised public utilities, who appear to have little control over consumer prices or managers' salaries, what regulation can there be over the pricing and investment policies of the transnational companies when they threaten to locate elsewhere? In fact the TNCs are more, rather than less, dominant than in 1918 or 1979, and once more as in 1918 more capital flows out of the country than is invested in Britain.

Some of these facts about the condition of the people were recognised by Tony Blair in 1983, in his maiden speech to the House of Commons, particularly as they affected his own constituency in Durham. But he appears to have forgotten his promises to his constituents made in those far-off days, when Labour leaders felt the need to give some time and attention to the interests of their own people. New Labour's programme so far gives no indication of doing this, either by posing any challenge to the tax concessions granted to the transnational companies or raising taxes on the rich, which would together provide resources for correcting some of the inequalities which have grown ever worse in our society under Tory rule. It is true that average incomes have steadily risen in the UK — at least threefold in the last 40 years. That is indeed a change for the good, but we saw that in the last two decades the distribution of income has also changed. And this change is very much for the worse so as to leave a larger share for the top 20% of incomes and a smaller share for the bottom 20%. The tax system has only worsened this inequality. Indeed the bottom 20% have seen no absolute improvement in these two decades in their real incomes at all.

How can it be that New Labour is not able to say, with a national income three times the size of that of 40 years ago, that it could raise the taxes on the rich and on corporations making large productivity gains, so as to maintain and expand expenditure on health and education, to keep up with modern needs and possibilities? The answer is only in part because the population is older and needs more medical care and because there are many more unemployed. That is an easy answer for New Labour, but the reality is that UK spending per head of population on health and education is below that of other countries. And the reason is that, as we have already seen, UK taxes are below all those of our European partners, and only a little above those in Japan and the USA, as a proportion of national income. Most of our European partners are now also cutting back their welfare spending — to keep *down* with the Brits. This is a downward competitive spiral that has to be checked and reversed. This can only be done by government intervention and public spending, which New Labour has turned its face against.

Rebuilding Belief in Common Ownership

So nothing has changed to justify the ending of the Clause IV commitment to common ownership. The aim of the Clause, it will be recalled by Old Labour members, was

'to secure for workers by hand or by brain the full fruits of their industry and the most equitable distribution thereof that may be possible *upon the basis* of the common ownership of the means of production, distribution and exchange, and the best obtainable system of popular administration and control of each industry and service.' (emphasis added)

Clause IV was not a commitment to *total* common ownership or to any particular form of nationalised industry, but to the *basis* of common ownership for securing equality and ending exploitation. To remove this clause was to attempt to terminate the Labour Party's history as a socialist party.

Although the new Clause of New Labour states that the party is a 'democratic socialist party', the subsequent rather obvious claim, 'that we achieve more by the strength of our common endeavour' than we achieve alone . . . to realise our true potential . . . and a community . . . of solidarity, tolerance and respect', does not say anything about how this is to be realised. The first set of intervening words about 'power, wealth and opportunity' being 'in the hands of the many not the few' explains neither who will be making the allocation nor how much will go to each. Nor does it explain the criteria of allocation. These criteria are hinted at in the second section of the new Clause, which states that a 'just society is to be judged by the condition of the weak as much as the strong'. But, surely, in a just society there would be no difference between the weak and the strong, because 'weak' people would have strong rights in order to ensure equality of outcomes?

The second set of intervening words about 'the rights we enjoy reflecting the duties we owe' reminds us of Mrs Be-done-by-as-you-did. Even worse, it may cause us to think of Mr Jack Straw declaring a holy war on beggars, squeegee merchants and wind-screen washers, to say nothing of graffiti artists , all of whom offend New Labour because their miserable existence is visible to their betters in the political establishment. This arouses feelings of shame, which New Labour appears not yet to have learned to dispense with. But it is making rapid progress every day in this respect. Of course, New Labour's balance of rights and duties might refer to the reciprocal rights and duties of collective organisations like trade unions or sports clubs, where all members are equal and rules are voluntarily agreed and self-imposed. But widening such collectivism into the social polity is called 'old fashioned' in New Labour Speak.

Such total collectivity belongs to the Kantian imperative and is impossible in a class ordered society with owners and wage slaves, masters and hands or even employers and employees. It is no more but also no less possible now than it was in 1918. But it is still possible to have that as the objective to work towards. That is why not only humanists but Christians like Archbishop Temple supported Clause IV. Ownership of capital must by its very nature give power to treat others as means and not as ends. This is not to say that having a savings account makes anyone into a capitalist. As Cohen points out, such savings are both useful and also egalitarian, if the savings are from one's own labour and there are reasonable limits on bequests.

Labour's commitment to common ownership was ended by Tony Blair not only because it was said to be irrelevant in the modern world but because it was said to be dishonest. No Party member really believed in it, so he claimed, and it could not be canvassed on the door step. All Labour governments had operated a mixed economy of private and publicly owned enterprises. Other social democratic parties were more honest, it was said, in having abandoned social ownership as an aim. This claim could, in fact, only be demonstrated by a selective choice of parties and a selective quotation of parts of their constitutions. Most such parties have both an interim statement of what is currently achievable and an ultimate statement of aspirations for an ideal socialist society. Usually the first were quoted by New Labour and the second omitted.

It was as if Christians should revise the Lord's Prayer, excluding the third and fourth sentences: 'Thy kingdom come. Thy will be done on earth as it is in heaven.' One must really wonder what Mr Blair is thinking about when he says that prayer. Does he feel that he is being dishonest? Or is it too far in the future, like the requirement of the old Clause IV, to be of concern today? Would he, perhaps, leave out the third sentence to make Christianity more 'electable'? He knows, after all, perfectly well that Christ's kingdom on earth is one in which all are equal in the sight of God and all goods are held in common.

Interim and Long-term Aims

William Temple long ago in 1908, before Clause IV was agreed in 1918 and denounced in 1995, argued in favour of common ownership:

> 'This is not an economic question. It is a question touching the human personality. It asks what are the deepest and most potent motives in the human soul. The question is not economic — to the Christian it is religious . . . If Christianity is to be applied to the economic system, an organisation which rests primarily on the principle of competition must give way to one which rests primarily on cooperation. . . .
>
> The question of the competitive principle is driven down into the labour market, so that men compete against each other for the right to live. Go and see it at work in the London Docks [today we might add 'or any job queue']. If one man is to secure the means of feeding himself and his family, he must be depriving another. Is that an exhibition of Brotherhood? Such a system embodies no principle but selfishness and mutual antagonism . . .
>
> As citizens we are guilty of a whole system of oppression: it is there: we tolerate it, and so become responsible for its results. There is nothing inevitable in it: it is all the result of human choices. I do not mean that anyone deliberately put it there; it is the greatest fluke in creation. But it is the net result of innumerable human choices, and by human choices it can be modified. Here lies our duty — and our guilt.'

There is indeed a real dilemma for socialists in having both interim and long term aims, which is that each is prone to conflict with the other. But without ultimate goals the intermediate ones are likely to be dissolved in the acid of opportunism, leaving an infragrant air of disappointment, if not a rich stench of betrayal. Tony Blair's aim of extending the 'stakeholding' in companies and in society at large could be acceptable to any socialist, if it were set within the wider aim of reducing the power of capital and strengthening labour. When it is not, it is mere rhetoric, or, as he would say, 'froth'. Mr Blair says that he wants to 'change our industrial culture', but without changing company law, as Archbishop Temple recommended, and challenging along with William Temple the demands of a competitive capitalist market with social demands, it is pure wishful thinking.

Industrial culture, as any politician must recognise, is embedded in material foundations. It does not float free from the brain of even ever so clever politicians. Company law is different in Germany. The culture of industry is different in Japan. In both countries workers are more involved in decision making, and conditions of work and incomes are somewhat more equal than in Britain. But unless such advances are seen as being directed towards changing the system, they will not be very effective and cannot be called 'socialist'.

Challenging Capitalism

It is necessary here to review the fundamental socialist critique of capitalism. It is not only that the ethos of the system is competition and money-making and not cooperation and caring. It is not even just that a profit is made by paying workers less than the value of the goods and services which they produce. There can be no objection to a company making a profit. It can be regarded as one test of efficiency. The great issue is — who decides to what use the profit is put? If the owners of the capital decide and pay themselves and the managers many times as much as any of the workers receive, and the workers are not consulted, the workers are being exploited and have a valid ground for complaint. But the capitalist system requires that much of the profit be reinvested in producing more goods and services to make more profit. Again, the workers are not consulted, but, if this means they are still employed because the goods and services are selling well, they will probably not complain, although they may regard the managers' salaries and the shareholders' dividends as excessive. But, if the product sells indifferently well, and jobs are undermined, workers will complain that they have worked themselves out of a job.

Companies are not isolated units, however. The whole of society contributes in some way to any one company's success. Yet, there is no consultation about decisions on the use of profits with the wider society any more than with the company's workers. A board of self-selected directors decides under the competitive pressures of the market, never forgetting the requirement of company law that the interests of the shareholders come first. It is quite irrelevant that some of the largest shareholders are pension funds because neither the pensioners nor any of the organisations which could claim to represent them are consulted about the use of their savings, or about the decisions which are taken in their names. Yet, company law could be changed to provide for representation of workers and the public interest on the boards of companies. If this was part of an effort to make real inroads on the powers of capital, and if it was supported by other actions to strengthen workers' and consumers' effective powers, it could be an interim socialist measure. If it were not, then it would either end up as irrelevant, or worse, be seen as a confidence trick aimed at gulling those who are the subjects of arbitrary rule in industry.

The arguments we have been considering that can be ranged against an economic system based on private ownership of capital are primarily moral, that people are treated in it as means and not ends and that competition encourages destructive rather than constructive elements in the human make-up. We have to face the counter-argument, which William Temple (echoing St. Augustine) discussed that private involvement is necessary to the good care of resources and also the assertion that some measure of competition is necessary to prevent idleness and encourage endeavour.

The very large number of franchises in all lines of business (Macdonalds is the most famous example) show that private management can be as exploitative as private ownership, but they also show that private ownership of capital is not necessary for efficiency. Social ownership does not preclude franchising. There is no reason why numbers of cooperatives should not tender for maintenance contracts, to take one example.

The mix of cooperation and competition in any enterprise varies very greatly according to the nature of the enterprise. The VISA card service, described as the highest turnover business enterprise the world has ever seen, is owned by 20,000 different financial institutions cooperating under a skeletal administration, and competing with other smaller card services (Mulgan & Briscoe, p.29). It is said that major technical inventions have all required conditions of intensive competition. Examples are found in the war-time struggle that produced Radar, new information technology and nuclear energy. In the nature of the competition, however, in all these cases there was widespread cooperation in the process of discovery. The Japanese industrial success has been largely dependent on a combination of a cooperative framework within which competing enterprises can work with a maximum of shared information and a minimum of waste. The framework has been supplied by the state. Beneficent competition does not necessarily imply private ownership and it does not follow from putting competition before cooperation.

It is fashionable to deride all alternatives to capitalist power in the market as less dynamic, less efficient and therefore less beneficial even to the people who are exploited. Workers' cooperatives are seen to have failed. Cooperative retail stores barely survive against the giant super-market chains. Mutuality in building societies is being abandoned in favour of private shareholding. The nationalised industries, although they were in fact quite efficient in capitalist terms, were little different from capitalist enterprises in the matter of their relations with their employees.

The so-called 'state socialism' in the Soviet Union and Eastern Europe became a bureaucratic sharing of scarcity, as more and more of the national product was allocated to the insane arms race. But before that race took off, it performed far better than other Third World countries both in its initial industrial development and later in post-war reconstruction, despite Stalin's madness. By the 1960s RHS Crossman and other Labour leaders, including Harold Wilson, thought there was a real danger to the West that the USSR might overtake them. Then Khruschev fell, and after the Cuba crisis the arms race took over the whole economy. China, by an ingenious combination of central planning and market capitalism, enjoys continuous rapid economic growth, as does Poland and the Czech Republic using a similar mixture.

Is there, then, no future for common ownership? Everyone knows that money making is not the only thing in life or the only motivation for effective activity. The best work that most of us do is not done for money but for love. Not all producer and retail cooperatives have failed. Some like Mondragon in the Basque Country in Spain and the Cooperative Bank are outstandingly successful. Not all mutual societies have become private banks. *Nationwide*, one of the most successful, has not made this change. Not all state enterprises have treated their staff inhumanely. The Post Office has a record of internal promotion second to none. There are literally millions of successful not-for-profit companies and associations for special interests in welfare, sport, conservation, cultural and religious activities, which rely on voluntary labour. Despite the new commercial requirements, Health Trusts do not make a profit for private owners, nor do most schools and universities. Alternatives to market capitalism in the wider field of industry have engaged us in earlier chapters. Here we must note the importance of opening up the discussion of these things in education and the media.

Education and the Media

The relationship of Labour to the media, as we saw earlier, lies at the very heart of the emergence of New Labour from Old. The emphasis on presentation rather than content — on admen's red roses and sound-bites in place of home made banners and branch resolutions, on charisma and spin-doctors in place of decency and honest expertise — is all designed to attract media attention. The admen's task is not to present but to invent the leader. His views appear as carefully rehearsed interviews presented like soap advertisements. They are sculpted to fit such popular prejudice as can be monitored in the opinion polls. But spin doctors do not always follow the polls. The one consistent finding in the years before 1992 was that Labour would do better with a different leader than Neil Kinnock. This insight was not even discussed, leave alone acted upon. In effect, the adman does not so much seek to educate the public as to run with majority opinion and turn it to his own ends.

Those who surround New Labour's leader are from a background in the media, at least one from a frankly salacious background in pornography. Perhaps Tony Blair will tell us that even Christ 'did . . . eat with publicans and sinners'. If he did, this would cover not only pornographers, but others for whose attentions Mr Blair is not apparently so enthusiastic. Publicans in the time of Christ were the collectors of taxes for Rome — another bit put in, like 'Render unto Caesar . . .', by the Second Century authors of the Gospels to placate the Romans. But, if we read 'media moguls' for 'publicans', we convey the doubts we have about the 'master' eating with such people. They say that you can tell a man by the company he keeps.

Winning the support of the media for any enterprise is a difficult game, often even dangerous. The public has become used to amorality and cynical about immorality. It may be bemused by salacious stories of the affairs of politicians and by titillating tales of royal scandals, but it knows a lie when it sees one. Government through the media, whether of Berlusconi or Murdoch — that 'sleek, serviceable, but still untamed monster', in Tawney's words, 'who owns five-sixths of the press', is a high risk enterprise. Even press lords have limited powers, and they might well fear that it could be revealed that New Labour had sold to the people a false prospectus. The higher the claim to moral rectitude, the greater the fall in trust, if the claim were found to be fraudulent.

What may be appropriate to the world of advertising and public relations, may not work in politics. For the emphasis on presentation at the expense of content has two particular results: the first is that it leaves to the professionals at the centre the responsibility in effect not only for the promotion but the preparation of the product (i.e. the policy). Mandelson and Liddle reveal that once Mr Blair has 'kissed hands with the Queen' (Do Prime Ministers still really do that in our post-feudal state?)

then an 'axis of no 10., the cabinet office and the Treasury' — through informal 'bilateral and *ad hoc* meetings' and a group of 'super-ministers' — will 'drive the central government machine'. (M&L, p.240ff.) This follows the Thatcher precedent of informal prime-ministerial decision-making, superceding the formal decisions of cabinet and ministers. It also continues the key role of the Treasury as both economic department and keeper of the public purse, which Gordon Brown, Labour's shadow Treasury spokesman, has been insisting that it should.

Popular Participation or Populist Leadership?

Although there is much talk in Mandelson and Liddle of 'decentralisation to the regions' and 'revitalisation of local government', this is to be done 'without at the same time making the *disastrous error of risking loss of control of public expenditure*' (M&L, p.198 — emphasis added). Of course, not! And the innovations for revitalising local government include suggestions for

> 'elected executive boards which might be paid a proper salary, and the US system of elected mayors . . . which could foster creative partnerships with local business that have done so much to revive American cities.' (M&L, p.199)

There is no mention of workers' representatives in this elitist scenario, let alone a 'popular planning unit', such as invigorated the GLC under Old Labour. Mr Blair has made a particular point of recommending an elected mayor for Greater London's government.

The second result of effective centralisation of policy making and promotion is that this really ends membership participation and indeed any wider popular consultation. Once Party members have elected their representatives by individual vote, and taken part in a referendum on the Party's manifesto, their job is then to go out on the knocker and canvass for support. The old methods of Party policy-making are now called 'bureaucratic' by New Labour writers including supporters like Stuart Hall (*Soundings*, i.1995). It is an interesting case of projection. If ever there was rule by a bureau it was not to be found in the convoluted structure of committees and Conference and the PLP of Old Labour, but is to be seen in the leader's office of New Labour.

Inside the leader's office, Mr Blair prides himself, we are told by Mandelson and Liddle, on being 'invariably confident of his own overall judgement . . . though he will of course consult — getting points and suggestions from others.' (M&L, p.53) This sounds like a populist dictator and not a democrat. Blair is generally referred to as 'the leader'. It is all many miles from the old ways of laborious but creative hammering out of ideas from different sections of the Labour Movement with its multifaceted links to unions, women's groups, youth organisations, unemployed centres, Asian and Caribbean communities, pensioners associations and so on. Of course, the Party leaders did not always in the past take any notice of what the membership had to say, but the members are not supposed to have a say at all in the future.

This is all very sad, because what is desperately needed in the present crisis is real discussion and argument among socialists — education in the best adult education tradition, where members of the group learn more from each other than from the tutor and the tutor learns as much as all the others. The main skill of such a group leader lies in locating and in posing the right questions for discussion. This book and the Socialist Renewal series are offered as contributions to such an educational process.

In time socialists will need a new agency or agencies, to enable them to join their forces for the reconstitution of the Labour Party as a party of labour, or, if that proves impossible, for its replacement by another. The first part of this job must lie in discussion, exchange of ideas and educational opportunities for study of the key issues of rising unemployment and deepening poverty. The trade unions have their education programmes and their schools, and these can play a major role, but in addition we have perhaps to start all over again with socialist discussion groups, not just for a select few but involving all the forces for change like members of trade unions, local needs pressure groups and the *Real World* coalition. Out of such discussions people will find their own way to build new associations - from below and not from above.

The discussion groups we need to form will not be just like those which existed a hundred years ago, first because we can now involve far more different interests and second because we have a new way to make our discussions international. We now have the INTERNET to join up our exchange of ideas all over the world. Already, as Hugo Radice reminded *New Statesman* readers in a long letter in March 1996, there is a continuous flow of information and ideas being electronically transmitted between socialist economists in many different countries. Socialists everywhere will need to log onto this and other networks — social, cultural, political as well as economic — if they are to challenge the media monopolies and plant the seeds for a real socialist renewal.

CHAPTER 13

Conclusion
After New Labour, What?

'Stop not your ears against the secret mourning of the oppressed . . . lest the Lord see it and be offended and shut his ears against your cries, and work a deliverance for his waiting people some other way than by you'.
A Letter to Parliament from Gerrard Winstanley, 1655

If New Labour deserts the working people of Britain, they will look elsewhere for their deliverance. It was the same three hundred and more years ago, when Winstanley and his Diggers established their commune. It is the same today. The British Labour Party did not fall from the sky, but shaped itself painfully over the years in a prolonged effort to give voice to the needs and sufferings of that immense part of the British population which was oppressed by poverty, and largely excluded from political life. The suffering and the shaping go back well beyond even the Quaker, Gerrard Winstanley, but of all Labour's forebears he perhaps expressed most keenly that search by the people for deliverance, which Tony Blair says he is responding to. If he fails them, as it seems he must, then Winstanley's message is that they will find another way than by him.

Command Politics or a 'Broad Church'?

Tony Blair has staked his claim to our confidence on his Christian socialism. He says repeatedly that he is returning to the ethical values of the Labour Party after a period of aberration. But what he has done — abandoning Clause IV, undermining Labour's links with the unions, prioritising efforts to build confidence with the richer members of the professional classes and with the owners of capital, and hi-jacking the making of policy into the leader's office, has seemed to many Party members to have put in question the whole basis of Labour as a broad church for the people. A party in which members could participate and share in the making of policy, starting from below and working upwards,

N.Corb.
top down
party

is being replaced by a party managed from above with messages carried down by messengers from spin doctors and their masters on high.

This command politics was, of course, nothing new for those who had continued to accept Communist Party discipline long after the Khruschev revelations and had come by way of *Marxism Today*, which had been generously funded thanks to Brezhnev's largesse to the British Communists, to join the Social Democratic drop-out intellectuals in the Blair 'Revolution'. But for old Labour members it is an affront to all they have ever believed in, and all that was open and liberating in their Labour Movement. The Blair 'Revolution' is truly an agonising moment for Labour people and in writing this book to share with others our own feelings, we have tried to go back to the roots of our Party and to discern what it means to have those roots pulled up. For what New Labour's spin doctors term 'modernisation' of an old party we have seen to be nothing less than demolition, the destruction of key commitments and repudiation of essential beliefs

Modernisation = betrayal

Contrary to the thoughts of the modernisers who along with Henry Ford reject our history as 'more or less bunk', we have recalled the words of Gerrard Winstanley and revisited the crisis of Britain in the Seventeenth Century. Why? Because in a very real sense that is when capitalism in our society was established with all the supporting pillars of Church and Monarchy and a new post-feudal aristocracy. One of the major obstacles that remains in Britain to the political advance of ordinary working people and to building a more democratic and humane society is still, as it always has been, the hang-over of that settlement three hundred years ago that ended the challenge in a great civil war of the people against the divine right of kings and the unelected power of their ministers. The challenge was never completed. The oath of loyalty of Her Majesty's ministers, of the civil servants, the army and the secret service is to the Crown and not to Parliament, and the Queen is still the head of the Church of England. Her successor may not be a Catholic or marry a divorcee. For such was the settlement between Crown and Parliament in 1688. And Mr Blair should be reminded that you cannot have a community of subjects.

Oliver Cromwell while he lived claimed his legitimacy as the servant of the Parliament, narrowly based as it was, and of a commonwealth, however little of its wealth was held in common. The restoration of the monarchy in 1660 after two turbulent years was accompanied by the re-establishment of the authority of the Church as the arm of the king's writ and even when 28 years later the 'Glorious Revolution' made sure that the king would rule only through Parliament, the Church remained as the agent of the king's writ. It was this which the dissenting churches and much later the Christian socialists challenged and which Archbishop William Temple in the 1930s sought to reorder in his effort to return the church to its earlier role as a force for social good. It was out of this challenge that the Labour Party was born.

We have to go back these three hundred years not only to recognise the foundation of what we very properly call the 'British Establishment', but to understand the scale of what has been lost in the rescission of Clause IV and what is at stake in the attempted destruction of the old Labour Party. When Party members talked of Old Labour as a 'broad church', it was not just a metaphor but a true harking back to what had been the religious freedom of the Commonwealth. Qualified as this freedom was, all kinds of wild and interesting ideas had been set free and all sorts of institutions were formed to spread these ideas — Anabaptists and Quakers, believers in a 'Fifth Monarchy' and many others. They survived the Restoration as local dissenting communities, meeting in secret, facing heavy penalties if they were caught. It is to these people that Archbishop Temple looked in the 1940s in order to draw strength from them, along with the trade unions, as the real custodians of Britain's democratic traditions. Their successors founded the Labour Party not as a centralised uniform instrument of authority, but truly as a broad alliance in which many ideas could coalesce and people could work out their own salvation, rather than having it provided for them, with the king's privy seal attached.

The Agony of Conscience

The predicament for Old Labour Party members today can, we believe, truly be compared to that of those who 300 years ago were faced with the Act of Uniformity proclaimed on May 19th 1662. Of course there is not now the rounding up and imprisonment, even execution, of dissenters. To establish conformity in 1662 4,320 Quakers were thrown into prison. The hangman led 212 of them through the streets in Ilchester and two of them were put in fetters. The Fifth Monarchy leaders were hanged. 2,000 ministers were ejected from their churches because they would not conform to the new Act. From then on dissenters were excluded not only from the official Church but from all public life, including attendance at the universities. Such exclusion is quite enough to make any man or woman consider how far he or she can go in conformity or in protest.

It is an agonising moment of choice, when conscience indicates one direction and self advancement, even self-preservation, another; and it is an agony that many in the Labour Party are facing today, without quite the same dire consequences attending their choice. We have found ourselves encouraged during the locust years of the Blair usurpation, by the words of one non-conformist who lived near us, but three centuries ago, in the little village of Carsington in Derbyshire. He was a member of the Wirksworth Classis, several of whom had been ejected from their ministries. His name was Oldfield, a common Derbyshire name, and this is how he expressed his agony. His words seem perfectly, even in their archaic English and religious language, to express the very essence of our own sorrow:

> 'When thou canst no longer continue in thy work without dishonour to God, discredit to religion, foregoing thy integrity, wounding conscience, spoiling thy peace, and hazarding the loss of thy salvation; in a word, when the conditions upon which thou must continue (if thou wilt continue) in thy employment are sinful, and unwarranted by the word of God, thou mayest, yea, thou must believe that God will turn thy very silence, suspension, deprivation, and laying aside, to His glory, and the advancement of the Gospel's interest. When God will not use thee in one kind, he will in another . . . He can do it by thy silence as well as by thy preaching: thy laying aside as well as thy continuancy in thy work. It is not pretence of doing God the greatest service, or performing the weightiest duty, that will excuse the least sin though that sin capacitated or gave us the opportunity for doing that duty. Thou wilt have little thanks, O my soul! if, when thou art charged with corrupting God's worship, falsifying thy vows, thou pretendest a necessity for it in order to continue in the ministry.'

Telling the Truth

Surviving socialists have not yet been ejected from the Labour Party, and such dissidents as Mr Scargill or the Militant Tendency have not yet been executed or led in fetters through the streets. But our dilemma is exactly the same as Oldfield's. A Christian cannot abjure the dictates of his own conscience. A rationalist humanist cannot abjure the truth. So it is necessary, now more than ever, to insist that the first duty of every socialist is to tell the truth, no more and no less. We should recall those words from Christ's Sermon on the Mount, which the Quakers have always appropriated:

> 'But let your communication be, Yea, yea: nay, nay: for whatsoever is more than these cometh of evil.' (Matthew, 5.37)

How much more, and how much less, than the truth is being said in the communications of New Labour! It is not at all impossible that to proclaim the truth may be an obstacle to a 'continuance in the ministry'. More significantly for many, it may also be an obstacle to association in the effort to create employment, improve hospitals and schools, build houses, and give aid to the organisation of victims of exclusion. But the doctrines of New Labour do not envisage much activity in these areas.

The easiest form of escape from telling the awful truth in these circumstances is by sending smoke signals. These provide a form of communication which only those in the know can understand. They have become quite an art form. It is not new for politicians to identify distant opponents when they wish to denounce close enemies. Mr Khruschev used to spend strenuous hours denouncing the Albanians, who live in a small country with little international influence. But when he said 'Albanians' he meant 'Chinese'. It was not considered circumspect to say precisely what he thought. We may suspect that in the past, Labour leaders have not been averse to attacking the Conservatives when the real object of their criticism may have been other Labour leaders. Certainly Conservative leaders have mastered this trick.

Smoke signals may be acceptable in the day to day operation of a political system which is relatively stable and which observes predictable patterns of behaviour. But Tony Blair's henchmen openly speak about a revolution, the 'Blair Revolution', so that the present condition of the Labour Party is neither stable, nor permanent nor necessarily sustainable. In such a context smoke signals are an impediment to understanding. Everybody will read into them whatever they fancy. So when Clare Short tells us that the Leader is being manipulated by a small faction of latter-day Svengalis, but that she has no disagreements with him, she is in danger of choking on her own smoke. Brave though her outburst was, it does not clarify the situation. Other people in less influential positions have been more forthright, but usually within the same framework of ambiguity. We have decided that we must try to tell the truth, within the limits of our knowledge.

The Three Functions of the Labour Party

Why should this situation of ambiguous communication have arisen? None of those involved are foolish, and some are highly principled. We think that the problem lies in the three rather different functions of a party of labour and specifically of the historical Labour Party. These

3 purposes of Lab

overlap, but they are to some extent separable and must be described separately.

Firstly, the Party has been the keeper of a social conscience. Old fashioned people will say that it has defended a particular ideology. In fact, it has discharged this responsibility with a high degree of pluralism, reflecting the wide range of opinion in the Party. Men of ideas like Aneurin Bevan and Tony Benn on the left or Anthony Crosland and Roy Hattersley on the right, have embodied the principles involved. Men of opportunity, like Richard Marsh and Ray Gunther, have exemplified the vicariousness of such pluralism. A very wide debate has continued over the century in which the Labour Party went through its gestation, birth and subsequent development.

The ideals of democratic socialism have included strong commitments to common ownership and to democracy throughout society and industry. They have advanced the objective of equality, not simply in the sense of opening access to opportunities, but stringently in seeking to narrow the gap between rich and poor, and to create space for the assertion of common humanity. Christian socialists would adhere to these commitments at least partly as a matter of faith. Secular socialists would defend them as the outcome of a series of rational arguments based on observable evidence. Whatever the intellectual processes involved, however, the first function of the Party has been to maintain an advanced system of beliefs.

The second function has been the defence and improvement of current working and living conditions for all that part of the population which has suffered most from inequality and discrimination. This is an eminently hands-on engagement. It has ranged across the whole area of social action, from seeking to establish basic standards of wages, and working conditions, to the defence of the rights of women and of minority groups, to legislation for health and safety, to the development of housing and public amenities, to the provision of a universal health service, to the reform of the educational services in order to promote ever greater equality of access and achievement. These active commitments have united the Labour Party's members in trade unions, local government Councils, voluntary organisations, and a wide variety of caring professions, giving them their focus on direct practical action.

The third function of the Party has been an electoral one, seeking to win representation in democratic assemblies so as to advance the other two functions. Those who speak of a 'Blair Revolution' are anticipating significant electoral advances, for which they think it necessary to pay by accepting a very marked regression in the claims of the social conscience and in the practical defence of the condition of the people. We think that we have shown the likely costs of these concessions. The assault on Labour's political philosophy can only undermine the Party's cohesion and self-confidence. The acceptance of continued restraint on all forms of public expenditure, and the espousal of tax cutting as a core policy objective, will intensify the miseries of many who have already been reduced far below the threshold of decency in their living standards, will continue the attrition of the health and educational services, and will promote widespread disillusionment if not despair among those who used to see the Labour Party as their staunch defender, even when they disapproved of these or those actual policies.

Within this context, electoral gains, if they are realised at all, are likely to prove very transient indeed. In Britain, the widening chasm between riches and poverty demands urgent and resolute corrective action. The cumulative decline of the public services is already reaching the point of open crisis, and, quite unsurprisingly, the economy is in jeopardy, while the state of public finances may prove dangerously unhealthy. Many, perhaps most, leading Labour Party figures know all this and are in private profoundly concerned about it. Some signal their distress, but many are simply hoping that after the election, events will impose more resolute policies. However, the prospect of a Labour government returned on the votes of Middle England, and with the abstention of a great swathe of traditional Labour supporters, is enough to terrify even the most sanguine of Labour's ambitious leaders. And the sheer horror of it, combined with the erosion of the traditional forms of correction of leadership error, through the process of Party discussion and the Party Conference, is the cause of some of the smoke signals. In a nutshell, the fear is that, by displacing Old Labour's commitments, Blair will be able to realign British politics, bringing One Nation Conservatism into phase with parts of the old Liberal and Labour parties. If this washes better with a dash of 'ethical' rhetoric, the doctors will spin it.

The Electoral Prospect

The Labour Party, however, is a secular organisation and we still have secular means of association outside it. Indeed on the key economic questions, the more clamant the call for full employment, minimum work standards, free and efficient health services and educational provision and a decent state pension, the more vulnerable the New Labour orthodoxy of 'the enterprise of the market and the rigour of competition' will prove to be. If some leading Labour Party members believe that the need for equitable policies will quickly burst the Mandelson barriers, once Labour is in office, they may be right. Even if they are not, this hope will almost certainly prove sufficient to ensure that most true Labour people give their votes, so long as they go to the voting booths, to the apostates, at least in the Election of 1996 or 97.

On the whole we ourselves are pessimistic, because the very processes which have caused Tony Blair to proclaim himself a social democrat are the processes in which he has drawn his comprehensive compact with the mammon of unrighteousness, the transnational business world from Singapore to Fortress Wapping. There are no benefits to be anticipated for our people in this unholy contract. This must lead to the belief that, as the truth goes home, there will be big battles to come inside the Labour Party. But no-one can be certain of such developments. There could be a hung Parliament, and close alliance with the Liberals could conceal some of the realities which we have been uncovering. Or the continued offensive of New Labour to depress expectations may have the undesired effect of persuading millions of people to stay at home on Polling Day, thus achieving an otherwise impossible Conservative victory. Already the leadership has been working overtime in Scotland to ensure this outcome.

The Relevance of Alternative Policies

We have, we believe, been able to show in this book that there are alternative policies to those which suit the narrow short-term aims of the rich and powerful, whose interests Tony Blair has embraced. These policies could put millions of people back to work, give our pensioners a fair deal, strengthen our health service, widen educational opportunities, build more houses and create an environment that was safer and more sustainable into the future. But we have not concealed from the reader that these progressive measures would cost money and this would mean raising taxes on the richer households in our society. Almost, it would seem, at the eleventh hour, the 'think-tank' which has been advising Mr Blair in his social and economic policies, the Institute for Public Policy Research, has presented a radical programme for New Labour of increased public spending to be paid for by a higher tax band on incomes of over £50,000 per annum. The top 10% of income earners would still be keeping nearly all but £2 or £3 billion of the £15 billion in tax cuts they received under the Tories. But on the very day of the

IPPR publication, Tony Blair promised no increase in taxes on the higher tax bands.

If there is anything more to say than 'Amen' after joining in Professor Galbraith's *Requiem*, then it had better be said soon. Here is what the professor wrote of the requirements of good government and social cohesion in the United States:

'The only effective design for diminishing the income inequality inherent in capitalism is the progressive income tax. Nothing in the age of contentment has contributed so strongly to income inequality as the reduction of taxes on the rich; nothing, as has been said, so contributes to social tranquility as the screams of anguish from the very affluent. That taxes should now be used to reduce inequality is, however, clearly outside the realm of comfortable thought.'

He ends his *Requiem* by raising the possibility that

'a candidate for the American presidency will emerge who is committed to human needs and remedies briefly just mentioned. And perhaps if the electorate is enlarged to include the economically and socially now dis-enfranchised, he or she will succeed and bring along a favoring majority in Congress. As I said before the prospect is not bright.'

For many years the policies devised by John Maynard Keynes and espoused by Professor Galbraith did operate with considerable effect to maintain relatively full employment and to reduce inequalities throughout the advanced capitalist societies. We have given our explanations for the abandonment of these policies. As capital became more and more transnational in its operations it escaped the regulatory restrictions imposed by nation-states. It began to nullify the tax regimes which were designed to redistribute income and to slow down or speed up the rhythm of economic expansion. More and more of world trade and production took place within multinational corporations. Transfer pricing between operations in different locations rendered the tax contributions of these companies to the states where they operated almost a voluntary act.

The obvious solution is a regime of European wide or ultimately world-wide tax agreements. But we have seen that this has not been pursued as a practical policy. And we have to ask why, and in particular why Tony Blair is not proposing joint and common actions to this end with Britain's partners in the European Union?

We may perhaps learn the answer from past history. For most of the time that Keynes was preaching his doctrines, almost the whole world was suffering the terrible economic slump of the 1930s, deeper even than the current world economic depression. Yet Keynes found the statesmen to whom he addressed himself completely deaf. A few like Ernest Bevin listened and understood. But such experiments as Keynes inspired were overtaken by a more conventional solution to the crisis. This we know as the Second World War. If we are going to solve our crisis in the same way, nuclear technology will ensure that it is our last crisis. But Keynes had his day as a result of that last frightful global war. The reason was very clear: all the captains of industry, and all the most powerful financiers, listened at last because they were scared out of their wits. They were frightened by their narrow escape from Adolf Hitler; and they were all the more frightened, the day after victory, by the arrival of Josef Stalin, whose tanks were now deployed all along the River Elbe down to the Balkans.

Threats and Responses

Who is going to frighten these distinguished gentlemen at the beginning of the third millennium? The collapse of communism has, for the time being, given them the illusion that all is for the best, in the best of all possible worlds. History is ended. The poor need no advocacy, and the unemployed can be largely ignored. Divisions of left and right are now considered arguments of the past. That is why Tony Blair has been able to situate himself as a Labour spokesman first on the centre left and now, it seems, on the centre or centre right of our political stage. That is why old ballast like Labour's socialist constitution can be jettisoned. Meantime poverty flourishes.

Our civilisation has made possible immense social and scientific advances. Today, our machines can work by themselves, and our people could be free from economic compulsion. But because of our archaic economic arrangements, half our people slave continuously and the other half are locked out of the system. However clever our machines, they have been unable to maintain production when people have not been able to consume their products. There is a ghost at this tormented feast. It haunts Africa, where debt has destroyed most of a continental economy. It visits all around the Third World. In Finland it gives us the live sounds of its presence, among the 17% of the population who are unemployed in a land which was until recently among the most affluent. It is heard in Spain, only louder still. Across our British coalfields it strikes terror into old and young alike. But will *this* fear communicate itself to those who govern or would govern our societies? Will it make possible a modern Keynes?

When we wrote earlier of the need for socialist renewal, we deliberately left unclear the agency of change. Speculation about splits in New Labour and the forming of new parties are, and will remain, fanciful until after the election, when we presume that people will be able to see New Labour in action after forming a new government. Three facts are, however, abundantly clear to us.

The first is that the Blair project has nothing to do with socialism, or in fact with Christianity. What has become blindingly obvious is that it is not a New Labour Party, but a new conservatism that is being constructed. The abandonment of the unions is proof of that and with it the betrayal of the unemployed and the neglect of the state pensioners. And there is evidence also in the alliances being formed with 'wet' Tories, Liberals, social democrats and old reprobates like Lord (Roy) Jenkins.

The second is that the loss of a Labour Movement, and particularly the sharp decline in trade union strength, is a very serious matter for working people. The importance of the unions lies not only in the defence of their own members, but in establishing a framework of security for all employees, manual, non-manual and professional. The reduction of the unions has created insecurity for all — the unorganised who thought that they did not need a union and the organised alike. The liberation of the workers is in the end the liberation of all.

The third is that socialism cannot be handed down from above by parliamentary legislation. Parliaments and Local Councils are indeed needed both as a forum for generating public opinion and as rule-making bodies for giving legitimacy and authority and administrative effect to changes in public opinion. They cannot legislate social change; that comes from below. Chartists, suffragettes, socialists have all used Parliamentary representation to confirm and consolidate what was already being demanded. It would be the same with the demand for shorter working time. This will come from model local agreements in companies and local authorities and from joint actions across national borders. In this work, a much strengthened European Parliament could play a role both as forum now and ultimately as legislator.

The implications of these three facts and the considerations addressed earlier of the uprooting of the whole tradition from which the Labour

Party emerged is that men and women associated with the Labour Party in many different fields, will need to reorganise their activities. A serious effort will certainly be made to reclaim the Labour Party for its original purpose.

At the Trades Union Congress in 1996 a succession of inept interventions by Front Bench Spokesmen revealed the present leadership's medium-term plan for a divorce from the unions. Neither the unions, nor the overwhelming majority of active Labour supporters can accept such a divorce. Nor will they accept the implementation of a whole range of new policies which are calculated to make life more difficult for organised labour.

Assuming purely rational responses from those whose dreams of a better society, whose commitments and interests are threatened by New Labour, a leadership election is inevitable not too long after the General Election is out of the way. Unfortunately, Labour has no 'fast-track' procedure for replacing an unwanted Leader. Such a procedure is now urgently necessary. The present elaborate framework is much too complicated and long-drawn-out to be practicable or painless if Labour is in government.

It is only necessary to look back a couple of years to recall that, under John Smith's leadership, Labour was strongly committed to the priority of full employment, to modestly redistributive taxation, and to limited but significant improvement in labour law and workpeople's rights. The attack on 'old' Labour has meant the repudiation of John Smith's achievement, which made Labour highly 'electable' without betraying any of its deeply held principles.

Has the legacy of John Smith been totally forgotten? We doubt this. There are people right up to the top level of the Party who lived very happily with the Smith prescription. Margaret Beckett, Deputy Leader to John Smith, and all-too-briefly Party Leader, and Robin Cook, who managed Smith's election campaign for the leadership and brought him to Strasbourg to assure MEPs of his support for their efforts to achieve full employment in Europe, must surely be liable to occasional twinges of nostalgia. And without listing names — which would be invidious — there must be many leading figures who found Smith's package more palatable than what is now on offer.

When it comes to the wider Labour Movement, who can doubt that the Smith legacy is infinitely preferable? John Smith spelt out his specific programme for the trade unions at the 1993 Congress after months of discussion. Tony Blair has dumped much of this, and offers instead further anti-union laws, while the spin doctors trail the idea of a grand divorce in a manner reminiscent of the softening-up operation which was mounted to rubbish Clause IV.

A leadership challenge, once the election is out of the way, is the most rational method within a democratic framework to resolve the question of whether the Labour Party should be transformed into an alternative capitalist party. Those who have devoted their entire lifetimes to the Labour cause are unlikely to allow the vision which has inspired them to be permanently blacked out. If a challenge were made, it would almost certainly succeed, so wounded are the susceptibilities of so many Party members and supporters. The hordes of phantom 'New Labour' members from old social democracy, credit cards in hand, are extremely unlikely to blank out the anger and the anguish of so many people.

But, of course, it is just possible that such a bid may not succeed. If not, a new Party or new Association of Socialist Groups or a new Labour Representation Committee might come to be feasible. New agencies will be formed by people coming together on big issues and working out for themselves how to create a better society.

In this reorganisation of activity, the guidance of ideas whether Christian, humanist or Marxian, is only helpful in setting ultimate targets. Such guidance will not solve today's problems, except in generating the enthusiasm and steady commitment to struggle to make these ideals the norm. What ideas do tell us is that the way of trying to understand the world by disaggregating all-round human activities into fragmented categories like 'production' and 'consumption', 'work' and 'leisure' is self-destructive. We are whole beings, and labour, as something external, done for the enrichment and aggrandisement, and to the specification of, someone else, is alienating. We all have to struggle against the causes of that alienation, if we are to be fully human. We cannot do this as separated individuals on our own. It needs and imposes joint and common action at the local, national, regional and international levels.

Such actions for the right to work, for the defence and extension of the welfare society and the social wage, for the reduction of compulsory labour by shorter working time, for the advancement of women, for the protection of the disadvantaged and the satisfaction of unmet social needs, can renew the political process. They can serve to remind all those who have moved too far away from their common roots to feel what every victim feels, and to hold to that most simple knowledge of all — that we are members of one another. That was the message of

Christ and it is the message of all humanist thought. It is why the aspiration of holding goods in common, of common ownership, common wealth, real community still lives with many of us. It will continue to live. It cannot be taken away by any rewriting of constitutions. It cannot be written off, as old fashioned and out-of-date, by modernising spin doctors. What is spoken in the name of community cannot be taken in vain. It will always come back to haunt those who transgress that simple rule of our common humanity:

> 'Inasmuch as ye have done it unto one of the least of these my brethren, ye have done it unto me.'

When Gerrard Winstanley and his Diggers were driven off their communist colony, the common land of George Hill in Surrey, he told the politicians of his own day that he might lose 'the poor cows that is my living', and he might be imprisoned. But that would not begin to settle the issue:

> 'Alas! you poor blind earth-moles, you strive to take away my livelihood and the liberty of this poor weak frame my body of flesh, which is my house I dwell in for a time: but I strive to cast down your kingdom of darkness, and to open hell gates, and to break the devil's bonds asunder wherewith you are tied, that you my enemies may live in peace: and that is all the harm I would have you to have . . .'

> 'The world of digging still goes on and stops not for arrest,
> The cows were gone but are returned, and we are all at rest.
> No money's paid, nor never shall, to lawyer or his man
> To plead our cause, for therein we'll do the best we can.
> In Cobham on the little heath our digging there goes on,
> And all our friends they live in love, as if they were but one.'

References

Introduction

Peter Mandelson and Roger Liddle, *The Blair Revolution: Can New Labour Deliver?*, Faber & Faber, 1996.

Chapter 1
The Spin Doctors — Fabricating a Leader

Tony Blair, Maiden Speech, House of Commons, 6 July 1983.
Tony Blair, 'Forging a New Agenda', *Marxism Today*, October 1991.
Tony Blair, 'A Stakeholder Society', *Fabian Review*, February 1996.
Tony Blair, 'Why I am a Christian', *Sunday Telegraph*, 7 April 1996.
Stuart Hall, 'Tony Blair's New Labour', *Soundings*, Autumn 1995.
Peter Hitchens, Martin Jacques, 'Labour's New Leader: Tony Blair', *Sunday Times Magazine*, 17 July 1994.
Eric Hobsbawm, 'The Nation is Labour's for the Taking', *New Statesman & Society*, 3 May 1996.
Immanuel Kant, *Grundlegung zur Metaphysik der Sitten*, trans. T.K. Abbott, section 2.
Charles Kingsley, *The Water Babies*,
Peter Mandelson and Roger Liddle, *op.cit.*
John MacMurray, *Creative Society*, SCM Press, 1935.
John MacMurray, *The Form of the Personal, Vol.1. The Self as Agent; Vol.2. Persons in Relation*, the Gifford Lectures, Faber & Faber, 1953.
John MacMurray, 'The Early Development of Marx's Thought' and 'Christianity and Communism' in John Lewis, Karl Polanyi and Donald Kitchin (eds), *Christianity and the Social Revolution*, Gollancz, 1935.
Nyta Mann, 'Top Spinner', *New Statesman & Society*, 8 March 1996.
Karl Marx, *Contribution to the Critique of Political Economy*, Preface, 1864.
S. Matthew, *The Bible*, 18.21.
Patrick Rentoul, *Tony Blair*.

Chapter 2
Tony Blair and Christian Socialism

Ken Coates (ed.), *Common Ownership: Clause IV and the Labour Party*, Spokesman, 1995.

217

John Gray, *After Social Democracy: Politics, Capitalism and the Common Life*, Demos, 1996.

Amitoi Etzioni, *The Spirit of Community*, Crown Publishers, New York 1993, summarised in *DEMOS*, Winter, 1993.

Martin Jacques, quoted in E. Shaw, *New Statesman*, 26 April 1996.

Bronislaw Malinowski, *The Primitive Customs of Savages*, 1927.

Karl Marx, *Early Writings* collected in Penguin edition, 1975.

Jan O'Malley, *The Politics of Community Action*, Spokesman, 1977.

Ellen Meiksins Wood, 'The Uses and Abuses of "Civil Society"', in eds. Ralph Miliband and Leo Panitch, *Socialist Register*, Merlin, 1990.

F. Tonnies, *Community and Association*, 1887.

Raymond Williams, *Key Words: A Vocabulary of Culture and Society*, Fontana, 1976.

Julian Benda, *La Traison des Clercs*, Grasset, Paris, 1927.

G.C. Binyon, 'The Christian Socialists', in A. Barratt Brown (ed), *Great Democrats*, Ivor Nicholson & Watson, 1934.

Ken Coates and Tony Topham, *Trade Unions and Politics*, Blackwell, 1986.

Robert Cooper, *The Post-Modern State and World Order*, Demos, 1996.

Peter Drucker, *The End of Economic Man*.

Christopher Hill, *The World Turned Upside Down*, Penguin, 1975.

John Maynard Keynes, *General Theory of Employment, Interest and Money*, Macmillan 1936, 'Concluding Notes'.

Alasdair MacIntyre, *After Virtue: A Study in Moral Theory*, Duckworth, 1981.

John MacMurray, 'The Early Development of Marx's Thought' and 'Christianity and Communism' in John Lewis, *op.cit.*

John MacMurray, *Creative Society*, SCM Press, 1935.

Jacques Maritain, *Scholasticism and Politics*.

Karl Marx and Frederick Engels, *Communist Manifesto*, 1848 and 1948, Lawrence & Wishart.

William Morris, *Dream of John Ball*, 1887; reprinted in *William Morris: Selected Writings*, Nonesuch Press, 1937.

News from Nowhere, 1890, *ibid.*

Joseph Needham, *Time the Refreshing River*, Allen & Unwin, 1943, reissued by Spokesman, 1986.

Michael Novak and Ronald Preston, *Christian Capitalism or Christian Socialism*, IEA, 1994.

Michael Novak (ed.), *Reclaiming the Ground*, CSM, 1993.

Ronald Preston, 'The Moral Order of a Free Society' in Novak & Preston, *op.cit.*

Edward Said, *Culture and Imperialism*, Chatto & Windus, 1993, Verso, 1994.

R.H. Tawney, *Equality*, Allen & Unwin, 1931.

Religion and the Rise of Capitalism, Murray 1926 and Penguin, 1938.

The Radical Tradition, Penguin, 1966.

William Temple, *Christianity and the Social Order*, Penguin, 1943.

J. Howard Whitehouse, 'John Ruskin' in A. Barratt Brown, *op.cit.*

Matthew d'Ancona and Graham Stanton, 'Gospel Truths', *Prospect*, April 1996.

Michael Barratt Brown, *The Economics of Imperialism*, Penguin, 1974.

The Yugoslav Tragedy, Spokesman, 1996.

The Bible, 'Gospel according to St. Matthew', 25.

'Revelation of St John the Divine', 17.

Robert Cooper, *op.cit.*

Basil Davidson, *The Black Man's Burden: Africa and the Curse of the Nation-State*, James Currey, 1992.
John Kenneth Galbraith, *The Culture of Contentment*, Penguin, 1993.
Edward Gibbon, *The Decline and Fall of the Roman Empire*, ed. D.M. Low, 1960.
Elie Kedourie, *Nationalism*, Hutchinson, 1960.
Gilbert Murray, *Five Stages of Greek Religion*, Watts, 1935.
Archibald Robertson, *The Bible and Its Background*, Vol.II, 'The New Testament', Watts, 1942.
Sir John Squire, *Epigrams*, No.1, 'The Dilemma'.

Chapter 3
What's Wrong with Capitalism?

John MacMurray, *Creative Society, op.cit.*
Jan Pen, *Modern Economics*, Penguin, 1958.
CLARE Group, *National Institute Economic Review*, May 1996.
UNCTAD, *World Investment Reports*, 1993-4.
UNDP, *World Development Report*, 1996.
Labour Party, *New Industrial Policy for Britain*, 1996.
John Ruskin, *Unto This Last and Other Essays*, Dent.
Hugo Radice, 'Globalisation and the UK Economy' in Michael Barratt Brown, *Democracy versus Capitalism*, Spokesman, 1995.

Chapters 4 and 5
Success or Failure?: Labour in Government and Who Failed Old Labour?

Michael Barratt Brown, *European Union: Fortress or Democracy?*, Spokesman, 1993.
Michael Barratt Brown, 'By Their Deeds Ye Shall Know Them', *European Labour Forum*, New Year 1994.
Correlli Barnett, *Audit of War*, MacMillan, 1986.
Alan Bullock, *Ernest Bevin*,
CLARE Group, National Institute, *Economic Review*, February 1995.
Ken Coates (ed.), *What Went Wrong?*, Spokesman, 1980.
Ken Coates and Tony Topham, *Workers' Control: A Book of Readings*, Panther, 1970.
Elizabeth Durbin, *New Jerusalem: The Labour Party and the Economics of Democratic Socialism*, Routledge, 1985.
European Commission, *Economic Report, 1996.*
Milton Friedman, *Capitalism and Freedom*, Chicago, 1962.
Michael Hatfield, *The House the Left Built*, Gollancz, 1978.
Eric Hobsbawm, 'The Forward March of Labour Halted'.
Stuart Holland, *The Socialist Challenge*, Quartet, 1975.
Stuart Holland, *Out of Crisis*, Spokesman, 1983.
Will Hutton, *The State We're In*, Cape, 1995.
Grazia Ietto-Gillies, *International Production: Trends, Theories, Effects*, Polity Press, 1992.
Rudolf Meidner, Allen & Unwin, 1978.

Robin Murray, *Multinational Companies and Nation States*, Spokesman, 1975.
Eric Shaw, 'New Labour: All Right Now', *New Statesman & Society*, 26 April 1996.
Eric Shaw, *The Labour Party Since 1945*, Blackwell, 1996.
Tony Topham, *Planning the Planners*, Spokesman, 1985.
UNCTAD, *Trade and Development Report*, UN, New York, 1995.

Chapter 6
Will New Labour 'Deliver'? And to Whom?

Tony Blair, *New Fabian Review*, Issue 108, No.1.
Ken Coates (ed.), *The Right to Work*, Spokesman, 1995.
Ken Coates and Stuart Holland, *Full Employment for Europe*, Spokesman, 1995.
Ken Coates (ed.), *Dear Commissioner*, Spokesman, 1996.
Central Statistical Office, 'International Taxes and Social Security Benefits', *Economic Trends*, January 1995.
John Kenneth Galbraith, *The New Industrial State*, 1976.
Sir James Goldsmith, *The Trap*.
Colin Hines and Tim Lang, *The New Protectionism*, Earthscan, 1993.
Eric Hobsbawm, 'The Nation is Labour's for the Taking', *New Statesman*, 3 May 1996.
Will Hutton, 'Left with no Illusions', *Prospect*, March 1996.
National Institute, *Economic Review*, February 1995.
Martin Wolf, *Financial Times*, 19 January 1996.

Chapter 7
Rescuing the Welfare State

Michael Barratt Brown, 'Away with all Great Arches', *New Left Review*, No.167, Jan-Feb 1988.
Michael Barratt Brown, 'Commercial and Industrial Capital in England: a Reply to Geoffrey Ingham', *New Left Review* No.175, Nov-Dec 1989.
Ken Coates and Tony Topham, *Readings and Witnesses for Workers' Control*, Panther, 1970.
Ken Coates and Tony Topham, *History of the Transport & General Workers' Union, Vol.1. The Emergence of the Labour Movement, 1870-1926*, Blackwell, 1991.
M.J. Daunton, 'Payment and Participation: Welfare State and State Formation, 1900-1951', *Past and Present*, No.150, February 1996.
M.J. Daunton, 'Gentlemanly Capitalism and British Industry, 1820-1914', *Past and Present*, No.122, February 1989 and No.132, August 1991.
David Donnison, 'What Sort of New Labour?', *Soundings*, 1996.
J.K. Galbraith, *op.cit.*
Jose Harris, 'Political Thought and the Welfare State, 1870-1940', *Past and Present*, No.135, May 1992.
Will Hutton, *The State We're In, op.cit.*
Geoff Mulgan and Robin Murray, *Reconnecting Taxation*, DEMOS, 1993.
Peter Townsend and Alan Walker, *New Directions for Pensions: How to Revitalise National Insurance*, Spokesman, 1995.

Chapter 8
Unemployment and the Future of Work

Michael Barratt Brown and Hugo Radice, *Democracy versus Capitalism: a Response to Will Hutton*, Spokesman, 1995.

Ken Coates (ed.), *The Right to Work: The Loss of our First Freedom*, Spokesman, 1995.

Ken Coates and Stuart Holland, *Full Employment for Europe*, Spokesman, 1995.

Ken Coates and Michael Barratt Brown, *The European Recovery Programme: Restoring Full Employment*, 1993.

European Commission, *Annual Economic Report, 1996*.

John Hughes, 'How Deregulation Kills Jobs', *European Labour Forum*, 12, New Year 1994.

Paul Ormerod, *The Death of Economics*, Faber, 1994.

Jeremy Rifkin, *The End of Work: The Decline of the Global Labour Force and the Dawn of the Post-Market Era*, Putnam, 1995.

Michel Rocard, *A Reduction in Working Hours*, European Parliament, 1995.

Trade Union Congress, *Britain's Longer Working Week*, TUC, 1995.

Chapter 9
Responding to the Ecological Crisis

Peter Mandelson and Roger Liddle, *op.cit.*, p.164.

Jacques Delors, 'A New Model of Development', a paper for European Socialists, 27 March 1996.

Michael Barratt Brown, *Models in Political Economy*, 1995, Penguin, Chapter 11.

Pearce *et al*, *Blueprint for a Green Economy*, Earthscan, 1989.

Jonathan Porritt *et al*, *The Real World*, Kogan Page, 1996.

J. Altvater *et al*, *Alternative Economic Policy for Europe*, Free University of Berlin.

Chapter 10
The European Dimension

Michael Barratt Brown, *European Union: Fortress or Democracy?*, Spokesman, 1991.

Ken Coates and Michael Barratt Brown, *A European Recovery Programme*, Spokesman, 1993.

TUC, *The European Union: Trade Union Goals*, TUC.

Christopher Gifford, *Deregulation, Disasters and BSE*, Spokesman, 1996.

Wynne Godley, E.B. Kapstein, *Foreign Affairs*, May-June 1996.

Tim Lang and Colin Hines, *The New Protectionism*, Earthscan, 1994.

Ken Coates and Stuart Holland, *Dear Commissioner*, Spokesman, 1996.

Chapter 11
Labour and Internationalism

Michael Barratt Brown and Hugo Radice, *op.cit.*

Michael Barratt Brown, *Fair Trade: Reform and Reality in the International Trading System*, Zed Books, 1993.

Michael Barratt Brown, *Models in Political Economy*, Penguin revised edition, 1995.

Michael Barratt Brown, *Africa's Choices: After 30 Years of the World Bank*, Penguin, 1995.
Mike Best, *The New Competition*, Polity Press, 1990.
Stuart Holland, *Towards a New Bretton Woods*, Spokesman, 1994
Geoff Mulgan and Robin Murray, *op.cit.*

Chapter 12
Why Socialist Renewal?

Michael Barratt Brown with Hugo Radice, *Democracy versus Capitalism* (second edition), Spokesman, 1996.
Ken Coates (ed.), *Common Ownership, Clause IV and the Labour Party*, Spokesman, 1995.
Gerry Cohen, *Is Socialism Inseparable from Common Ownership?*, Spokesman, 1995.
Royden J. Harrison, *New Labour as Past History*, Spokesman, 1996.
Stuart Hall, 'Parties on the Verge of a Nervous Breakdown', *Soundings*, Vol.1, Autumn 1995.
Will Hutton, *op.cit.*
Lewis Minkin, *The Contentious Alliance: The Labour Party and the Trade Unions*, Edinburgh, 1991.
Geoff Mulgan and Ivan Briscoe, 'The Society of Networks', DEMOS, No.8, 1996, p.29.

Other Socialist Renewal titles

Is Socialism Inseparable from Common Ownership?
by G.A. Cohen   50p

New Directions for Pensions
How to Revitalise National Insurance
by Peter Townsend and Alan Walker   £1.50

New Labour's Aims and Values
A Study in Ambiguity
by Ken Coates MEP

Democracy versus Capitalism
A response to Will Hutton with some old questions for New Labour
**Michael Barratt Brown
with Hugo Radice   £1.50**

Feminism after Post-feminism
by Liz Davies   £2.00

May Day
Solidarity, Celebration, Struggle
written and illustrated by John Gorman

The Rights of the Unemployed
A Socialist Approach
by Anne Gray

Europe and NATO Expansion
by Frank Blackaby   £1.50

The Yugoslav Tragedy
Lessons for Socialists
by Michael Barratt Brown   £4.99

Also

Common Ownership
Clause IV and the Labour Party
by Ken Coates MEP   £5.99

Forthcoming

The Transport Crisis in Britain
by Philip S. Bagwell   £9.99